Presenting on TV and Radio

Presenting on TV and Radio

An insider's guide

Janet Trewin

ELSEVIER

AMSTERDAM • BOSTON • HEIDELBERG • LONDON • NEW YORK • OXFORD
PARIS • SAN DIEGO • SAN FRANCISCO • SINGAPORE • SYDNEY • TOKYO

Focal Press is an imprint of Elsevier

Focal Press
An imprint of Elsevier
Linacre House, Jordan Hill, Oxford OX2 8DP
200 Wheeler Road, Burlington, MA 01803

First published 2003

British Library Cataloguing in Publication Data
A catalogue record for this book is available from the British Library

Library of Congress Cataloguing in Publication Data
A catalogue record for this book is available from the Library of Congress

ISBN 0 240 51906 X

For information on all Focal Press publications, visit our website at:
www.focalpress.com

Typeset by Newgen Imaging Systems (P) Ltd., Chennai, India
Printed and bound in Great Britain

Contents

Acknowledgements

My sincere thanks go to all who helped in the compilation of this book. I hope I have done justice to the views they hold and the information they gave. I'm grateful also to the Radio Academy (www.radioacademy.org) which performs the increasingly important task of raising the profile of radio in a televisual world.

I

What it is and how to do it

1 Being a presenter

Being a presenter is either one of the most difficult jobs in broadcasting … or it's one of the easiest, cushiest numbers you could ever hope to get. Some presenters are expected to be intellectually brilliant, journalistically unsurpassed and capable of displaying these talents constantly on TV or radio with never a hint of pomposity. Others are *expected* to be pompous, infuriating and hated! Some are hired because they are experienced in all aspects of broadcasting. Others are wanted entirely because they are *inexperienced* and gauche. Some (a frighteningly large number) merely need good looks, bundles of personality, an ability to read an autocue and, in moments of crisis, to do what they're told. Inevitably, if being a presenter can mean being so many different things, becoming one is bound to be something of a challenge!

One of the reasons why presentation defies definition is that duties can vary so completely. News and current affairs presenters tend to be heavily involved in the whole news-gathering operation, while a features presenter on location may have to do little more than appear and read a prepared script. Either way it's not easy. Nor is it an end in itself. Channel 4 News presenter, Jon Snow, is quite clear on this point:

> *Presentation is secondary to all other skills. If you want to be 'a presenter', forget it. What you must be is a first-class journalist. You must be capable of asking questions. The right questions covering the issue and you must ask them on behalf of the audience you are talking to. Even if you are only reading someone else's copy, which is pretty depressing, you must still have enough of an inquiring mind to know what the questions are and what issues are raised. To be a presentational slave is to be a tedious operator. You must be able to write what you read. All this is true of absolutely any type of presentation. The success of Richard and Judy is based upon their understanding of the right questions for*

Figure 1.1
Jon Snow believes there is no such thing as presentation – only good journalists who communicate well

their audience. You can't be a great communicator unless you can do this.

Presenters are often accused of whinging about what a hard job it is. Understandably, they get little sympathy since if they do their job well they achieve the deceit that it is glossy and easy. You are paid to make complicated things seem straightforward, to look bright and be informative. In reality these are terrifically complicated things to achieve, particularly whilst everything is falling apart behind the scenes, a fact well recognized by Lis Howell. She rose through presentation in TV and radio to become Managing Editor of Sky News, Programme Director of GMTV and Senior Vice President of the cable and satellite group Flextech. A hirer and firer of the first order.

I don't think being a presenter is the job. I think being a capable TV professional and producer is the job. I don't think newcomers to the business realize that it's a skill. You get a lot of people who are actors or models manqué who think, 'Oh I'll be a TV weather person' or, 'I'll read the news' and they have no idea of the responsibility or the skill that's needed. It comes as quite a shock. It's a very hard job and it's part of a much bigger skill which is journalism on any level.

A PRESENTER'S WORKING DAY

There really isn't a typical example. Every production team will make different demands of their anchor. Compare two extremes, 1FM's *Newsbeat* and presenting on a pre-recorded features programme. I've done lots of both. It pays to be this flexible if you want a steady stream of work.

Presentation on *Newsbeat*, BBC Radio 1FM

The anchor on *Newsbeat* is a news reporter and a newsreader as well as being the presenter. You muck in with everyone else but have the added duty of being 'the voice' for the whole fifteen-minute news sequence. The shows run at 1245 and 1745 hours. I was the first female presenter of the programme. Today, once again, it's a woman: Georgina Bowman. Her day looks something like this.

1030: Arrive at 1FM's West London studios ready to rock! The other journalists have been there since 0800. The presenter arrives later specifically so she can bring a fresh perspective and prevent any tendency to following the mainstream news that everyone else is doing. She must have watched and listened to all possible news outlets, particularly the commercial sector, both analogue and digital stations, and she must have read the papers. Her first task is to talk to the day editor and offer new stories or angles on tales already underway. There will be six or seven items in the programme. She'll have to do at least one of them – get the background information, phone the participants, go out to do interviews or arrange for guests to come in or to attend outlying studios for 'down-the-line' interviews. Georgina then edits the interviews, scripts them, lays down the voice track and writes the cue. She must also be briefed on the other stories and interviews to be done.

1145: The presenter writes or re-writes all the programme cues working with the editor.

1240: The presenter bundles up the scripts and leaves for the studio which, being en suite, is about five steps away! There's a short time to give level (ensure the volume is OK) and read through the scripts.

Figure 1.2
Georgina Bowman: 'It's great fun, high profile, hard work!'

1245: On air. The presenter operates her own microphone and that of any guests. A studio assistant in the sound booth next door plays in inserts, the studio producer fires the jingles, the editor oversees the process.

1300: There's a post-programme debrief lasting anything from two to ten minutes. If work allows, there's time for a quick lunch before a completely new evening programme starts into production.

1430: The presenter is back in the studio reading the news after which another package and interviews must be completed for the next show.

1530: The presenter reads another news bulletin and banters with the DJ.

1630: Another news bulletin. More banter, some of it perhaps quite personal. Georgina has to think fast around a presenter like Chris Moyles, who may deliberately 'drop her in it'.

1700: A final news bulletin before rushing back to the office to write the cues and prepare for the evening programme.

1745: On air with the second edition of *Newsbeat*.

1800: Programme debrief. Go home and follow all the news happenings throughout the evening in readiness for the next day. Georgina Bowman is on air five days a week but her job requires being a news junkie seven days a week.

1FM's news editor, Rod McKenzie, insists that presenters on this show above all others on Radio One have to be journalists and hard-working ones at that!

> *They are absolutely news journos because they've got a big copy tasting role. You can't have a 'gob on a stick' in a tight team like this. We don't have 'producers' in the traditional sense. We only have reporters and senior reporters who are also output editors. Everyone employed is on-air capable. We try to recruit into* Newsbeat *at the age of 25 so that we're as close as we can be to our target audience. They go out clubbing in the evening and so on, which is important. We used to find a lot of people from the independent stations but they don't do news packages like they used to so they don't have the reporter craft skills. So now we're looking through the journalism colleges. It's not just about finding good journalists; it's about trying to find good journalists with a young head on their shoulders … with a young outlook.*

Presentation on magazine and features programmes

Making movies as a presenter on programmes like *Countryfile*, *Holiday* or *Top Gear* which include filmed features, involves a very different schedule. Whilst presenters will sometimes devise, research and film the story, they may also only be needed to front an item that's been produced and scripted by others. The latter requires much less work in advance but heaps of energy and concentration on the day.

Pre-shoot: The producer will call to tell the presenter the story and arrange times and places and will e-mail or fax a draft outline.

Day 1: The presenter meets with the crew on location and is told what questions to ask. The interviewees have been told in advance the point they are expected to make. The presenter does the interviews and the producer listens to ensure the necessary sound bite is obtained. The presenter is given a script to be performed as a series of pieces to camera to wrap around the inserts. Each chunk has to be learned by heart immediately. Such an item would take a few hours to complete – weather and light permitting. At the end of the day the producer returns to base for the cutting and final scripting.

Day 2: When the item is ready, the presenter is again called to lay down the studio voice track. The producer or presenter writes the cue.

Thus a simple four- or five-minute item might only take a couple of days of the presenter's time – on occasions even less. The presenter's responsibility is to make the story appear to be his or her own and to give it the relevant programme style.

The more adept you become at handling diverse presentation styles the better. Ian Gilvear, Development Adviser for BBC Training, has been a reporter, presenter and producer for 25 years. Ask him what his greatest memories are of presentation, done either by himself or others, and you'll see what I mean about variety … and the frightening demands of the job.

> *I did a long report for Radio Forth in Edinburgh when the city's dead were returned from the Falklands. There was a service in St Giles Cathedral. The OB engineers captured all the actuality and I wrote the script, produced, packaged and presented it myself from the Landrover, which I was glad about, because I was close to the events and wrote it simply, capturing the emotion without becoming over-sentimental. Other memories … Rod Sharpe flawlessly ad libbing cues for a fifteen-minute radio news bulletin during a power failure which deprived us of the scripts … Archie MacPherson filming a sport piece with me while being spat on from above by hostile Dundee United fans … Kirsty Wark trying to stay awake at four in the morning for a satellite link with the US Secretary of State … Mark Goodier doing a breakfast show on his knees because it was the Queen's birthday … me doing live commentary on water-skiing at short notice without knowing the first thing about it … a You & Yours*

reporter doing a package about a gentle, elderly man who'd lovingly looked after his profoundly disabled wife; she'd lost all power of movement and speech, and could only blink once for yes, twice for no.

QUALITIES OF A PRESENTER

Even if we can't say what it is we can at least list some of the qualities you need to be a presenter.

A presenter is... a great communicator

... at least, should be. Good presenters can turn the complex into the comprehensible. They should have great command of the language and an ability to write well (see Kirsty Lang's experiences in Chapter 8). There are relatively few presentation jobs where you won't be expected to do at least some writing and if you want to 'make a script your own' you really must be able to string a decent sentence together. Erstwhile Conservative Member of Parliament, Edwina Currie, who has made such a successful second career as a radio presenter, gives as her top tips to presenters:

> *Learn good English and read a lot. Read everything. You're a wordsmith.*

Lis Howell, who after nearly 30 years in front of and behind microphones is now teaching television journalism, is keen to impress on aspiring presenters the importance of the story-telling art:

> *If you're a good journalist you can present anything pretty well because your role as a journalist is to clarify things for the general public. If you're doing presentation because you're good at something else like sewing or being a chef, or being a footballer, there is a role for journalism here too. You become, for example, a 'gardening journalist', sort of. You must have that ability to explain complex subjects without patronizing. You've got to be able to say, 'This is how you make a roux sauce' or, 'Beef Wellington', without making listeners feel stupid. So that's journalism. All journalism is about making things clear and universal.*

Of course, simplifying is not enough. Shows have light and shade. A presenter needs to turn from tragedy to comedy without sounding crass. TV

Figure 1.3
Getting young children to say something useful is as difficult as it gets. Only recalcitrant politicians are worse!

and radio can distort things that would have sounded OK in other circumstances. For example, sitting at the breakfast table, you might get away with a conversation about a close friend who has been knocked over in a car accident and then follow it up with a complete *non sequitur* about a one-legged, talking parrot. Those who know you may accept your strange disparate thoughts and your swift, apparently unsympathetic, transition from sadness to silliness. How different it is when your listeners are strangers and you talk to them through microphones! On air you must use pauses, deliberate tonal changes and breaths to separate a tragedy from the 'and finally' story.

It goes without saying that you need to relate well to anyone from any walk of life, any age group, any nationality and any religion, and then, as if this isn't enough, you must ensure that what they say is accurately transmitted to the audience. This, I confidently assert with no shadow of doubt, is a lifetime's work and a wonderful mental challenge.

It clearly is possible to learn communications skills but from his position in the BBC's Training Department overseeing young hopefuls and those already presenting, Ian Gilvear is cautious:

> *Presenting can be taught to a certain extent ... but some people are more natural communicators than others and no amount of coaching will turn a weak or wooden performer into a star. Enthusiasm goes a long way – Sister Wendy on art and Fred Dibnah on buildings are both passionate communicators in their field but wouldn't transfer easily to a different genre.*

New presenters can be forgiven for being unsure as to whether they're suited to the task when it's clear that editors and producers have difficulty choosing the right communicators. Lis Howell has been on both sides of the choosing process:

> *Not everybody can do it. Out of twenty students I might find seventeen are capable of it and want to do it and three are mortified by it and can't stand it. The fact of the matter is that nobody knows how to pick presenters. I mean we've tried everything. Going round the country looking for a presenter. Getting people that are apparently absolutely guaranteed because they have a specialism or have done it before. But there is no formula. There is absolutely no way of knowing. There are two reasons for this. People can have done it elsewhere very well but change the environment and it doesn't work any more. Or the other thing is you don't know what is going to be flavour of the month, what the public will want.*

Enthusiasm is a real aid to successful communicating. Simon Schama has transformed dusty history into a glittering relevance for millions of TV viewers. However, he is at pains to point out that whilst some in academia interpret his style as vulgarizing complex issues, in reality the enthusiasm can only be built on fiercely high standards of communication:

> *Because you've done television history there's an assumption that you're dumbing down the content of what you're doing. I defy anyone to say this is a Mickey Mouse version of the Irish hunger or Orwell in the 1920s. It takes a huge amount of craft and care. Making complicated ideas understandable to a large number of people is amazingly exacting work.*

One of the most over-the-top enthusiasts is the (now retired) veteran motor-racing commentator Murray Walker, once memorably described by Clive James as commentating as though his trousers were on fire! The excitement came from a huge love of the sport. He went to his first bike race meeting when he was just two years old and had a lifetime of knowledge to call upon when he took up Formula One commentating:

> *My style always came from the heart because I think a commentator's job is far more than informing. Anyone can drone away about what is actually happening in front of you. I knew that the anoraks were going to be listening whatever happened and whoever was talking but I regarded my remit as to entertain people.*

A presenter is…an expert at something else!

This may sound mad but it is true of all the best presenters. Innate talent, personality, natural affinity for the camera, a great voice – all of these are desirable but they will not earn you a living for life. Stated simply, the theory is 'be good at something – presentation comes later'.

Some of the most highly respected presenters insist that there is no such thing as 'the art of presentation'. They see themselves first and foremost as journalists, reporters, sportsmen or academics. They have a core skill or specialism and in order to inform others about it, as a matter of necessity, they present. Alan Titchmarsh says he got into presentation by mistake really only because he was a committed gardener:

> *It is about sharing the passion. It's about passing something on. You can't keep it to yourself. Getting into TV happened when swarms of*

greenfly invaded Margate. I was asked to go on Nationwide. *So I did. And it was like tasting blood! I remember the cameras homing in on me and being able to explain all about it.*

Jon Snow, that unflappable and intelligent driver of Channel 4 News, says with real conviction:

I do not believe in the art of presentation. If you do you should be in advertising. I'm happy to admit that I am an indifferent presenter but a good journalist and one who has to present every night.

BBC presenter and reporter, Wesley Kerr, is convinced that if you want to stay in the game you have to underpin it with something else:

There are three routes to presentation. One is journalism, one is celebrity and one is specialism, like being Handy Andy. The first and the last are the best. I'm only half joking when I say that the other way to get in is to get involved in some tabloid scandal. Cleverly managed, it can get you there. You can build a career just on being a celebrity. I think, to some extent, that's what DJs do and why they can have a long career. But your best bet is to become a damned good journalist before you start thinking about being a presenter.

In truth, any self-respecting presenter wishing to make a career in any part of broadcasting cannot afford to be only a 'voice on a stick'.

A presenter is ... calm

It's a presenter's job to stay cool and keep going. The Rudyard Kipling quotation about keeping your head when all around are losing theirs, seems entirely appropriate for a presenter. You need highly developed powers of concentration. Presenters talk calmly to the public while people are screaming to them through earpieces about entirely different things. They remain impassive come hell or high water.

There is probably no situation you could imagine that hasn't already happened to a presenter somewhere. Jan Haworth has had twenty years presenting, reporting and producing in radio. She is now a lecturer in broadcasting:

Always be able to think of something to say. When I was news-reading regularly I had nightmares where all the letters on the page would suddenly get up and march off in little rows like ants. I wouldn't be able to get them back and would have nothing to say. A lot of presenters have this kind of dream and lots of students do. The scariest time can be when you're out on location commentating and it's all going wrong. Like when the royal personage hasn't turned up to cut the ribbon and you're still having to keep going. Your crib sheets and colour sheets are running out. This is more important even than having a lovely voice ... being unflappable and able to ad lib. I've had to read the news during a total black out at Invicta radio. An emergency generator powered just one small light in the studio which was, of course, the one above the disc jockey! So I read by the light of my bicycle lamp. I've read with only one contact lens because the other fell out on the studio floor. A most awful time was when I had to do a twenty-minute bulletin and, with five minutes to go, the husband of my best friend phoned up to tell me that she had taken an overdose and had died. I shall never know how I read that bulletin. At the end of it, I just totally collapsed. Before you put a presenter on air you've got to know that they have the kind of temperament that can go on.

Most presenters can relate such experiences. I myself was presenting a chatty and amusing item live on Radio Four whilst I was miscarrying my first child. At the end of the programme I left for hospital and, of course, neither the production team nor the public ever knew.

A presenter is ... powerful

The somewhat fantastical and manufactured position of a presenter gives them enormous power. Power that can go to your head. Don't let it. You really can be here today and gone tomorrow. More significantly though, this power can be used unfairly against the vulnerable. I advise students to cultivate what Shakespeare terms 'the milk of human kindness'. It means having respect for all points of view and all people. You don't have to agree and you still test their arguments to destruction. It simply means that in a democracy such as ours you have to allow others the right to believe and say what they like, within the law.

When, some years ago, I was shooting one of the first films ever made about child pornography for BBC2, I had to interview a convicted pae-dophile. It is distasteful to come into close contact with someone like that but nothing will be achieved if an interviewer allows disgust or anger to colour the interview. I needed him to explain how he enticed children to do his bidding. He knew that I despised everything about his behaviour but he also knew that he would be treated fairly. Having secured the interview, the upper echelons of the BBC at the time wished to excise it claiming it was, in effect, teaching others how to become paedophiles. My argument, which won the day eventually, was that unless innocent parents knew what they were up against they could never protect their children. The outcome was that extra information and knowledge was placed in the public arena.

It goes without saying that everything you utter must be right and fair. You should understand the laws of libel (see Chapter 7) and follow your own broadcasting organization's guidelines which will cover issues regarding secret recordings, interviewing children, dealing with political bias, sponsorship, racism, sexism and so on.

Once in the business you can become inured to the impact on ordinary citizens when the cameras come to call. During a BBC2 documentary about a teenager who had died from cancer after turning, unsuccessfully, to alternative health therapies, I was given much access and help by the boy's father. Angry at health professionals, he wanted the story told. He knew the power of TV and wanted us to play the dying boy's tragic, tape-recorded diaries. However, the rest of the family also knew about the power of TV. The divorced wife and other children were worried about re-living the trauma and were frightened about the reaction from the medical profession which might even affect their own care. It took weeks of discussion to get everyone on board. In the end the programme was made. The family had their say, the medics and therapists had their say and, as usual, we the TV crew congratulated ourselves on a job well done and never met any of them again. You can't carry the weight of the world on your shoulders but it's only decent to be aware of the power you have.

A presenter is ... to blame!

Certainly, presenters are in the front line. They get all the plaudits when it goes right and all the brickbats when it goes wrong. It's tough when others lose the scripts, the autocue goes down, the researchers have got the wrong interviewee, your information is incorrect and the lighting explodes in the studio, but still you have to plough on holding the show together.

It may look as if you are to blame but, of course, broadcasting is a team effort, particularly on television, and the team won't ever work well unless the post-mortems are left until after the show and conducted with tact. If you haven't got a sense of humour and can't laugh at yourself, give it up now!

A presenter is ... a marketing tool

Once you are in front of a microphone you are a marketing tool and a financial asset reinforcing brand loyalty. Think Terry Wogan, think BBC; Chris Tarrant, ITV; Trevor McDonald, ITN; Graham Norton, Channel 4. It is no coincidence that the links are there in our minds. This is the result of hard contract negotiation by agents and broadcasters who know their image value. The Radio Academy's research into the significance of presenters on music stations (*Presenters – Who needs 'em?*) shows just how vital they are to the building and retention of an audience. Eighty-one per cent of listeners in the 15–45 age group want a presenter rather than segued

Figure 1.4
DJ Leona Graham abseiling. Presenters are called upon to do weird antics in the name of raising station profile

music. The presenter provides entertainment, humour and character – two-thirds of respondents believed that. Only 1 per cent thought they were annoying. More significantly to station chiefs was the statistic that nine out of ten people agree that presenters offer a brand identity for their station, making it distinct from rivals.

A presenter is ... thick-skinned

As a presenter, you're safe only as long as the audience wants you and the boss can afford you. Be prepared for the old heave-ho. It's a remarkably fickle world. TV and radio studios are hard-nosed business places. I have myself worked on a series for which the production standards were necessarily compromised to bring it within a very low budget limit. The production team argued that this approach would lose audience over a period of weeks and the show would eventually be axed. The management argued that it wouldn't matter since what keeps audiences high is constant change in the schedule. So by the time the public realized they didn't think much of the programme, there would already be another cheap alternative on the drawing board – complete with a new, glitzy presenter. Of course, if you do your job well, when they do feel tempted to chuck you out, your talent will already have been recognized by others. You are your own advertisement.

The presenter must also be prepared to be the 'hate figure' in the newspapers. Lis Howell has had her fair share of adverse press comment:

The press will always hate you if you're a presenter because there is a senior service attitude of the printed press – they act as if they are superior to anybody in broadcasting. So you can't get through without having a thick skin and being prepared to take criticism. You'll get it from your neighbours and friends and you'll get it from the press. It is not a comfortable life. I used to live in a block of flats in Manchester and you could bet your bottom dollar if I'd had a good night on Granada Reports *I wouldn't see anybody and if I'd had a bad night on* Granada Reports *there would be two or three people chatting in the foyer and they'd all say, 'Oh we saw you. That was awful wasn't it?' TV presenters are still seen as people who have a glamorous and easy life, so they get knocked.*

A presenter is ... a team player

This can't be emphasized enough (see Chapter 3). Simply stated: you can't get on the air without everyone else doing their bit to put you there. In any case it isn't about getting *you* on the air, it's about making a good programme. Getting on with everyone is particularly important for presenters because some of them are astonishingly self-obsessed (see the views of cameraman, Dave Jones, in Chapter 17) which gives every presenter a bad reputation. Those who can't be team players don't last. Your motto should be: never fall out with anyone. It's not just this show that counts – it's the next one they may offer you!

A presenter is ... being yourself

Most people would tell you that honesty to yourself and to your audience is a key attribute. They say you must 'be yourself' because you can't live a lie for very long – the camera, the programme format or the audience will find you out. The trouble is how do you know who you are? And if you know that, can you bear to be that person in public? Many people come into broadcasting to *avoid* being who they are. What's more, many of the top reporters and presenters I know are actually quite insecure, shy people. I would put myself in that category, except that years of strutting my stuff has allowed me to act in a confident manner. Ironically, if you want to find yourself, stop looking. Concentrate on the subject matter you are dealing with and the audience. Don't fuss about yourself and the impression you're giving.

Olenka Frenkiel has been a foreign correspondent and documentary film-maker for many years. Here's her take on the issue:

> You will always be told to relax and be yourself. That only works if 'yourself' is the persona which works on the screen. Jill Dando was like that. If 'yourself' is a slightly subversive, foul-mouthed, irreverent, cynical type (which many of us are), it will be useless unless you're really prepared to take a gamble – and then you may become late-night cult viewing with health warnings! It is more likely you will suffer a split personality syndrome, being faced with a constant supreme effort pretending to be the girl (or boy) next door. I think many presenters in news and current affairs create a TV persona for

themselves to become. As the years go by they become more and more like that persona until it eventually takes over. They think they are 'being themselves'. Actually, they have become a 'self' which is acceptable to the public and to themselves. Some never manage to reconcile the two personalities. You hear stories about presenters being sweet on screen and filthy off. There is some hilarious footage of one famous television news presenter yelling furiously at some Greenham Common women who were being silly behind her while she was trying to do a piece to camera, yet on screen, of course, she had an image of gentle kindness. Still, it all makes great out-takes!

A presenter is ... a star

... and let's face it that can be fun. Sometimes the presenter becomes a celebrity. Sometimes the celebrity becomes a presenter. Sometimes there's a bit of both. Increasingly there's pressure to seek fame to bolster your career, hence the sniping at the concept of *I'm a Celebrity – Get me out of Here*! But beware! Here's Wesley Kerr's reflection on this after two decades of presenting and reporting in news, current affairs and features:

> I was offered a thousand quid to go on Ruby Wax for a late-night chat show she was doing a few years ago. I was invited in to talk to her about the possibility. She immediately asked me all the difficult questions and quickly established I was a black, gay, foster child. You could see her casting the show. It was going to be with Julian Clary and Boy George. I suspect it would all have been about orifices and so on! But you saw that potentially it was a way to market yourself. It would be 'here are my unique selling points', not 'here am I, a good journalist'. You could advertise yourself as a sort of famous, slightly outrageous black gay who knows the Queen. Another time I was asked to pose for the cover of Gay Times. I thought then, 'Oh no, I'm not going down that celebrity route'. But I realize now that I would be more marketable today if I was involved in some tabloid scandal. The trouble is that what you have to do for a scandal is much more now than it used to be!

Despite all the pitfalls, there is glamour. You may not be a huge star in the firmament, you may be a very small one that gets only rare opportunities to twinkle in public, but still you will enjoy the kudos and fame it offers.

Figure 1.5
A presenter can be a celebrity with an audience of complete strangers across the globe. In this case, the broadcast booms out to late-night shoppers on a street corner in Hong Kong

What can match the pride of being congratulated on a report well done, an interview well executed, a sports commentary full of excitement and explanation? Few in everyday life get the open admiration of even friends and family, let alone complete strangers.

I shall never forget the evening in the *Newsnight* office when my investigation into child pornography had just been transmitted after weeks of research. It had had constant lawyering and internal viewings by heads of news, ethics, even the Director General of the BBC himself, all of them concerned at the controversial nature of the movie. When it was finally aired, intact and uncensored, we were exhausted. Then the phones started ringing. It was immediate. Viewers wanted to say how moved they were, how shocked. One woman phoned up in tears to thank us for doing it. She simply wanted to know what she could now do to protect children – not just her own but those of others too. The police asked for copies of the film so they could learn from the material. 10 Downing Street asked for copies so that the Prime Minister, Margaret Thatcher, could view it at leisure. This is the glamour. It doesn't last long and, like an iceberg, is just the dazzling pinnacle emerging from the unseen foundation. Then it's back to the grindstone but now with the knowledge that your standards have to be even higher to achieve anything more memorable the next time round.

IN SHORT...

- Being a presenter is about being a good communicator of your core skill. Make sure you've got one.
- Presenters are in the front line, being used as marketing tools. They must be tough when the going gets rough. Don't be surprised to be moved on. It's not necessarily your fault!
- Listen to the advice of others whom you respect and trust.
- Be confident but not bumptious. You can't work without a degree of self-assuredness – but nobody wants to work with a know-all.
- Be a team worker. The more you do it, the more you'll see how much you depend on everyone else.
- Be yourself – just as soon as you've worked out who that is! The simplest method is to think about the subject, the programme, the research, the audience – in short, the job in hand – and not about yourself.
- Get heaps of experience wherever you can – even if it's unpaid.

2 Your voice and how to use it

Your voice is one of the most powerful weapons you have. It is insane not to train yourself in the ways you can use it. It seems obvious that you must be able to speak well if you are embarking on a lifetime in broadcasting but, strangely, this is often overlooked. Your voice will be your unique, identifying trademark and a selling point. It will be recognized by everyone who hears you. Incredibly, people still recognize mine from my *Newsbeat* presenting days years ago.

As you compete for jobs and positions throughout your life, you will find that others may be able to achieve the same quality of presentational skills but no-one (except, perhaps, Rory Bremner and his ilk!) will be able to match your voice. Its quality may recommend you for certain positions. News voices tend to have a hard edge with an urgent quality about them; on the other hand, featurey, day-time discussion programmes require softer, more relaxed tones. Work on how to use your vocal cords and you can do both.

A GOOD VOICE

A 'good voice' is simply one that is suited to the job in hand, so the requirements will vary. Broadly, though, it must be strong and have a predominance of middle tones. Squeaky, high or 'toppy' voices are not favoured. Women can be at a particular disadvantage here, although training can lower the pitch. Voices that have peculiarities or speech defects are often frowned upon but, as always, it's a matter of degree. A lisp may be utterly irritating or quite endearing. It might hinder your chances at news reading but get you an afternoon TV chat show. Jonathan Ross has

Figure 2.1
The first female presenter of *Newsbeat* hit the airwaves twenty years ago, yet still listeners recall the voice. The power of radio! (Reproduced by permission of the BBC.)

certainly not allowed his speech quirks to stand in the way of a glittering presentation career.

Jan Haworth, radio presenter and director for the postgraduate Broadcast Journalism course at City University in London, admits she never was sure what a 'good broadcasting voice' meant:

> *The other way to think of it is, 'What's a bad microphone voice?' – which is one that bores. It's the ability to engage the listener, either*

because it's a peculiar voice or it's distinctive in some way. Warmth is a very important thing, for radio particularly. When I started at 21 I had a very squeaky voice which was fine for pop shows on Piccadilly Radio but it had to change and become more authoritative for commercial news which was trying to sound 'ballsy'. They told me I would have to work on the voice to get on. So I smoked a lot! It was recommended by fellow reporters as a way of lowering the voice. It did make my voice deeper but it damaged my breath control. I wouldn't recommend it!

The audience empathizes with and reacts to a voice, albeit unconsciously. Hearing a nasal, 'tight' voice makes the listener feel physically tense. This can be so subtle a reaction that even the person who turns you down for a position may not be able to put a finger on what it is he or she isn't quite happy with.

Remember too that, like an actor, you must be prepared to alter your voice to suit not only the occasion but also the audience. My career has benefited tremendously from being able to read fast, highly projected, energetic scripts for 1FM and moments later change to the more measured and calmer renditions required by Radio Four or the World Service.

ACCENTS

The days are long gone when a presenter's aim was 'BBC pronunciation' which was regarded as 'the Queen's English'. If we want to be honest, our sovereign has a positively appalling broadcasting voice. It is tight, affected, wooden, self-conscious, lacking in inflection and emotion, and most important of all, utterly without authority. If you avoid all of these pitfalls, you'll be OK!

Received pronunciation today is simply the accent that can be most easily understood by English speakers throughout the world – which is a very flexible concept. The limit must be that any accent that interferes with intelligibility is unacceptable.

The man whose job it is to find the right voices for BBC Radio Four is the much revered Chief Announcer, Peter Donaldson. It clearly can't be just anyone who presents the 'bits in between'. These junctions give the network its image. However, despite the fact that he himself is thoroughly 'RP', it is clear that attitudes have changed even in this well-defended bastion:

> *Speaking 'the Queen's English' is no longer required. You only have to listen/watch to realize that. As long as your accent isn't too broad, it shouldn't hold you back, even if you can't roll your 'Rs' or speak with some other slight impediment. Obviously, it depends to some extent whether you want to broadcast locally or nationally. It's quite simple really: you need to be easily understood by your audience, otherwise you will create a barrier and their attention will wander.*

Independent TV producer, Paul Freeman, who's had many years of experience directing presenters for lifestyle shows, says, somewhat radically:

> *Look cute or zany/bizarre (either will do) and develop or acquire a regional accent. Adopt a style that sets you apart from the rest. TV*

Figure 2.2
BBC Chief Announcer, Peter Donaldson, has become the 'voice of Radio Four' and the trainer many anxious presenters have come to rely on to improve their delivery

is looking for larger than life characters. Much of it is to do with fashion but regional accents seem currently to be all the rage. Just listen to Radio Five Live – full of Scots, Liverpudlians, Brummies, Mancunians – all actively encouraged to flaunt their regionality.

Fashion is certainly involved. The Lowland Scots accent is perceived as trustworthy. The accent least associated with success is West Country. Bristolian, Norfolk and Suffolk accents are not regarded as authoritative.

So, if you're blessed (or is it cursed?) with an accent, should you change it? In her early days at Piccadilly Radio, Jan Haworth witnessed the voice transformation of one now famous network radio presenter:

I listened to people who I admired. One of them was Winifred Robinson, who was working at Radio City in Liverpool and used to hang out with us. Winifred has a completely different on-air voice from her social conversational voice. Twenty years ago she had an extremely thick Liverpool accent and as soon as the mic went on she changed it completely and it was almost the Queen's English! We used to take the piss out of her mercilessly whilst secretly doing it ourselves! But as well as this positive role model, there was a warning role model. Another female reporter, who had fantastic news sense, always got great exclusive stories and had marvellous contacts, was not wanted on air because of a nasal, heavily accented voice. The bosses always got me to voice her stuff. It was a warning to get my voice right. Now she's a high-ranking BBC editor but doesn't appear in front of the mic.

Winifred Robinson, radio presenter on *Today* and *You and Yours*, admits that she did once have a Liverpool accent 'that you could cut with a knife'. Her father was a docker and she grew up on a council estate. The change came when she did elocution as part of her regular English lessons at school and thus understood how to achieve 'received pronunciation'. So when, in her first job at Red Rose Radio in Lancashire, an executive warned her that if she didn't 'get rid of that accent you'll never work outside of the north west region', she began to do just that:

I did set about getting rid of it ... well, really, more to soften it. I'm not very proud of that. I think it should be possible to have a thick Scouse accent 'cos, let's face it, it's only associated with class. When

I was presenting the Today *programme I got a letter from a bloke who said, 'Do you realize your accent is an affront to educated people everywhere?' That's because I have kept my way of saying 'bath' not 'baahth'. I haven't done the total Home Counties makeover. I describe my accent now as 'posh northern' but even so it causes such comment! Someone said to me that you can't have a real voice and a radio voice because when you're under pressure, covering a big story or you're in danger, you'll revert to your natural accent. So you have to speak with one voice or it's pointless. Now, though, the reverse is true. My northern accent is valued. It's a huge asset. I received a very insulting letter which said, 'If you weren't a Scouse woman you wouldn't get a sniff of the* Today *programme.' And I thought, 'Yes, quite true. How right you are ... mate!'*

THE POWER OF THE VOICE

Your voice is the ultimate power tool to *drive* a script and hold the audience, particularly in radio. Presenter and reporter, Jenni Mills, is also the professional broadcasting voice coach behind many of the most famous voices you hear:

In radio the listener only gets one chance at grasping what you're saying – they have no visual clues to help them and they can't go back and read the words again. So clear speech and intelligent intonation (what a lot of broadcasters refer to as 'getting the emphasis right') is key. It's also important in television, of course, particularly when the presenter is out-of-vision, but in radio it is everything – your voice does all the work and it is what will engage or alienate the audience.

Your voice also has the power to *control* a broadcasting situation, just as shouting makes others shout back. I once made a very contentious investigative film for *Newsnight* on BBC2 about the treatment of animals used for experimentation in the UK. One of the key interviews was with the Head of the Medical Research Council which had put a great deal of money into work being carried out by a hitherto internationally respected award-winning scientist. We had got secret footage of this same man, at the MRC's headquarters, using poor laboratory techniques and outdated anaesthetics on rabbits which were squealing and kicking during operating procedures. The interview was clearly going to be crucial. My interviewee was, to say the least of it, reluctant. I knew that the slightest edge in my voice, the tiniest ill-considered hint of aggression, would have him walking out. I shall always remember the effort and concentration I put into controlling the tone and level of my voice on that day. The more he attempted to evade the questions, the more I was bound to repeat them but, oh so carefully, so that they came out as persistent but not harrying, as inquiring but not judgemental. The interchange lasted about fifteen minutes and on a number of occasions I was aware that having to insist on an answer was pushing him frighteningly close to wrenching off his microphone and leaving. Empty-chairing is the worst of all outcomes. No information is given: one-half of the story is lost. Never had I felt so surely that it was that secret weapon, the voice, that had the power to hold this man in his chair *and* it allowed us to be civil to each other when it was all over.

This power is also about pace. Don't jump in too fast or too loudly (unless it's part of your strategy). You may think you are simply being 'energetic' but you can appear aggressive. This will make interviewees frightened, hostile or suspicious and they may clam up altogether. Worse still, the same effect may be visited upon the listeners and you will lose *their* support too.

VOICE TRAINING

This is a controversial area, not least because of the price. Professional voice coaches can charge £100 an hour. There are many who say, like presenter Jonathan Hewat, former Head of Radio at the University of the West of England, 'Don't take elocution lessons. You either have a suitable voice or you haven't.' It's true that many top presenters I know have never done any voice training. Neither have I – even after I was told at the age of 21, by a radio station manager, that my voice was so bad he didn't want me on air! I assumed that he was indulging a purely personal view or being vindictive, or both, and ignored him. No-one else ever made such a comment and my voice has been my living for 25 years. However, my belief today is that whilst professional training can't cure the *truly* unbroadcastable, it may deliver amazing solutions to a wide range of problems, some of which the presenter is unaware of. City University's Jan Haworth takes a similar stance:

> *If you've got a good voice, then you've got a good voice and you won't need any training. That's definitely true. But we get a lot of*

students who've not achieved their full voice because they haven't practised enough. They haven't listened enough and they don't care enough about what they're saying. You need warmth and that comes from caring about what you're saying ... from having worked on the story from beginning to end, from being interested. The voice training we do on the postgraduate diploma in broadcast journalism aims to make the best of the voice that you've got – not change the accent or the pitch or the basic characteristics. It's organically linked with news writing. Students must write so that they can

Figure 2.3
Jan Haworth, course director of the postgraduate diploma in broadcast journalism at City University in London. She believes strongly in the value of voice training

perform at their best. If they've got any self-consciousness about a lisp or a dialect or dyslexia which hampers their oral fluency, we send them off for special coaching. Under the new Disability Discrimination Act it's illegal to reject an applicant to a broadcasting course because of a vocal impediment. Legally speaking there is nothing now that should stop you from being able to present... but of course this is showbiz. Somebody can always say, 'Yes you've got a lisp but I prefer the voice without the lisp... and I'm the boss!'

After a lifetime of reporting and doing regional TV presenting, Winifred Robinson found herself, four years ago, presenting national radio and felt she needed help to improve her delivery. She had a series of sessions with Jenni Mills and came out of them convinced of the benefits:

I wanted to improve the range and pitch of my voice. Training was hugely helpful. You get set in your ways. I was doing that dramatic pause that you hear all the time: 'The news is read by [dramatic pause!] Peter Donaldson.' There's no reason to pause there. Training can help you get rid of all those ticks you get into.

RELAXING

To speak well and confidently you must be in control and calm. Jenni Mills' advice is this:

I'd say the most important thing to do is relax – mentally AND physically. It's harder said than done. Even now I sometimes catch myself leaning forward with my muscles in knots! But once you understand the tricks of using your body to help your voice and your mind-set, you can sound amazingly confident even when you're tired, terrified or under pressure. I always recommend three deep breaths before you go on air, really filling your lungs and emptying them again. It relaxes you and wakes your body up.

Try relaxation exercises too. They can be done quite swiftly and unobtrusively on your way to the studio, in the toilet or even in the studio itself, so factor them into your routine.

Here are a few suggestions for keeping calm and improving the voice quality:

- Put the tips of your fingers onto your shoulders and draw really big circles with your elbows so that they reach up high on either side of you and come together and touch in front of you. Do this forwards and then backwards.
- Relax your arms and attempt to push your shoulders down really hard. Then, with your arms still relaxed, push your shoulders up as if you were trying to touch your ears.
- Turn your head to the left and look as far as you can over your left shoulder. Do little pulling movements at the most extreme point. Then gently turn your head the other way and do the same towards the right.
- Now, tip your head upwards and look above and back as far as you can. Then lower your head until your chin touches your chest.
- After you've completed the cycle jiggle your shoulders up and down and nod your head as if settling everything back into position.

These procedures can be done as quickly or slowly as you like. Just remember that if you don't allow time for them, the exercises themselves will *add* to anxiety levels.

BREATHING

Correctly controlled breathing is absolutely key both before you go on air, to relax the vocal cords and, while the transmission continues, to ensure you read intelligibly.

You must use your diaphragm and your lungs. Frightened, shallow breaths won't do. They don't allow the big injections of oxygen you need. Really opening the throat and lungs helps to give the voice a much deeper, more resonant quality. This is especially relevant to women. When the BBC first used female announcers there was quite a reaction against it. Their voices were said to be too high and painful to listen to! Fortunately, the BBC forged ahead regardless. However, the fact remains that women's voices do tend to be more highly pitched and when passions rise, they can be squeaky. They sound more authoritative if they are 'relaxed down' a few tones.

I once had to read the news into a John Peel show on Radio One without a breath in my body. The subs were late finishing the copy. Newsreaders are warned never to use lifts in case they get stuck in them. So a breakneck sprint down about ten flights was the only answer. I flung myself into position as the jingle started. I had to read a three-minute summary. I swiftly changed the running order so that the first news story also had a tape, allowing me a valuable 30 seconds during which I had to force myself not to pant which would have resulted in a coughing fit. You have to *insist* that your body calms down and control your air intake. I muddled through. I've heard worse. One newsreader in similar circumstances actually gave up all together. The anchor had to take over again until the news presenter could speak!

POSTURE

Make sure you are sitting comfortably. You can't present with your legs crossed or hunched up. Your spine should be erect and your shoulders

Figure 2.4
Good posture and relaxed shoulders help voice quality

back, allowing plenty of air space for the lungs. Your voice will sound richer and you will feel more in control.

Some American newsreaders have experimented with standing up and even walking around radio news studios to deliver the news. Rod McKenzie, now 1FMs Editor of News, did just this when on *Newsbeat* many years ago. It elicits a greater sense of drama and immediacy. Unfortunately, it also leaves you nowhere to put your script pages and requires headset microphones if it's to be at all practical. Perched on the edge of a desk, as on Channel 5, would seem a possible half-way house that can work on TV, thanks to radio mics and autocues!

PROJECTING

In layman's terms, the art is to 'speak up' but not shout. At the same time, you must sound natural. Actors talk about 'stage whispers'. You can, in fact, appear to be whispering whilst speaking loudly enough to reach to the back of an auditorium. Similarly, you can appear to be bellowing whilst not actually raising your voice very much. Newsreaders do not shout yet they command your attention. Projecting successfully comes

Figure 2.5
1FM's Georgina Bowman must project her voice strongly to match the fast-paced pop output

with the coalescence of all the other vocal features, i.e. relaxation, controlled breathing, good diction, posture and understanding.

The amount you project must depend on the outlet that you are serving. In a commercial music setting where ads abound, you will find yourself projecting more to match your surroundings. Sound engineers will add to the effect by using compression on the output to 'squeeze' the voice and make it sound 'tighter' and punchier.

DICTION

Do not be embarrassed to use your mouth to shape words. Make your lips frame the syllables accurately and don't rush. Speak out strongly and clearly. Here's an experiment. Get a tape recorder and say into it, 'Edinburgh area'. Listen back. Did it sound like 'Edinbererarier'? If so, it's high time that you improved your clarity.

I had a mature student who appeared lively and confident but was inclined to mutter the ends of sentences through a half-closed mouth. Off air, he frequently spoke with a hand across his mouth. It turned out that he had always hated his 'weak jaw line' and wanted to hide it. He'd grown a beard and moustache as soon as he could. Now his speech reflected that insecurity. Of course, this is not to say that beards and moustaches are unacceptable in broadcasting (except, it seems, amongst some TV folk in the extraordinary tale related by presenter Nigel Roberts in Chapter 13!).

Remember too that for the purposes of TV, the audience relies to a surprising degree on lip-reading. This lesson was brought home to me when, as a news reporter on Radio One, I used to record *Newsnight* so that I could edit out clips for news summaries. I was astonished when, having cut the sound bites, I discovered they were, on occasions, barely comprehensible. The reason was simply that, in general, TV pays far less attention to the importance of sound and once you've removed the speaker from view it's hard to catch the words, particularly if there is insistent background noise like traffic or crowds.

PACE

Pacing your speech is a vital part of being able to read comprehensibly. If you rush the meaning will be lost. Even worse, you'll swallow final syllables.

You can give the impression of speaking at a normal pace even although you are hurrying or slowing up. Maybe the sub-editor beside you is writing a new line to the story you are reading live. You need to play for time, so you simply use bundles of emphasis and carefully chosen breaths and pauses. Similarly you can lose seconds from a script without appearing to, using emphasis.

The normal formula is that you speak at three words per second. If you want to know how long it will take to present that last paragraph out loud, I can tell you that it is 69 words – which means it will take about 23 seconds. I can read the same paragraph in only 18 seconds and still make it comprehensible. I drop certain pauses but make others more emphatic. I say 'you're' instead of 'you are', 'and' instead of 'similarly'. I can lengthen it to about 32 seconds by adding pauses, reading slightly more slowly and adding 'and' or altering the phrase to 'What you need to do is ...' just before the words, 'play for time'.

EMPHASIS AND INTONATION

Your voice must go up and down as it interprets a script or addresses an interviewee. It's an acting technique. Imagine a Paxman interview without that smiling face, the body flung back in the chair and the voice expostulating with incredulity, 'This is utter nonsense, isn't it? You always knew this policy would never work!' It stings the interviewee into a swift response, which may be defensive or attacking, but will, in either case, be ear-catching for the audience. The ploy may backfire with the interviewee becoming aggressive and unhelpful but the point is that a good presenter is not simply relaying questions. The presenter is also considering *how to use the voice* to achieve the required end.

When reading a script, don't be formulaic. It's particularly noticeable with novice news or sports presenters. One student of mine lay down a film commentary emphasizing every fifth word. It sounded awful – and meaningless. When I asked why he was reading like this, he said he'd heard sports reporters doing it on the radio. And, sadly, he was right. Many do. But it detracts from the meaning. Always think about the meaning of the script – you can't read what you don't understand. Broadcaster, Jan Haworth, had this impressed on her by a voice coach even though she'd been presenting for years:

> *I had some fantastic voice training when I was news editor at Invicta Radio in Kent. It was basically a lot of ego-stroking, quite a lot of*

Figure 2.6
You can hear a smile! LBC presenter Sandy Warr

*'pastoral care'; 'How are you feeling today? Let's see how that
makes your voice sound.' She'd bring a recording from last time so
that you could hear for yourself. She taught me a lot about how your
emotions get suppressed and then, when you go live, your voice can
suddenly behave in a certain way due to the pent-up strain or pressure. She used to make you lie down on the floor or lean against the
studio wall so there was nothing blocking your breathing and your
throat wasn't constricted. You'd have to think where the breathing
was coming from. There was a lot of physical and emotional stuff as
well. She gave us permission to be a performer without going over
the top. I'd done loads of amateur acting but never connected it with
broadcast journalism. You'd have to read news stories. If it was a fire
she'd say, 'Smell the smoke. Someone is in that building.' You can feel
the tension rise in your head and you're thinking about what each
word actually means, for example what it means to the fire fighter.
That kind of total immersion in your story is vital, especially if you're
doing two-minute headlines with five stories, all completely different*

*and ending on a light-hearted note with a bit of sexual innuendo and
banter with the DJ. It takes a lot of doing, actually. In some ways it's
much more difficult than presenting an hour-long show. I think she
produced the best voice I ever had.*

EXERCISES

1. When did you last do the nursery-rhyme tongue twisters? Do them
   now. The challenge is to speak the ditties fluently, without stumbling,
   not to see how fast you can do it. Speak them meaningfully and
   with emphasis and you will find them much easier to perform. Try
   reading 'Peter Piper' as if it was the top story in the bulletin:
   - Peter Piper picked a peck of pickled pepper. If Peter Piper picked a
     peck of pickled pepper, where's the peck of pickled pepper Peter
     Piper picked?
   - Round the ragged rocks, the ragged rascal ran.
   - Red leather, yellow leather.
   - She sells seashells on the sea shore. The shells that she sells are
     seashells, I'm sure.
2. Try reading the following news story in as flat a way as possible,
   removing all inflexions:

   *House prices in the UK are soaring despite fears that a property
   crash is on the way. According to the Nationwide Building society,
   the cost of the average property rose by nearly 4 per cent in April.
   It's the biggest monthly increase in ten years. The figures mean that
   homeowners have seen the value of their property improve by a
   massive 90 per cent since 1996.*

   - Now mark up the most important words in the story and read it
     again. Be careful to consider where you will need to breathe to read
     smoothly.
   - Try reading it while smiling and notice how different it sounds (and,
     of course, in the case of this story, how inappropriate). If you want
     your voice to sound warm and friendly, you literally have to feel that
     way. If you smile the audience can hear it.
   - Finally, try reading it at different levels to improve your projection.
     Read it too softly, then too loudly. Record some instrumental pop

music and play it back to yourself in headphones. Talk above it but without shouting. The music beat will force you to project more.

3. Record this news bulletin and listen back to the result:

Britain's highways are cracking up and drivers face an eight-year delay before local roads can be restored to adequate condition. A study by the Institute of Civil Engineers claims that cracks and potholes are worse than ever and £7 billion needs to be spent to rectify the damage. The Department of Transport has admitted that it is 'concerned'.

Scientists at Tohoku University in Japan say that the use of mobile phones on trains could damage your health. Experiments show that radiation bounces around the carriage and can exceed safety limits. In a standard carriage with 151 people, if 30 or more use their cell phones at the same time exposure to radiation can be unacceptable. It's claimed that the same problem can arise on buses and in some lifts.

The first official report into Britain's urban parks in half a century has called for a 5 hundred million pound cash injection to revive them. The Government's 'green spaces task force' says parents are increasingly turning to indoor play areas and paying for leisure centres which creates a two-tier leisure culture for the haves and the have-nots. They believe that people won't use parks for fear of crime, vandalism and antisocial behaviour.

Young people in Britain ARE patriotic and that's official! A survey of 20- to 30-year-olds, conducted for a marketing consultancy, shows that traditional symbols of Britishness are more popular than the 'cool Britannia' ideas promoted by the Blair Government. It seems that national pride is still inspired by the Royal Family, Buckingham Palace, the Union flag and Marks and Spencer... and three-quarters of those asked said they were proud to be British.

- Do it in different styles – first for Radio Four and then for a commercial pop station. Think 'relaxed' and 'in control' while reading – even for the high-energy version. It should give your voice a more authoritative quality.

- Read the bulletin as fast as you can and as slowly as you can. How many seconds difference is there?

IN SHORT...

- Your voice is vital. Listen to it.
- The clues to a strong, reliable on-air voice are confidence, breathing and posture, relaxation, diction and projection.
- Do everything possible to become mentally calm e.g. get your script early and read it through. Check for difficult pronunciations. Get to the studio/location early.
- Do breathing and relaxation exercises before going on air.
- Project but don't shout.
- Concentrate on clarity and don't worry about accent or dialect.

3 How to look and how to act

As a presenter, appearances, in every sense of the word, are all. Primarily, of course, you are trying to do a good job of work but at the same time you are selling your own capabilities to your audience, your interviewees, fellow workers, your employers and, last but by no means least, you are trying to convince yourself that you can do it so that you build up your own confidence. What you look like and how you conduct yourself are fundamental issues.

DRESSING FOR RADIO

Some will say it doesn't matter how you look on radio. This is baloney!

How you look affects how you sound and sound is more crucial here than anywhere. You will find that being smart makes you feel more confident and that enables you to speak better and to liaise with your team with more authority.

The chances are that you will be meeting guests and interviewees. You need to look good for them. They may interpret a dishevelled or tatty appearance as being amateurish and inexperienced. They can't perform well if they doubt your ability. It will make them feel nervous.

What's more, you may be on the airwaves but the advent of web cams can mean that your image is being digitally beamed around the world.

Your choice of clothes must be suitable. You do not turn up to 1Xtra or Power FM wearing a twinset and pearls! Conversely, there is a difference between being casual and being unkempt.

Like it or not, bosses are impressed by dress. Your attire says a lot about you. Remember, too, that many presenters start out in radio but may move to TV. The people who count i.e. those who hand out contracts, may be around you every day. Don't leave it to their lack-lustre imaginations to picture you on screen – give them a daily preview. You must be your own shop window.

In studios, I always find jackets useful because they have pockets and allow you to carry notes, pencils, discs etc. without being in danger of losing them.

Don't put on heaps of jangly jewellery; the noise will be picked up by the microphone. When I interviewed the pop band Third World some years ago, I had to ask both the men and the women to remove tons of bangles

Figure 3.1
Appropriate dress may mean a hard hat! An earpiece for the producer to monitor sound is vital because of the background noise

before doing the interview. They were piled up in the middle of the table as if we'd just robbed a jeweller's but at least there was no clattering! Rings can also cause unpleasant clicking noises when you hold the metal stem of a microphone.

If you are out on location, use your commonsense to choose the appropriate clothes. Raincoats in the rain, umbrellas if necessary, light clothes in summer. Have pockets. Comfortable shoes are a must. Don't be seduced into wearing winkle-pickers or high heels if you are about to tramp about streets all day talking to the public or if you are going to interview a hill farmer on a Scottish mountainside.

DRESSING FOR TV

On TV it's even more important to have clothes appropriate to the occasion but they must also be of good quality. If jeans are genuinely what you need to wear e.g. for a youth programme or for out and about location shooting, just make sure they are well fitting and flattering. There are smart denims and scruffy ones. If you need to look casual, it must be smart casual. You may not be in the habit of wearing suits but get used to it, you could get through a lot of them from now on.

Lis Howell puts appearance as one of her top tips for presenters. In fact, she inspired a storm of outrage in the tabloid newspapers when, as Director of Programmes for the emerging GMTV, she talked about presenters for the station having to have the 'fanciability factor'. She became known as the 'F factor' woman. In truth, her comments were an extremely toned-down version of conclusions from an American group of marketers. They had studies to show that audience figures were higher if presenters had, as they crudely termed it, the 'F—ability factor':

> *Some people don't make it because they can't or don't want to communicate in the way necessary and some don't make it because they look wrong. This is where I got into such trouble about the F factor. Because it was all about appearances. I've got a cupboard full of cuttings from the press who thought this was terrible. They said, 'Fancy saying somebody's looks matter on TV!' But they do! It doesn't matter that they're ugly. But they've got to look well turned out. They've got to look confident and they've got to look accessible ... approachable. Of course there are exceptions. The*

astrologer Patrick Moore, for example, perhaps, defies the rule! But
for 90 per cent of ordinary jobbing presenters and reporters they've
got to look presentable. They've got to look the sort of person that
if you had to travel to Carlisle in a train with them for five hours
you wouldn't think, 'Oh My God, who is this?'

The right look at the right time

Your look must always be suitable for the show, the company image, the
location and your own comfort. Clearly, there is a difference between
being on the road and being in the studio – not least because the chances
are that away from the set there will be no make-up person to help.
Presenter Kirsty Lang admits she was surprised at how much she had to
smarten up when, after years of reporting on the road, she started studio
work (see Chapter 8).

Andrew Bailey, now Head of News on Virgin Radio, broke into presentation after doing a postgraduate broadcast journalism course. He'd done the
usual unpaid dogsbody stint at Radio City in Liverpool and had
the normal student cash shortages. But, unbeknownst to him, his determination to make a good impression, even for such a short spell, was to
prove key:

Eventually I got my first proper job at Radio City and funnily
enough, I discovered that they remembered me because I wore a
suit every day of my work experience. So there's no doubt – the
small things matter.

Some programmes have specific demands. One daytime, live, network
show used to specify no jackets, no ties and shirtsleeves only. They also
demanded colours rather than white. This was because they were attempting to achieve a certain 'branding' for the programme and everyone on it.
Interviewers and interviewees alike had to be part of the image. The BBC
has recently decided to opt for a similar approach in their political coverage in the hope that it will be more accessible to the viewers. Incidentally,
if shirts or blouses without jackets are the order of the day, make sure you
have a good deodorant. Lights are very hot and nerves can make sweating
a real problem. Also don't wear plain white – it glares in the lights and
looks ugly.

Suits

For news work, suits are usually best for both men and women. They look efficient and convey authority. Make sure the suit is roomy so that the jacket doesn't pull across your back and make you feel uncomfortable when you are stretching to put on microphones or gesticulating on air. You would not normally do up the buttons but if you do, make sure the fabric doesn't stretch in creases across your chest. Choose material that hangs well and doesn't crush – so linen's out. It looks awful unless you never move. Your lapel microphone may well be pinned to the jacket so fabric with body is important – fine silk will be dragged down in an untidy way. Choose clothes that can withstand the necessary pins and clips used to fix pieces of equipment to you.

Jackets are also useful because they hide the cables of earpieces and microphones. Those all-important jacket or trouser pockets can be used to carry a battery pack for a radio microphone. A belt is useful for this too. If you're likely to be doing this kind of work carry one with you.

If you're outdoors remember you may have to wear a coat in vision. Often, you can jump in front of the camera, say your piece and then wrap up warm again out of sight. But not always. The traditional hack-mac, the beige, belted thing with a turn-up collar, can look rather tacky unless it's a really good one. Worse still, these are usually in off-white colours that show every spot of dirt. This is very impractical for a presenter on the road in all winds and weathers. Have a coat that is going to do what a coat should do i.e. protect you from the weather – not just look fancy. It should be hardwearing and, once again, it must have pockets.

Colours and patterns

Television cameras are much more forgiving than in the early days when it comes to colour. Once, you would have been advised not to wear red because it would 'bleed' on the screen which meant that the outline of the garment looked frizzy. With video this is not now the case. However, solid blocks of colour can be distracting or fierce. Be colourful, if you like, but think how the clothes will look when placed in the studio. Sets are built with colour and commercial branding uppermost in a designer's mind. When you sit in such a set you do not want to clash and ruin it.

Don't wear checks, houndstooth or narrow stripes. All of these will 'vibrate' on film. Pure white in blocks, like a shirt with no jacket or tie, reflects too much light and is blinding. Large expanses of black absorb so much light that detail is lost and it looks like a big blob. Charcoal grey is a good alternative to black.

Studios, particularly for news programmes, use equipment that projects pictures onto a coloured screen behind the newsreader. The picture, usually over the right or left shoulder of a newsreader, can't be seen in the studio. The same is true of weather maps where the forecaster sees nothing but a blank screen. The technology has different names but colour separation overlay (CSO) is one recognized term. The background colour onto which the projection is done is different from one place to another but is often blue. If you are sitting close to a CSO and there is a danger that you might stray into its path you would be well advised not to wear blue since you might find bits of film projected onto your arm. Not that you would be aware of that yourself although the viewers at home would certainly know about it. It has been known for errant footage to wander up a presenter's blue tie!

Accessories

Jewellery in moderation is fine but make sure it's not too glittery and distracting. Things that bobble about, like very long earrings, can be a nuisance. They might also interfere with an earpiece. Bracelets and bangles should be carefully vetted to make sure they aren't going to jingle. They can also be uncomfortable if you are having to hold news copy on a desk in front of you with your wrists resting on the table.

At some times of the year and in some countries it is *de rigeur* to wear certain extras e.g. poppies for Remembrance Day. This usually means you should wear a poppy for an unspecified period beforehand and should stop wearing it as soon as the day itself has passed. If you are recording something that will be transmitted at that time it may be sensible to get a poppy to wear. By contrast, do not start recording an item at the beginning of November in which you are wearing your poppy when the item won't go out until January!

Hats don't look good for reporters on TV. If it's raining have an umbrella and make it a large one. You want to protect, at the very least, your whole torso from the wet so that you won't look like a drowned rat on camera. There are times when there will be enough pairs of hands for someone else to hold it high for you so that it is not visible whilst you do your piece to camera. Nobody need ever know it's raining. On the other hand you may have to hold it yourself and the brolly will be in shot, so get one that is unobtrusive and has no advertising on it, unless, of course, it's the logo of the company you are broadcasting for. Make sure it's got the kind of handle that you can easily clutch whilst brandishing the leaked Ministerial report in the other!

Hairstyles

Get a good haircut and keep it cut regularly. One student I taught appeared on TV to read the news with a strange zig-zag centre parting. When I suggested it should be tidied up, she told me it was supposed to look like that! Maybe, but if it looks a mess on television, change it.

Don't have your hair in your eyes or a style that allows it to flop across your face whenever you do a piece to camera. If it's very short around the ears, you'll have nothing to hide that all-important earpiece. A clever pair of hands can do a good job of concealing the wire but hair can be useful.

Coloured hair, by which I mean green streaks or purple plaits, can look zappy in certain situations but it's unlikely to go down well with mainstream network news organizations. Foreign broadcasters tend to be even more conventional than those in the United Kingdom. Another of my students who was particularly talented, with a refreshingly alternative view of life, sported bright green dreadlocks as a fashion statement. My advice was that if he wanted to get into news and current affairs he would be lucky if he found an editor who wouldn't tell him to do something else with his hair, pronto. He'd be limited to working behind the scenes. In a news environment particularly, the important thing is not you but the information you're relaying. You shouldn't distract from it. My student went back to nature. He returned to his real hair colour and cut it startlingly short. Another fashion statement perhaps, but, by the end of the year he was in the news room at Channel 4.

Short hair was the best decision I ever made as a woman in TV. I never have to fuss about tying it up or worry about wisps blowing in my face. It's quick to wash and dry for those early morning starts and there's no need to take hair tongs, slides and grips with you!

Hands

Manicure your nails…and that means you too, chaps! If you've been biting them since childhood now is the time to break the addiction. You will be doing close-ups where you're demonstrating how gadgets work or you'll be pointing to charts or holding someone's hand in big close-up. What's more, every person who meets you sees you as a representative of your broadcasting company. You are a person belonging to that privileged club of people who are 'on the telly'. You are expected to look professional. What do *you* think about a person whose nails are bitten to the quick? The details count.

Carry spares

Sometimes circumstances contrive to disrupt the best of plans, so having a fall-back arrangement can get you out of a pickle.

I arrived at the studios once expecting to be safely under the lights indoors, only to be sent out on location to a pig farm. I had to do a piece to camera standing in a pigpen wearing a silky, printed dress. As I crouched (carefully!) down and spoke cheerfully to the camera, I was aware of a number of piglets munching happily on the skirt.

Take a change of clothes in the car. A pair of Wellington boots is handy. You never know when you might be expected to report from the burnt-out wreckage of a building, the flooded banks of a river or the top of a rubbish tip.

If everything goes pear-shaped you may even need a complete change of clothes. I once had to do a piece to camera while holding in my arms a fully grown, somewhat disgruntled peacock. I was warned that whatever happened I should on no account (a) let the peacock go because they fly brilliantly if they haven't had their wings clipped and (b) allow this bird to evacuate its bowels over me since peacock poo is incredibly foul smelling (excuse the pun) and almost impossible to remove. This last is, of course, not an issue you can control, particularly if you are holding the peacock closely to your bosom so that the camera shot will include the two of you in close-up! The inevitable happened and I stank to high heaven for the rest of the day despite much scrubbing and heaps of perfume.

Make-up

Make-up is an essential ingredient for TV studio presenters ... but, surprisingly, not perhaps as much as you might imagine particularly if you're a man. Nigel Roberts presents on CNBC from London:

> *Chaps shouldn't panic about make-up. It takes only a couple of minutes and it's only done because there are so many lights that you end up looking very pale. There's also a lot of blue in the set so you need to be darkened up a bit. At CNBC in London we don't use much. In the US they have a proper make-up artist.*

If you have coloured skin it might be worth your while taking a little more interest in the technicalities. Black presenter Wesley Kerr has:

> *I've never worn foundation on air. Just some Clinique powder which I take around with me when I'm on the road. Even make-up do very little with me in the studio. Again, just powder. When there weren't many brown people in studios, we were lit rather badly. So I think you should have knowledge of backlighting etc. The trouble is, the piece to camera is usually the last thing that's done, so it's hurried. I know one black reporter who has a darker skin than me and he had a reflector issued by news which he carried round with him, otherwise he'd look like those pictures you see in Third World newspapers of African statesmen where you can barely see them!*

For female anchors make-up can take half an hour or more. You can usually choose when to go so don't do it just before you go into the studio because you should be thinking about the programme. On the other hand if your session is too early the make-up and hair will be ruined before you get in front of a camera. You can take your scripts into make-up with you and revise as you sit there. Often make-up is done a couple of hours before the programme and you pop back again to have it refreshed just before the show.

When you're on the road make-up is usually up to you – unless it's a big production. It's tempting to skimp on it because there is so much else to do and also because you may feel embarrassed to be putting on lipstick or foundation while the camera operator taps a foot waiting for you. Don't cut corners. It may seem vain but it is an essential part of today's television. You clearly do not want to look like a catwalk model if you're in a war zone but looking in control will raise your profile.

HOW TO ACT

How you act when you are literally on air is covered throughout this book. But there is an important aspect of performance that applies to broadcasters when they are not on air. This is team-working. It affects both radio and TV, although it is even more crucial in the latter. I talk about it to students but they seldom understand the concept until they've actually made programmes. Then they are amazed at its significance. Some will never have the temperament to achieve it and may leave the profession altogether. Others will spend their career trying to get it right.

Team-working

Being a team player is one of those indefinable qualities, the parameters of which can hardly be overestimated. It pervades everything you do from the moment you begin a project.

It involves doing your damnedest to get on with everyone. It means accepting orders, sometimes without question. Post mortems come AFTER the show, not during it. As the front person, it's vital that you know, and show that you know, that you are only in the hot seat because other people have put you there. Wesley Kerr presents and reports for BBC factual programmes. He has spent years in news, current affairs and features in TV and radio. He's unequivocal:

> *It's all teamwork. Never think you're special because you are fronting the thing. Be nice and patient to everyone. Help carry the gear, get the tea … anything. You need them to help you look good!*

An appreciation of the nature of everyone else's job will help. Brush up your diplomacy skills and learn how to bite your tongue. Take time to consider every angle of what is going on before you jump in and start throwing your weight around. It is particularly important for presenters to be good at this aspect of the job. People are all too ready to paint the front person as selfish and thoughtless if things go wrong. Too many presenters we have known and loved are actually a nightmare to work with and don't make any attempt to meld with the team. One very famous front man was recently making a movie where he simply turned up on location, did what was required and left without lending a hand or putting in anything like a full day's work. He was travelling first class and eating like a lord while

Figure 3.2
A director has to muck in – here, holding a cumbersome monitor for the cameraman and wearing
a heavy belt for extra power

the crew had to travel on long-haul flights in economy and scrimp at every turn so that they didn't blow the budget. His manner was offhand and sometimes insulting. He got away with it because he was the name, what is often euphemistically termed 'the talent'. This is not a talent I would care to have working on any project. It caused tremendous bad feeling during shooting which was scheduled for a whole month. By the end of that time everyone was at each other's throats and the whole film was badly affected. Such presenters may be able to continue to trade on their fame but be sure their sins will find them out eventually!

Try to involve yourself in the whole programme-making process without getting so close that you are actually interfering. Get into this habit right from the start. Such a policy has the advantage of allowing you to learn everyone else's job as you go along. This is a vital element of team-working.

When I first started reporting for television I used to get immensely frustrated at spotting shots that would be great for the film yet which the cameraman never appeared to see. He was always looking the other way or taking another shot. I thought the person behind the lens was just not *thinking* about the story or didn't understand it. I would stand about gritting my teeth but smiling while getting totally stressed out inside. After a while I began to see the truth and then thanked my lucky stars that I had never had a stand-up row about any of the pictures *I* wanted not getting in the can. Here are some of the things I learned about dealing with everyone else's pressure.

First, did you (or your producer/director) explain to your camera operator at the start not only what the story was about, but also what you were trying to say and what you expected your interviewees to come up with? If you simply rush to a location and say, 'Get GVs of houses', you will get just that – probably rather boring wide general views of the kind that are usually termed 'wallpaper shots'. Medium-length pans and tilts. Statics. A few people walking past the house to give a bit of movement but nothing more. In the editing suite the shots will look uninspiring. But you got what you asked for. If, whilst filming these GVs, you suddenly start hopping about or, worse, talking whilst they're rolling, telling them to turn and film a man mending a brick wall, the shoot tends to get snappy and grumpy. You will get a bad reputation and the camera operator will probably be unnecessarily bad-mouthed by you back at base.

If, however, you tell the operator at the start that the story involves a close-knit community which has struggled against a government road-building scheme for ten years and that it has finally lost the battle, you can imagine that the shots are going to be very different. It's important that the camera operator knows that all the houses on 40 streets are under compulsory purchase orders and will be bulldozed in a few months. Suddenly your shots will have purpose. They will be big close-ups. They will reveal those telling signs of domestic care and loving attention that the community has showered on its homes. There will be shots of people cleaning their windows, of children and toys in play areas, of flowers and trees planted in gardens, of dogs and cats sleeping in the sunshine, of road signs like 'Eternity Way', soon to be no more, of lined elderly faces that may have been here for a lifetime but which will now be relocated and of your

DIY enthusiast mending brickwork or roofs which, in a short time, will be mown down. These shots will not necessarily take much longer to shoot but will lift your film out of the doldrums that is very often the fate of a fast-turnaround news or feature piece. Now your camera operator knows what you are trying to achieve. He or she will take delight in hunting down those details. You have allowed the operator to do what he or she does, and loves to do, best – observe. If you now see a couple of good shots, you can suggest them and everyone will know what you are up to. You may still be unlucky in that the camera is already doing something else. But it may also be the case that a suggestion from you will have the operator abandoning the shot being set up because what you saw was better. Now you're working as a team.

Secondly, are you aware of how a camera operator takes footage? On some professional video cameras there is a 'run up' of a few seconds. The camera cannot start taking pictures the moment you turn it on. Usually the operator will 'turn over', wait a moment and then say 'speed', which means that from this moment (and not before) the tape is rolling at the right rate and can record properly. However, even with the commonly used smaller digital cameras where the run-up is non-existent, there is much preparation to be done before you start rolling. The beginning and end of the shot and its framing must be chosen. The operator may check the sky to see if the sun is going to go in or come out during the shot which will destroy it. They may need to watch the traffic to ensure a lorry isn't going to come down the road and obliterate the view. If that happens the sound-track will be wrecked too. What is the sound like? Is there a fountain play-ing in the background but not in the shot? That may well sound as if someone out of vision is having a pee! Perhaps you should move away from the water or change the shot to include it. Are there any people com-ing along the street? Maybe the picture would look better if there were shoppers wandering through. It might be worth waiting for a moment until that family with the toddler comes by? Perhaps a pan would be good? If so, the camera move needs to be decided. What does it start on and where will it end? What is the speed of this move? Is it a slow, contemplative look along the street? Or is it a violent whip pan? Maybe the shot would be better if you lowered the legs of the tripod so that the lens is down by the curb. Now the shot will look more threatening. Once all this has been sorted out the operator needs to settle so that when he or she turns over, the shot is a good, usable one. Experienced photographers can make all these decisions fairly quickly ... but snatched shots are useless. They waste tape and time both on location and in the cutting room when you have to look through disastrous rushes. Be helpful. Offer to stop traffic, watch scudding clouds, usher people in front of the camera – work as a team.

Thirdly, are you aware of how the editing process works? A camera operator worth his salt will understand that pictures are unusable unless you have related shots to knit them together. The obvious example is the interview. You cannot simply film the interviewee answering the questions without, for safety's sake, doing a few 'noddies', as they are known with the interviewer. The noddies are those shots of the presenter looking wise and interested or smiling faintly in response to the answers. Since you almost always have only one camera on the shoot, these pictures will have to be taken afterwards. They are necessary so that if you want to reduce any of the answers in length you can cut the sound of the interviewee but cover the messy picture cut that will have resulted with a suitable reaction shot – the noddy – from you. Clearly, if you are to do noddies, it is best if they are done in the same location as the interview, with the same background sound and, preferably, the interviewee still there so that your eyeline will be at the correct level. This is another technical process that can't be unduly rushed. It may be a pain but be patient.

Figure 3.3
Editing can be laborious and frustrating … and spine-tinglingly wonderful – sometimes!

Fourthly, do you appreciate what's known rather splendidly as 'the grammar of film'? Many presenters and reporters, particularly those new to the job, may be unaware of this phrase and all it stands for. It means that there are things that look good and will cut well, and other things that will look messy or will give the wrong impression to the viewer. A simple example is over-use of the pan. You may be insisting to your camera operator that you want yet another sweeping view of a street full of houses. If you already have loads of pans and if those pans are all left to right, you are going to have a very ugly sequence of pictures indeed. Nor will you be saved by deciding to throw in a few tilts since the viewer will feel positively seasick! Shots need to be arranged with a flow and a pace in the same way that good, absorbing music has light and shade, loud and soft, fast and slow. It is for the team to establish the 'composition' of your piece and it is for all of you to decide how this is to be done. Even with straightforward news items there should be at least this degree of artistry.

You can begin to see how deep-seated a phenomenon team-working is. The presenter who can't do it makes a stressful job much worse.

Being producible

Allied with the team-working is the need for all presenters to remain 'producible' – which means that they can willingly take advice from others and act on it. In a career dealing with hundreds of presenters in ITV, Sky, cable and satellite channels, Lis Howell has seen the need for this again and again:

> *I think the most difficult thing about presenting is having to abdicate some responsibility to the producer. Presenters become difficult to work with and become divas and finally get the heave when they don't accept that it's a collaborative venture. Sometimes they simply don't accept that they're just the front. It's collaborative and it's transient.*

I was asked recently by an executive producer to help train a presenter who had been given a contract to do an entire series of light-hearted, human-interest programmes, each of them half-an-hour long. She had never presented before in her life and had been offered no training when she had been signed, all of which is a sad indictment of the so-called professionals who hire talent for shows. One of the producers contacted me saying 'unfortunately her fame has made her quite egotistical and she is satisfied with far less than we are. We've tried pushing and coaxing without success but it seems the best technique is to treat her like a puppet and just get her to memorize her lines.' Being producible is about discussion and flexibility.

There are times, though, when you should simply grin and bear it – even though you think the producer is mad! Five Live presenter, Richard Evans, knows the score:

> *Don't become 'difficult talent'. Rule One of presenting: only give your opinion if you're asked for it. Rule Two: if the producer gives you his shopping list to read out … read it out!*

EXERCISES

1. Look closely at your wardrobe and pick out your favourites. Consider them objectively and decide whether you would feel confident to wear them in a TV or radio studio.
2. Choose suitable clothes and make-up for the following shows: an early evening TV news bulletin; a live pop radio station broadcast at a seaside resort; an afternoon chat show on television.
3. Look at presenters on TV (e.g. newscasters, weather presenters, quiz show hosts). Are they wearing appropriate clothes and hairstyles? What image do their clothes portray? How could they be improved?

IN SHORT...

- Smart clothes are important for TV or radio. They give you confidence and authority.
- Wear things that are appropriate to the programme, occasion, network style and location. If it's casual be *smart* casual. Jackets are good for hiding leads and holding microphones. Wear minimum jewellery and not too flashy. Wear sensible shoes, suitable for walking and for carrying equipment. Have a good coat with pockets and a large brolly. Carry spares, particularly stockings and ties.

- Don't choose an outrageous hairstyle unless it fits the role you're playing.
- Manicure your nails for those close-ups.
- Act as part of a team. No presenter can make it alone.
- Learn about the jobs and stresses of others so you can understand more about your own.
- Never become an unproducible diva!

4 Interviewing

If you are presenting, you will probably spend a large proportion of your time interviewing people. The idea is usually to elicit information from the interviewee or to get the interviewee to be entertaining. The interview is *not* a vehicle to make you, the presenter, look good. There are, as always, exceptions to this rule, as when a comedian or a model is given a chat show. In that case, the guests are often regarded as cannon fodder to feed the star. In the main, though, your job is to make the interviewee feel at ease, ask appropriate questions and most important of all, *listen* to the answers. It's easy to be so overwhelmed with other thoughts that you stick to your prepared questions even though the answers you are getting suggest that a very different game plan should now be used. There are a million ways to interview the same person. It's as much about your personality as it is about theirs. It's not always necessary to be 'tough' to get revealing answers. Sometimes that attitude has precisely the wrong effect. The best interviewers think hard about what they want to achieve and most importantly, about the psychology of their guest.

CELEBRITY INTERVIEWERS AND PRESENTERS

Those who are not themselves journalists but who have become presenters because of a knowledge of gardening, cooking, comedy, acting etc. can have a real advantage. The audience loves to see someone famous joshing about with an interviewee; being curious, risqué, or even, on occasions, a little bit rude or dismissive. Interviewees, who are, after all, simply members of the public, will often respond more readily to a celeb. However, be you ever so famous, it is the armoury of clever ploys, learnt as part of your journalistic skills that will raise any interview to a higher, more riveting and entertaining plane. Fortunately, being a good interviewer

Figure 4.1
Interviewing may be hard for you but it's even more scary for the interviewee. It's your job to over-come their nerves and your own!

requires only experience and intelligence. Anyone can do it as long as they put in the groundwork.

HOW TO PREPARE FOR AN INTERVIEW

Your first task is to gather as much information as you can about your guest. The amount of research is bound to be dependent on the time and budget available. Use all sources – books, newspapers, websites, your colleagues, your guest's colleagues, TV and radio programmes, company reports – but always be sure of the integrity of those sources. As you make notes about your guest, write down your sources. You may think you'll remember where a fact came from but, I can assure you, you won't!

My own approach to research is that there is rarely any such thing as a fact. There are only points of view, opinions and perceptions based on evidence of varying degrees of reliability. Even what is widely quoted as 'scientific fact' is only what scientists have been able to prove to date. Such 'facts' are only as sound as the scientist themselves. It may be that the boffin you relied on today will be exposed as a charlatan tomorrow. I am not advocating groundless scepticism, only reasoned uncertainty and open-mindedness. This is surely the home base of the journalist. It is also by far the safest and most objective place for an interviewer to inhabit.

This attention to detail should prevent you from getting into a vulnerable position that could undermine your whole interview. You do not, for example, want to refer your interviewee to a statement they made some time earlier only to have this quotation rubbished. Imagine that you say triumphantly to your guest, believing yourself to be dealing the killer blow, 'But it is true, isn't it, that in 1999 you claimed "the project will cost only £30,000 and will be finished by Christmas?" Yet here we are, years later, with an estimate of £1 million and we are still nowhere near to completion.' Your interviewee may do one of a number of things:

1. Demand to know where you got that information. If this happens you will be hard pressed to cling on to whatever advantage you have in the interview if you can't cite the source.
2. Deny that this was ever said. In these circumstances your position is seriously undermined unless you can be sure of your facts. Many is the time a presenter has suddenly had to veer away from hard questioning simply because of the fear of being exposed on air. It may not be that you are actually wrong it is simply that you can't be sure.
3. Agree that this had indeed been reported in 1999 but the correspondent and the newspaper concerned were later successfully sued for libel.

Half-hearted research is dangerous!

Choosing your angle

A golden rule which should be applied to any story to establish its worth is the 'So what?' or 'Who cares?' test. This is how news editors choose priorities. These tests help to reveal an angle i.e. the most significant part of the event. Is it the biggest, longest, oldest, most dangerous, shocking, immoral or amusing? Will it affect a large number of people?

Will a large amount of money be spent? Or, more perversely, will it cost a lot but affect only a few? Perhaps it is just a curious oddity.

The 'so what?' test also helps you choose your line of questioning. Consider, for example, 'Miss Muffet frightened by spider shock'. So what? Millions of people a day are frightened by spiders. But was Miss Muffet a famous film or pop star? Was she 104 and then suffered a heart attack outside the offices of Help the Aged? Was the spider a tarantula in a case at a zoo? Was it a tarantula *out* of a case at the zoo? Had Miss Muffet recently undergone therapy for arachnophobia at a top Harley Street clinic for which she paid £3000?

Choosing the questions

When dreaming up questions, start at the beginning and establish a logical order. Any interview, even the squashy-couch, chat-show variety of celebrity banter, needs a structure. It's simply more obvious when the interview has a clear news edge.

You don't want to ask the old lady with the cruelly famished dog, 'So what are you going to do now that the RSPCA is lobbying to have you prosecuted?' It would be more sensible to go to the beginning and ask her how it was that she allowed the dog to starve. She will probably explain, 'I went to the cupboard to get the poor dog a bone but when I got there, the cupboard was bare and so the poor dog had none.' Your follow-up could then be, 'So why, Miss Hubbard, did you not seek help at this point, instead of leaving the dog until he became skeletal?' Finally comes your question addressing the situation as it is at present, with today's possibility of impending legal action.

An interview needs a beginning, a middle and an end. It may be helpful to think of it in terms of past, present and future. Consider what happened to get us to this point, what is going on now and the present effect of the event, and finally, what the future consequences will be.

Always write the cue material or introduction immediately. You will find that the top line of the story is the main question you need to ask. Think about the first question and the first answer to it. You or your researchers or producers should already know the most likely responses to any questions. After all, if you don't know what they are going to say, why have you got them there in the first place?

Write questions down. I always put them in the order in which I will ask them so that I have a proper game plan. Where the answer is uncertain, consider what the likely responses will be and have questions prepared for all eventualities. You may or may not be able to hold your clipboard or notepad with the questions but at least you'll have a checklist to refer to afterwards to ensure that you did hit all the right buttons. It's usually possible in recorded situations to do retakes. This method of notation also covers you in the event of a catastrophic brain failure which can happen to the best of us through nerves. The danger here is that you rely on the notes instead of listening hard and responding spontaneously. Listen, think and make connections. Above all, you are duty bound to ensure that what is said is comprehensible to the public. Interviewing is about asking the questions *they* want to know the answers to.

The question is...why are you asking the question?

The golden rule in my view is: there is no point in asking a question unless there is a point to asking a question. To translate: a question, comment or rhetorical remark may relax the interviewee so that he or she is given the chance to shine, explain, defend or offer witty responses. Alternatively, it may serve only to promote the persona of the interviewer. Does it reveal something about the interviewee that the audience should know or is it simply a cheap jibe that achieves nothing?

A question can have all sorts of objectives. In the first instance it can be intended to get practical information e.g. 'Why did you start eating fried grass for breakfast?', 'How do you do it?', 'What's the best oil to use?', 'What do you eat with it?', 'Are there any notable health benefits?', 'Could it be harmful?'

It can also be used to get a broader picture of the interviewee's personal views and thus reveal his or her character. For example, 'Is this a deliberate rejection of multinational cereal manufacturers and consumerism?', 'To what extent is this a statement of solidarity with cows?'

A question can also be used to *make a point*, as in, 'Don't you feel really bonkers doing that?' To which the answer is probably going to be 'No, not really. But I don't care anyway!' So the viewer is given the indication that it could, justifiably, be seen as mad but that this person is committed enough not to be concerned. That's quite a lot of information and background to be gleaned out of one, apparently jokey, remark.

Framing the questions

All interviewees have an in-built escape mechanism. They instinctively know how to speak for the shortest time (unless they are politicians, in which case they will drone on for as long as possible to prevent more tricky questions being asked). Usually they will run in a verbal straight line and escape under the wire if you don't stand in their way! This is why you should not ask, 'Do you?', 'Will you?', 'Is it?' or 'Has it?' because the answer to all of these is 'yes' or 'no'. End of interview!

Always frame the questions so as to achieve the maximum amount of information with the minimum amount of prompting. The golden rule is to ask 'Who?', 'What?', 'Where?', 'When?', 'Why?' and 'How?'.

Not only are these questions the kinds that stall the escape attempt but they are also good for jogging *your* memory into thinking up the kinds of things that need to be asked. The who-what-where-when-why-and-how

Figure 4.2
Watch the body language. When the interviewee looks away from you with this kind of expression, he may have had enough!

questions are much more demanding. Thus, it is not: 'Has the headmaster resigned?' but 'Why has the headmaster resigned?', 'When did he do that?', 'What is he going to do now?' and so on. It is not, 'Will there be disciplinary action?' but 'What kind of disciplinary action is likely?' If they say 'None', there are obvious follow-up questions about the reasons for inaction and apparent complacency. This then moves the interview into new territory and a deeper explanation of events.

Your command of grammar and language is vital in framing questions. The aim is to maximize the information flow from the interviewee and minimize the interruptions. Never end up having to explain the question through your own lack of clarity and don't use long words that your interviewee won't understand.

It's worth remembering that an interview is not just about the questions. Sometimes a bit of banter, a joke, a barbed observation is more revealing than a straight question. It's a power the presenter has and should be used fairly. If the point you want to make is really worth making, then do it. Do it gently, or with a smile on your face, or deadpan, but do it. What will happen is a gamble but the more you take risks the more you win and the better you get at psyching out your subjects.

The length of the interview

You will develop a mental clock that sometimes forces you to leave out questions you thought you'd get in. It's the pressure of time that often gives live interviews that purposeful edge. Even recorded interviews can't go on forever. The more you record the harder it is to edit and the less accurate the interview becomes since you often end up cutting one answer from the front, one from the middle and one, that was said perhaps ten or even twenty minutes later, from the end. You should be as disciplined as you can be in sticking to the areas of interest. Prioritize your questions. If you have time to fill you will have plenty of spares. Tell your interviewee in advance how long the interview will be. Make it clear, too, how much of it is intended to be broadcast. Warn the interviewee to be succinct. It is only fair that an interviewee knows that you only require a twenty-second sound bite, if this is the case.

As a guide, you should expect that each question will receive an answer of about 30 seconds. Longer answers are obviously fine, if they are a good listen. News demands clips that are as short as fifteen or twenty seconds, so it's no good allowing your guest to embark on complicated explanations when you know they will be cut. Develop techniques to prod people onwards. Paraphrasing the answer that they are in the middle of and talking over them (as politely as possible!) is one way. Cutting in with another question that spurs the story on is an alternative. Thus: 'And I gather you did eventually see the rescuers at the bottom of the mountain. So how did you make yourself seen through the blizzard?' Yet another method is simply to be brutally honest and say, 'I'm sorry to press you but we are running out of time ...' Ugly but sometimes necessary.

PREPARING THE INTERVIEWEE

Put your guests at ease. Shake hands. Smile. Greet them using their name. Interviewers frequently use first names almost instantly, rather than the more formal surname. It helps create the illusion that is being built up for the interview itself. In a few moments you may be asking a total stranger all sorts of personal questions. You will be sitting right next to them, possibly with bodies touching so that you can both use the same microphone or be in a close shot. Despite the contrived situation, you are wanting this person to behave in a natural way. You want them to gesticulate, smile, cry or get angry as if he or she has known you forever. Interviewers attempt to achieve this by being calm and friendly (even when it is to be a hard, critical interview), explaining the set up and ensuring that they provide everything the interviewee needs.

Make your guests physically comfortable. If it's a studio, is the chair OK? Is there enough room to put down any notes they may have with them? If it's television they may well not be allowed to have papers in front of them because they will be seen on camera. In this case explain why you are about to remove their crib sheets! Get them a glass of water.

Explain the technicalities. Interviewees often think they have to lean towards the microphone. This will distort the sound and on screen it will look dreadful. Tell them to relax, sit in a comfy position and reposition the microphone to suit. Tell them they don't need to shout and that the red light will come on when you're live so they mustn't speak from the moment you give them the sign to be quiet.

Let them know, in general terms, what the interview will cover and how long it's going to take. You or a researcher or producer should already have done this but that may have happened over the telephone a couple of days or weeks ago. In any case it helps to concentrate the person's mind if you just say, 'So we'll be chatting about how you first realized that going to Sainsbury's standing on your hands was a good way to do the shopping. I'll probably ask you how you make sure your dress doesn't fall round your arms revealing your knickers and you can tell me how you got the idea in the first place, what your family thinks of you and how you've calculated that you are saving £389 a year on shoe leather, OK?'

This is a good opportunity to 'bond' with interviewees. It lets them know that, although you are a whizzy-looking celeb with an entire production team in tow, you still have a brain on board and are in command of the situation. People need to be given confidence. If they feel comfortable psychologically and physically they'll respond to your questions, laugh at your jokes and offer much more in-depth stuff than you could have hoped for.

If you are live, the first opportunity to see and speak to your guests may be the moment when they are brought into your studio during a recorded item. This means that there's little time for pleasantries. Nevertheless, they must be done – even if it's only a reassuring smile.

The warm-up chat you give to an interviewee is not 'small talk'. It is packed with essential information. It might go something like this:

Thanks for coming in at such short notice, George. Bad news, I guess, for the City not to have got the City of Culture status they were seeking. We've got a couple of minutes while this film report's on. Take that seat there. Your microphone's hanging above you so you don't have to worry about it at all. No need to shout or anything! There's some water just there. In a moment when I wave at you it'll be because we're going live. Just so that you know what's going on… I'll read the introduction to our item about City of Culture status for Belfast. Then there's a very short bit of film showing some of the sights. Then I'll introduce you and we'll start the interview. Just look at me throughout the interview. Don't look at any of the cameras and don't take any notice of anything else going on in the studio. It'll be about three minutes long. The first question I'm going to ask is what your reaction is to the news tonight that Belfast didn't make it into the last five finalists and then we'll want to know what went wrong, what you think about the other cities that did get through, what damage (if any) has been done by not getting into the finals… all that kind of stuff. The kind of thing we talked about on the phone this afternoon. OK? Not long now. Are you comfortable? Right. Looks as though the film's coming up now. Here we go.

If you are on location, making interviewees comfortable may be harder. Try to ensure that they are not standing in the wind or rain. On radio, moving will not be quite so arduous as it can be for television where the picture and the light are important. Nonetheless, even on TV, it is possible to alter the angle so that the rain is not lashing into their faces or the sun blinding them into a squint.

Explain basic technicalities like how far they can move from the microphone. If you want them to point out something behind them they may naturally turn away. Tell them that's OK as long as they don't talk a lot looking in the other direction.

If it's TV, explain how big the shot is so that they know whether their hands and feet are in frame. If guests are holding a prop, a document or something to demonstrate, tell them at what point it can be seen on the camera. There's no point in them waving it about if all the viewer can see is the top edge of it!

Figure 4.3
You must look each other in the eyes. Radio interviewing often means invading your guest's personal space. It can make them feel uncomfortable

Warn them about unnecessary rustling, jangling of pocket-change or tinkling of jewellery, particularly if you are on radio where such noises are even more inexplicable and distracting than on TV.

It is vital that interviewees are told to look at the interviewer. As a cub reporter I interviewed the head of the National Coal Board, as it then was. This powerful industrial magnate never once looked at me. He had spent days being interviewed by people about the long-running coal strike and had rehearsed his answers thoroughly. In fact, he conducted the entire interview with closed eyes! And when I say *he* conducted the interview in this fashion, I mean it. The interviewer can hardly hope to engage guests or divert them from any tack they've chosen if you can't see their eyes. Apart from anything else, you need to be able to give them visual warnings that they must begin to wrap up as time is running out. This is usually done by faster and faster nods of the head.

Interviewees often try to look elsewhere out of embarrassment or uncertainty. Their eyes wander to any person who looks interested. If you're not doing your job that might be your producer who is standing to one side. It means they won't see that you are looking aghast, angry, querulous, friendly, any of which might give them an indication of the way things are going and could inspire them to perform better. From a televisual point of view, the eye-line will be wrong. What's more, if they either look away or stare directly down the lens they will look shifty and evasive. Looking straight at the camera can only work if a guest is appealing directly to the audience and is doing it intentionally for either dramatic or comic effect.

AVOIDING INTERRUPTIONS

Make sure your guest has turned off all mobile phones, pagers, alarms and their normal telephone line. Is the doorbell likely to be rung? Does the cat wander constantly through the cat flap? Does the dog that sits so sweetly on the knee now start to attack the microphone when it's brought near? (There is a great filmed example of this where the dog of the TV chef, Rick Stein, virtually demolished a perfectly good boom microphone!) Is that humming the air conditioning system and can it be turned off? Are you next door to the office loo which will be flushed constantly throughout the interview? (This has happened to me!) Will the clocking-off siren start up in two minutes and the entire factory walk through the back of shot whilst you are trying to get sense out of your victim?

Such interruptions could even cost you the interview itself. It's sod's law that at the very moment you have got the interviewee to admit to stealing the cash, an ear-splitting alarm will go off and you'll have to stop the recording. By the time you re-start the moment is lost and the confession retracted.

If you are interrupted for a short time, explain the stoppage and try to keep the interviewee's mind on the relevant points but without discussing them and thus losing spontaneity. If the stoppage is longer you become adroit at using a series of 'you-ain't-seen-nothin'-yet' stories! I remember a nervous interviewee standing in a field who had to be stopped three times. First it was because of a low-flying plane. Then, an entire pack of hunting hounds erupted through a hedge behind him. Finally, a convoy of three enormous pea-harvesting machines began grinding their way up a steep zig-zag road so that the roaring of their engines stayed with us for fully fifteen minutes! It's at times like these that you discover how very tiring the job can be!

INTERVIEWING TECHNIQUES

1. Look at interviewees and maintain eye contact.
2. Listen closely to what they say and try to understand what they really mean. It takes a lot of concentration and it is not helped if you are constantly looking for the next question on your pad instead of participating in the discussion you are instigating now.
3. React with obvious interest. It will give interviewees the confidence to carry on.
4. Don't keep saying, 'Hmmm', 'Yes' or, 'Oh, I see'. It's distracting to listen to, makes editing impossible and makes you sound silly.
5. Interrupt if you want to but not too frequently – let interviewees make a point somewhere, otherwise you will lose the sympathy of your audience. If you must persist in asking a question, do it with good grace and, above all, with good reason. At some point, if guests will not answer, it will become obvious that they are prevaricating. It is for you to decide if that point has been reached. The obvious example is Jeremy Paxman on BBC2's *Newsnight*, when he repeatedly (fourteen times) asked the then Home Secretary, Michael Howard, whether he had sought the resignation of the Head of the Prison Service. Michael Howard at first found ways to side-step the question. When it was put

yet more times, he began to repeat his original formula and by this stage it was clear that both men knew the game was up. Interestingly, Michael Howard did not walk out and at the end both men were smiling – although in the Secretary of State's case one suspects it was through gritted teeth!

6. Think about your next question while interviewees are answering the last. This means you will be ready if they suddenly stop talking but also you will be forcing the pace of the interview and taking it along the path you choose.

7. If you mess up a question during a recorded interview, simply take a breath (which will be long enough for an edit) and start again to get a clean take.

8. Don't encourage interviewees to do the same. It's often better to do retakes with interviewees later rather than stop the camera and lose the flow. If they mess up an answer, either help them out with a prompt e.g. 'You mean you actually sat down in front of the car?' or say, 'Don't worry. I'll just ask that again.' Leave a pause so that it's clear where the usable take is and start again.

9. Silences can be significant. You don't have to keep talking just to keep the microphone busy. Sometimes you will ask a question that some-one would sooner not answer. Keep quiet and it will put the pressure on the interviewee to talk; if he or she doesn't do so the continued silence is revealing. Keep your wits about you. Sometimes a person will say something so moving or emotional that for you to say any-thing would be crass.

10. Try to listen to and watch the interview as if it is an out-of-body experience. As if you were floating outside yourself looking in. This is particularly important in an interview that will be cut into a longer item. Imagine what it's going to sound like to the audience once it's cut and assembled. Edit in your head as you go along. *You* already know what you are trying to achieve. *You* know the game plan. *You* know all about the rest of the interviews you've done for the pro-gramme. The interviewee only knows what you are asking right now. This means that you must ask questions that take account of other interviews you have done and other knowledge you have.

11. Play devil's advocate. Interviewees deserve (and are legally entitled to) a fair and honest exposition of their motives and intentions. They may not know that they will look daft in the light of others' criticisms in the programme about which they are, of course, unaware. That's why, in the absence of the accusers, you must do the pushing. Even if

it is an interview that will stand alone, you must put the views of the detractors. Nor is it for you to judge whether those criticisms are valid. There may be relatively few people who disagree but they may just be right.

12. If you don't understand something that's said, ask. Don't be afraid of looking silly. If you really do look dim as a result it will be cut out but the likelihood is that if you don't understand it, neither does your audience. Never be embarrassed to admit ignorance. Even the most experienced journalist is not expected to be an expert on all matters. You are the representative of the wider public. Be bold and don't be browbeaten into *not* asking a follow-up. Politicians are particularly cute at this technique. They might say, 'Well, Janet, as you'll know from the 4th revised edition of the statutory instrument 691 published last January, that whole issue was dealt with quite satisfactorily!', which is a ploy to shut you up.

13. On the other hand, don't be tempted to show off your own specialist knowledge. It will appear pompous and may well leave the audience without an adequate explanation.

14. Control your tone of voice. You can get loads of information out of people by pushing gently but politely and without malice. Keep your face inscrutable – deadpan. If you get excitable at the critical moment they'll take flight and go for the wire (see above!).

15. Treat your interviewees with respect. They may seem bonkers, criminal, violent, devious, liars. They may seem funny, lovable, innocent, charming. They may, in fact, be none of these things. They may be some of these things for some of the time. Your job is not to judge them but to find out how they tick. Don't patronize, discount, bully or ride roughshod over people who are frequently not as capable as you at communicating and who don't have the power you wield with the might of the microphone. As I mentioned before, I warn students they'll get nowhere unless they have about them 'the milk of human kindness' mixed with the steel you need to have the courage of your convictions.

THE AFTERCARE SERVICE

Doing an interview may be hard work for you but it is often a million times more stressful for interviewees. They not only have to perform in this alien and false environment but they will be aware that their friends

Figure 4.4
American gay activist 'Sister Boom Boom'. People may look odd but you'll not find out anything unless you treat interviewees with interest and courtesy

and family, their bosses, fellow workers and neighbours will see them. They may have been worrying about it for ages. The adrenalin rush of the event itself can keep everyone on a high whilst it's going on. When it's over there can be a terrible sense of anticlimax. Interviewees worry that they didn't say what they wanted to say in the way they meant to. Often you can reassure them that they did do a good job. Outsiders cannot be expected to understand how an interview will come over, so you can explain how the mere fact that they said 'umm' a few times at the beginning is irrelevant since that answer is going to be cut out anyway. If the interview is an emotional or disturbing one, ensure that there are people around who can help. Do they need professional counsellors? Can they get

71

back home easily? Do they need to make a phone call? Give every reasonable assistance. They didn't have to do the interview. Even if they were paid to do it, you probably need them as much as they need the money. To be brutal, if you can't be bothered to be civil for any other reason, remember, you may need them again.

EXERCISES

1. Write out a selection of questions for the following stories. Remember, it will be useful to write the cue or introductory material first to clarify issues.
   - A long-running campaign by workers and management to prevent the closure of a local hospital has finally lost its battle. The Health Authority has decided the building will close in six months and the 120 patients will be removed to other facilities in the area. You are interviewing the head of the Health Authority.
   - A new autobiography has just been published by a sixteen-year-old British female fashion model who features widely in tabloids and magazines. Her career started when she was talent-spotted in a drama school at the age of six for a TV advertisement. Since then her parents have given up their jobs to escort her on dozens of foreign trips to experience catwalks around the world.
   - A top comedian is arriving in the locality for a one-night show. He is on TV a lot and has done a few small parts in movies. His agent and the press officer for the theatre where he will perform have been pressing hard to get on your show. Your producer has agreed.
   - A ten year old child has just passed a maths GCSE. The girl was taught at home by her father, a lorry driver, and her mother, a nurse who works night shifts. You have the whole family coming in to the studio.
   - A famous pop star has brought out a new record. The record company's PRs have been doing their usual job of putting the star forward for every available slot. Your show is one. The star will sing the song in the course of the show.
   - The parents of a child killed locally in appalling storms have agreed to speak. Their tragic story has been all over the local and national news. Their seven-year-old son was crushed to death after pushing his five-year-old brother to safety, out of the way of a falling tree. The family had been walking their dog in woods during gales that had been sweeping the country with winds gusting up to 100 miles per hour. Their three-year-old Labrador dog was also killed.

2. Which of the questions you have prepared would you concentrate on asking if you had only one and a half minutes to do the interview?
3. Record an interview from radio or television and devise a different structure for it so that you would achieve different and perhaps better answers.

IN SHORT...

- Research your interviewee diligently and be sure of your sources.
- Write the intro or cue material to focus your mind on the main points.
- Write your questions out. There can never be too many but ensure you know which are the most important ones.
- Put your interviewee at ease. Explain the process and be confident.
- Dare to ask the questions you wish but in a polite way.
- Listen closely to the answers.
- Look your interviewee in the eyes.
- Silences can be telling.

5   Television essentials

Whilst much of presentation is similar whether it is for radio or television, there are a few things that are peculiar to the visual medium. The three areas addressed here cover reading, writing and performing for the camera. First, handling the autocue or teleprompter allows you to communicate a script without your having to memorize a single word of it. What a lifesaver this gadget is! Secondly, writing for television is a skill that requires good command of language, well-developed powers of observation, disciplined timekeeping and much practice. Finally, performing a 'piece to camera' or 'stand up' is increasingly a necessary part of a day's work. You must know when and why you're doing it and how to do it quickly. As a television presenter you might be able to get through life without being spectacularly good at every one of these crafts but it is not possible, particularly in a multi-skilled world, that you won't have to do at least one of them well.

READING THE AUTOCUE

The autocue is simply the machine that allows you to read the script while looking directly at the camera. Your words are typed into a computer which relays it to a screen under the lens. The back-to-front gobbledegook is then reflected up onto a glass panel mounted over the lens of the camera. In this way you are looking directly at the lens whilst apparently speaking off the top of your head. It is worked either by an operator sitting to one side in the studio or, in many regional news studios particularly, by presenters themselves using a foot pedal or hand control. The self-op method is even used when there are co-presenters so each has to be sure to take over the autocue without spinning it on too fast for their colleagues.

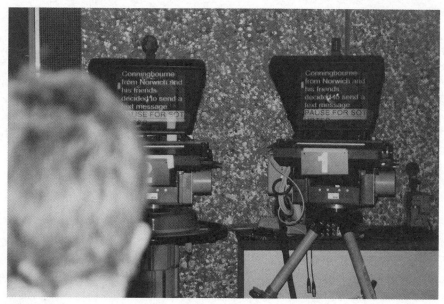

Figure 5.1
Anglia News presenters operate the autocue with a foot pedal. Note the directions – not to be read! SOT means 'sound on tape'

> And finally, some rogue motorists
> in West Wales are using cooking
> oil in their car engines to cut
> costs. Persistent offenders
> could face up to seven years
> in jail, because they are
> dodging paying fuel tax.
> It's reported that the fumes
> smell like chips cooking!
> The police – dubbed frying squad
> officers – are, apparently,
> sniffing out these tax dodgers.

Figure 5.2
Autocue lines are short so you must pace yourself carefully

Autocue operators listen to you speaking while watching the monitor in front of them which is a replica of the one you are seeing. They move the script up to match your pace, so that the words you've just spoken disappear off the top of the screen and new ones appear at the bottom.

The technique

Beware the glazed-eyed expression borne out of massive concentration and fear! Get acquainted with the script so you aren't surprised by what comes up. Read everything beforehand. You may even be lucky enough to have rehearsal time which has the added benefit of allowing the operator to get used to the way you speak. Relax and work at putting in all the mannerisms and movements that you would if you were speaking your own words naturally.

The positioning of the autocue is important. If it's too high or too low it will be more obvious than ever that you're reading which will destroy the deception.

It's a fact of life that the autocue screen has to print words big so that you can read them at a distance of up to five or six metres. You can alter the size of the words and, in some circumstances, negotiate to change the position of the camera but the effect of it is that there can only be a few words on each line.

Figure 5.3
It's all done with mirrors! Notice how the name *al Qu'eda* will be split over two lines. You have to keep your wits about you

Inevitably the sentence is broken up and, if you're not careful, the sense is broken too. Reading ahead is impossible so the pace at which you talk is vital. Give yourself enough time to understand the meaning but don't be tempted to stop in the hope that the end of the sentence will appear. If you stop so will the autocue. The speed of the scrolling is entirely dictated by the pace of your speech. If you slow down, the words slow down. In fact, there is a terrible tendency, at first, to hurry because it feels as if the words will disappear before you reach them. They won't (or shouldn't!). Choose a pace that allows you to see at least one line above where you are reading so that there's no danger the script will disappear off the top of the screen.

The script that goes up in front of you will also warn of impending video tape. It will say what the name of the item is, what the first words are, what the 'out' (or final) words or sound effects are and how long it is. Make sure you don't try to read these bits too!

If you have a co-presenter, your name or initials will alert you to which bits are yours.

If you ad lib for any length of time without warning anyone in advance, you had better expect a sharp intake of breath in the studio and don't be surprised if the autocue operator starts scrolling the script frantically, looking for the place you have apparently jumped to.

When the autocue goes wrong

As you speak to the camera, you should also be moving the hard copies in front of you so that if the autocue goes down you won't be left speechless. Using your typed script and looking at the camera is tricky, requiring you to read a long way ahead and concentrate hard on the story.

A failure is usually pretty obvious to the audience. Raise your script slightly from the desk so that you don't have to drop your head so much. Plough on. It may not have happened to *you* before but the *audience* has seen it dozens of times!

If you can't now proceed with an item, change direction or ad lib. Make it clear to the gallery what you are doing. For example, you might now be unable to finish the cue for a piece of VT (video tape) so instead you can say, 'I'm sorry there's a technical hitch. We'll try to get back to that item later.' At this point, you'll probably get instructions in your earpiece from the director. If this doesn't happen, you must make your own decisions.

You could continue, 'In the meantime, I'm pleased to say that here with me is Joe Bloggs who recently returned from a round-the-world tour on a pedal bike ...' and so on. You may be able to give the autocue operator enough time to whizz on to this item.

TELEVISION SCRIPTS

A full television script for a recorded item or programme will have a great deal of information of relevance to many different people. As a result there is no uniform format. There are, however, a few guidelines.

Script layout

The convention for film scripts is that they are written in two columns with the shots always described on the left and the words on the right. This means that when you look at a script, by casting your eye down the left-hand side, you can picture immediately in your mind's eye what kind of action you will see and how long each of the sections lasts. Often you will see 'time codes' written beside the description of the shot. This is to allow the picture editor to locate the shot on the original tape. In the right-hand column is the soundtrack comprising the words the presenter must speak and the words of interviewees. The latter may not be transcribed in their entirety but at the very least the opening words (known as the 'in words') and the final phrase (known as the 'out words') will be shown.

Throughout there will be durations for individual segments. Often there is also a 'running time' inserted every now and again so that you can see how long the movie is at any point. Sometimes each track or section that the presenter must speak will be lettered or numbered for easy reference.

You may have to present a script that you wrote yourself or one written by somebody else. In many areas it is common for a producer or researcher to put the story together, get the footage, oversee the editing of it and then hand the cut copy to you for tracking i.e. recording the commentary track. Top correspondents in news often have to be elsewhere working on another story. The programme editor, however, may require that the item is given their stamp of authority and so it will be finally vetted and voiced by the specialist correspondent. Similarly, celebrities may have almost nothing to do with the production process. They can simply arrive at a pre-arranged time to lay down a voice track.

NO MORE EXCUSES.

1 Fairground pics 04 16 34 Music (with echo?)	Synch 07 00 45ish "She wanted to go to the fair with her friends." 07 02 33 "They were actually coming home and these two girls had followed them" 07 03 09 - 03 16 "And then the two girls turned on Louise kicking her to the head and killing her."
2 Photos of Louise	VO. 00 00 29 - 00 00 40 **2 years ago this month 13-year-old Louise Ellen from Corby was beaten to death by girls aged just 12 and 13. They got 2 years and were released exactly one year on.**
3 Ellen Alien in vis.	Synch 07 03 54 "I couldn't believe that it was children that had actually done this. That had so much violence in them "07 04 38 - 05 08" and being two years on doesn't make it any easier they've got all their lives in front of them and Louise is dead."
4 Slamming prison doors keys. 08 29 02 08 30 18; 08 32 40; 09 34 05; 09 35 27;	FX AND TITLES VO. 00 01 09
5 CCTV shots intercut with moody night shots round Thetford.	**The growing public anger at child criminals has become an unstoppable tide. So now the government is embarking on the biggest and most controversial shake-up of juvenile justice in 60 years.** (pause at 00 01 19. Glass smashes) (in again at 00 01 23 - 00 01 34) **The Crime and Disorder Bill will be law by the summer. Tough new measures will tackle the very youngest troublemakers and are intended to prevent the epidemic of youth crime.**

Figure 5.4

The opening part of a half-hour documentary film script. The shots are summarized on the left, words on the right. Notice at '5' the voiceover is broken to allow for a sound effect

Writing the script

A film script is written and re-written constantly. This is because when the item is first mooted a 'treatment' is drawn up which is an outline of what the issues are and who should talk about them. The treatment follows a logical progression from the opening thought, through the complexities of the tale to the conclusion. You may have to do this alone or in conjunction with the production team. As each interviewee and location falls into place, what has to be said becomes clearer and the treatment becomes a draft script. There will be many versions of it before everyone's happy.

The art of scripting is the art of précis. Be concise and precise. Change sentence constructions. Remove words. Use a synonym dictionary to find others. You will be astonished at how much you can shorten the script and how much it is improved. Despite what anyone might say, let me warn you that it is a time-consuming and challenging effort. Expect to write each track at length and then spend ages paring it down until it contains the feel you want and the information you need.

Writing the opening lines

Ironically, the opening lines will not be yours to speak! No script should be started until the cue material has been written. A horribly common mistake is to repeat the cue, word for word, in the first lines of the film. Get used to thinking of any film as a whole item with the cue as the first part of it. Too often presenters or reporters try to save the best opening lines for themselves. This is nonsense since the first mention of a story, which should galvanize the public into watching, will be spoken by the anchor. Include your most mind-boggling facts. Think back to why you started this film and what you set out to do in it.

Suppose you are working on a film commissioned to investigate the re-emergence of Dutch Elm disease and the damage to the environment. In the process you have discovered that over a three-month period four people have been injured by falling, rotten trees owned by a local council. You might be tempted to state in your opening track:

The hedgerows and woods in this county are, according to some, fast becoming death traps as a result of negligence and ignorance by local councils. In recent months, our investigation has revealed that no fewer than four people have died as old elm trees have crashed down on them … trees that were, literally, rotted to the core by the re-emergence of Dutch Elm disease.

It sounds wonderfully dramatic but what is there left to introduce the film? All this would be much better handed over to the studio anchor. The script can then launch straight into the core of the story with real drama. A classic opening shot might be one of the bereaved relatives near the spot where the tree fell or, perhaps, a furious local residents' committee baying for action. The cue and the piece are all part of the same work of art, so treat them as such when you begin to write.

Writing to picture

Once you've started scripting for the film, have a care that every word fits with the pictures you've got. If the shots show angry people at a meeting, it is not appropriate to be talking about the dead trees or the dead people. With experience you develop ways of mentioning facts and thoughts in the script even though you don't have the right pictures, but that is a last resort. Commentary that does not match the pictures is said to be 'fighting the shots' and it's confusing for the viewer. If it goes on for too long, there will be an irresistible desire to switch off. On the other hand, don't repeat in script what can be seen in vision. Added value is what you're looking for. Over pictures of trees, don't say, 'Trees around a quiet, rural village', say, 'The trees here are only months from being destroyed.'

If the worst comes to the worst and you don't have the pictures you need, the art is to refer initially to the pictures you *do* have whilst incorporating the information for which you have no shots. Suppose you only have pictures of the angry meeting. How are you going to illustrate what the trees look like when they are diseased? You might have to say:

The anger of the residents spilled over at the campaign meeting. Dozens of those in the hall bemoaned the growing number of leafless and lifeless trees. One environmental activist said that once the condition took hold the wood deteriorated to a dangerous degree in a surprisingly short time. Others were appalled at the fatalities and there was outrage too that the council seems to have been either unaware of the problem or unwilling to act.

Unlike radio scripting, writing for TV does not always allow you to follow what appears to be a logical progression. In radio it might be fine to start by describing the first tree that fell and then how the council got involved but in TV you must always start your film with the very best pictures you have. So if the most astonishing thing you have is a council officer physically attacking you for trying to ask questions, a weeping relative or an angry meeting, that's where your story begins. Perhaps start with a few seconds of rural peace shots. The camera tilts down a dead elm tree as birds twitter. Then mix the sound of crying and cut to a woman in vision weeping, a furious meeting and the mayhem of a fight. Over this the presenter says:

> *It seems remarkable that the beauty of this rural vista could turn no fewer than four families to grieving and bereavement… [pause for shots to establish and hear sound]… inspire local residents to become raging campaigners and activists… [another pause for shots]… and move this formerly law-abiding council official to turn to violence against our camera crew.*

Timings are critical. If the script says there are twenty seconds of tree shots then you have about seventeen seconds for the voiceover because you must allow a moment for the audience to assimilate what has just gone and also leave time before the next interviewee or changed location comes up. It's called 'allowing the film to breath'. If you don't, the whole project becomes frenetic and tense. You also lose your audience because you must lead them gently through the complexities of your story, not hit them about the head with it!

The usual formula applies for the speed of reading. It is three words per second. You can speed it up and slow it down to a surprising degree with pauses or the lack of them but it's a good general guide.

The only way to judge whether a script is good is to read it aloud. You'll suddenly find repeated words, poor grammar and confusions unnoticed before. Even if the circumstances only allow you to whisper it, I cannot emphasize enough that since your script is to be spoken, you can only test it by doing just that.

Laying down the track

When the final decisions have been made about how the script should be and how the film should be cut, you will go into the edit. There are a number of ways to get your voice on the film. One is to record the script in its entirety in another studio and simply hand it to the editor who will cut the pictures to match it, ensuring the shots are the right length to cover your words. This means the script takes priority over the pictures. The editor may have to use poor pictures because there is nothing else to cover your track. It may also mean that some of your best shots will be thrown on the floor because you haven't written enough script to merit using them. If you know your shots well you can avoid this happening.

Another method, frequently used in fast-turnaround news situations, is to record each track on a lip microphone in the editing suite as the cutting is being done. A lip mic is simply one that has a bar across the top of it set about an inch away so that you can place this against your top lip and speak into it without popping or distorting. It is a mic for close work and will cut out most background sound so it can safely be used in the editing suite. It is the equipment sports commentators use in noisy environments like football grounds. It does not offer the best sound quality for your film by any means but where speed is vital it may be the only answer.

The other way is to cut the entire film with the outline script to hand but without the presenter's voice. This allows the editor to make the best possible use of the greatest shots. To some extent this is a vision-led method. Once again, it works best if you know your footage well. In this case, when you have a 'cut story' you go into a studio where the film will be run. It now consists of shots, sound effects and interviews but has gaps where there are pictures but no commentary. These are the bits you will have to fill.

There will be a time code on the master tape and your script can be annotated so that you know precisely when you must start speaking. The dubbing, as this is called, is done in a darkened studio where you sit at a microphone with a monitor in front of you and headphones on so that you can hear the film sound and also talkback from the producer in the sound suite. You have a cue light in front of you which will come on a few seconds before you have to speak, to warn you that it is almost your turn. You watch the film following the script with your finger so that you can keep your place. With only a couple of seconds to go your microphone will be faded up and you speak whilst keeping an eye on the footage so that you can see whether your words are hitting the right pictures.

Figure 5.5
When dubbing to picture, hold your scripts up so you can read and see the monitor at the same time

Sometimes there will be effects (FX) on the film mid-sentence, during which they want you to remain silent. There might be a sudden bomb explosion or a burst of laughter that the producer wants to hear clean.

Never rush your pace to squash all the words in. Instead, shorten the commentary. Be prepared to take advice about the tone you are achieving and to do as many retakes as are necessary.

THE PIECE TO CAMERA

This is often called a stand up or a PTC. It is the part in any film where the presenter or reporter addresses the audience directly. It is not there so that you can get your face known by thousands. This may be the spin-off but it's not the purpose. It must be an integral part of the story.

PTCs are an important part of today's television style. It's felt that if the public recognize the presenter/reporter, they will trust them and tune in with more dedication. Clearly, if celebrities are reporting, the public will want to *see* them, rather than just hear their voiceover. In news operations PTCs are encouraged, especially at the end of a report ('... Jo Bloggs, ITN, Kabul'), because it justifies a series of as many as a dozen station idents in the space of only half an hour. How else could you get the phrase *BBC News* or *ITN* repeated over and over? Sadly, due to sloppy reporting, many of these pieces add nothing to what has gone before. The art is to find something relevant to sign off with whilst not setting up a whole new line of enquiry.

Why do a piece to camera?

Pieces to camera are particularly useful in certain situations:

1. To explain complicated facts or statistics. Sometimes a graphic would be boring whereas a picture of you standing in the appropriate location and explaining things can make the message more palatable.
2. To demonstrate. A PTC describing a piece of machinery, a garden layout or how to drive a vehicle means you can point to the relevant parts and even experience the object at first hand. A PTC on a sailboard, for instance, really demands that you demonstrate the complexity of the sport by falling in! It gives the camera operator the chance to get big close-ups of the thing in question which otherwise would be static and very boring to see without you being involved.
3. To add drama. In investigations a PTC can be a handy tool when you need to brandish a leaked report or make accusations.
4. To turn corners. Frequently an item will start off with information about how an event began and what happened. However, the end of the story may be about how the issue is to be solved. There is, then, the corner in the middle of the movie that needs to be turned. A piece to camera is ideal. Here's an example:

> *It's clear that everyone on the project has been convinced all along that the new rules and regulations are too onerous. The paper work is mountainous. The question yet to be answered is, 'What on earth can anyone do about it?' The Government has recently brought out this Green Paper [raise document to chest height for camera] but already many in this community doubt it will change anything. [Interviews with community members speculating about the future follow.]*

5. To comply with stylistic demands. Frequently programmes require as part of their branding that presenters speak to the camera rather than voiceover shots. It may be because the presenter is a celebrity, it may be because it adds a warmth and direct familiarity with the audience.

6. To overcome lack of shots. This is a very practical consideration. Sometimes you won't have time to get the necessary shots e.g. waiting for a Blue Tit to land on someone's bird table. A piece to camera in these circumstances will save the day. If you haven't got pictures of the poor conditions in the hospital because the local health trust won't let you in, then the obvious alternative is to talk about the situation in a PTC outside. It may be a 'last resort' but it often adds drama:

> *It is within the walls of this hospital that the allegations have become the most alarming. It is claimed that patients entering by the door behind me, into the casualty department, might get no further into the building than that corridor for up to fourteen hours, no matter how ill they are.*

7. To overcome lack of editing time. Any filmed item takes time to edit. In the space of five minutes it is easily possible to have to cut more than 50 shots. How much quicker it is to pop in one good PTC lasting 30 seconds?

Where to do a piece to camera

Choose a place that is as relevant to the story line as possible in the time and within the budget. News reporters inevitably dash to the front doors of government buildings where the plaque outside clearly states 'Department of Health', for example. This does not mean it is actually the best place. Given half a chance they might have preferred to do a PTC in a helicopter hovering over a hospital where they could demonstrate dramatically how swift and vital an air ambulance can be.

Choose a place where the background sound is not going to obliterate your words or external elements make you look awful. The helicopter is a good example. Such a PTC would have to be carefully rehearsed to ensure that the chopper blades and the draught weren't going to drown your voice and distract from the information you are trying to get over.

Figure 5.6
Angus Walker's (ITN's Business Editor) PTC about power cuts after the storms of October 2002 has an audience of electricity repairmen. It can be off-putting. Note how he holds the mic just low enough to be out of shot. His cameraman, David Harman, will watch for traffic or people behind the presenter that might spoil the shot

The most common error is to stand at a roadside that is too busy. Traffic noise is very disruptive and you can be sure that the moment you begin your piece the biggest pantechnicans will appear around the bend. Sod's law follows TV crews everywhere!

However apt the location is, it may be technically impossible to achieve a PTC so be prepared to make compromises – but don't give up too quickly. For example, you may wish to stand outside an estate agent's shop on the High Street to talk about the difficulties of getting a mortgage but when the cameraman looks through the lens he can see himself reflected in the glass behind you. Perhaps the only way to get rid of that reflection is for him to move to a different angle which means that it is not now obvious that it is an estate agent's shop. Perhaps he must change the shot size so that it cuts out the reflection which may mean that you become more significant in the frame and the location again loses its effect.

Always be safe. In your enthusiasm to get the best shots it is easy to forget personal safety. I have done PTCs in front of speeding stunt cars doing handbrake turns so that grit hit me and the camera. I've done them standing on a ladder balanced a metre above the ground on a sheet of reinforced glass, perched on crumbling castle battlements and even driving on a dual carriageway with a cameraman lying upside down on the passenger seat filming me. All made great TV. All were insanely dangerous. It is only TV and not worth injury. Make cables and equipment obvious and divert passers by. For doubtful ventures take advice and most importantly, check your insurance.

Make sure that you are allowed access. Shopping malls are usually privately owned and have a management body that must be consulted. They will inevitably want to know what you are going to say to ensure that you are not going to be giving them bad publicity.

You are entitled to do a PTC on any public area as long as you aren't creating a nuisance or causing a breach of the peace or in any other way breaking the law. A suspicious shopkeeper or angry residents have no right to force you away from the street outside their property although you would be wise to tread carefully rather than upset people however justified your journalism is. Compromises are what we make every day. There is always another solution. Do some 'fancy footwork', as I always call it!

One last thought – although it should really be the first thing you think about: taste and decency. I leave you to make your own decisions about what is right or wrong for you. Reporter Wesley Kerr explains ...

I probably missed a great opportunity to become extremely famous in front of 50 million people at the Heysel Stadium when the cameraman was saying, 'Do a piece to camera where there are all these dead people behind you.' And I didn't because I felt the story was more important than my own celebrity, although I think that if I was doing it again, I probably would do a piece to camera. I did the story about 39 dead people but not the PTC. Then another reporter was sent to Brussels the next day and I noticed that he spent his whole day doing pieces to camera in different locations in the hope

*that one or two of them would make his package. And I thought,
'Ah, that's how you do it.'*

Performing a piece to camera

Before you can decide finally whether you are going to be sitting, standing, walking, running or whatever whilst doing your PTC, you must have
the script settled. It is essential that it slots in neatly with the material that
has gone before and flows into what comes next. There are two advantages to this. First, it will create a seamless argument with no repetition
which is clearly the ideal. Secondly, if it is well knitted into the item it will
be almost impossible for a programme editor to demand its removal
because the item is over-running. Obviously, if your film is too long and
someone is intending to reduce it, they will excise the bit that contributes
little or nothing and one of the first places to look is the PTC!

It's helpful to know the exact words of the previous interviewee and what
will be said afterwards. It sounds awful if you use the same words.

Now think about whether it would be good to wear a radio microphone
and walk towards the camera through the crowd. Would it be better to be
standing on an escalator coming towards the camera? Or should the camera be on the escalator with you? Clearly the more inventive the idea, the
longer will be the set-up time. Sadly, it is the habit with all crews to leave
the PTCs until last if possible as you can always do without them.

Learn your lines as quickly as you can. Go away from the crew and
wander about. Go to the toilet for a bit of peace if necessary. Don't be
embarrassed about talking to yourself in public and acting out the moves.
Keep the script simple and if you can't remember bits of it, change it or
cut it.

Some people use small tape recorders and a concealed earpiece. This
restricts your movements and repeating the words fractionally behind a
recording requires practice to do convincingly. Your eyes can lose contact
with the camera and your emphasis may be less effective. It is clearly
much quicker to become skilled at being able to do a PTC on any subject
at the drop of a hat. Directors and crews have great admiration for presenters who can do this, so it raises your profile tremendously.

Walking and talking to camera are surprisingly difficult things to do
together. The first time I did it the director had to endure an incredibly

slow amble towards the lens because I was concentrating so hard on the lines. Any walking must be done with a sense of purpose whilst not scurrying. Decide where you will be standing at the start and at the end of the PTC and change the words until they fit the walk.

Perhaps you will actually walk into the opening spot looking around you (shots that would be covered by commentary) and then raise your head to start speaking. Maybe you will finish speaking and walk out past the camera. You will have to practise at precisely what angle you must exit dependent on whether you are to get out of frame quickly or slowly. Yet another alternative is to do part of the PTC walking and part of it stationary.

You will need to have a few run-throughs. Try to ignore people who are interested and all the idiots who want to greet their mothers! Children are always fascinated. If you don't want them in frame, tell them what you're doing and guide them to a place where they can watch but not be in shot. Point out that if they do get into frame the film will be cut anyway, so there's no benefit in attempting it. Simply shooing them away is asking for trouble!

When you fluff, as inevitably you do at times, don't curse. Back at base someone might put that take on air by mistake … yes, it has happened! Simply stop, say 'sorry, go again' and walk back to where you were.

Often a PTC is terribly rushed. The light may be going. There may be only one chance to get the necessary background shot e.g. the last wrecked vehicle being removed from the motorway pile-up. This all adds to the strain on you. If you have missed the shot, so be it. Go to plan B. (Always have a plan B.) No-one at home will know what might have been.

If you find yourself getting more and more distracted stop and calm down. Don't be embarrassed about it. All sorts of things can throw you. It can be the place, your script, a lack of commitment on your part or the fact that out of the corner of your eye you can see the producer staring intently at you. Change things if you can. If not, try again and if it's still not good, be brave enough to cut and run. It's not professional to waste time.

Remember, if you're feeling the pressure of all this, so is the crew. Here are some pertinent observations by Dave Jones, a highly experienced and very creative lighting cameraman who's worked in news, features, documentaries and events for all the big broadcasters and with dozens of famous presenters. His views may sound uncompromising but I would only say that, as a presenter, you are the first to appreciate the beautiful pictures such a technician can achieve for you. It's interesting to see the rigmarole from the other side of the lens:

Remember the bloody words! Especially if you've written them. No crew likes standing about in snow flurries because some precious presenter can't get it right. If it's a long job and continuity is required, remember what got worn when. It's not the crew's fault they have taken the PA off most shoots! Likewise, remember with which hand you started the electric saw or drank that glass of wine. So much has to do with teamwork. I remember filming for Songs of Praise *on Blakeney beach on a foul stormy day with an inexperienced presenter reciting a passage from the Bible; 300-mm lens and the shot back-timed so he finished in close-up before he left the screen – for a presenter, one of the most difficult challenges. It was freezing cold, soaking wet and with a gale blowing. It took half a dozen takes but the director got it in the can. I recall, too, a warm sunny day in the hills and hollows at Barnack, with TV historian Bryan McNerney miles away out of vision, walking towards camera delivering a long explanation of why we were there, which again had to finish in close-up but he was unable to see the lens for most of the link as he was in 'hollows' for half of it. Edgy for the radio mic, extremely difficult for focus but we pulled it off. I remember PTCs done boat-to-boat with presenters driving, helicopter links where the background is of prime importance, craned links miles away from anywhere, where only a crane shot can tell the story. All these complicated links depend on team effort and trust. Practise, practise and yet more practise. Check yourself in a mirror and smile. Take advice, from producers, directors and the crew – they will often spot things production miss. Listen especially to a good recordist when it comes to delivery. Talk to make-up and wardrobe too. They have an instinctive feel for what will suit you. Get to grips with what presenting is all about and familiarize yourself with what goes on in studios and on location.*

Your shoot may be a nerve-shattering first for you but camera operators have seen it all before. It's that experience that you need to tap into. Good ones wouldn't dream of speaking out to you as Dave just has … that comes only when you kindly carry the legs and ask, humbly, for advice and I suggest you do just that!

EXERCISES

1. Tape a news bulletin and study the scripting of the items. Do the words fit the shots? Are there shots missing? What alterations would you make?
2. Type some newspaper stories onto separate pages of A4 using double spacing. Practise reading them as if to camera whilst looking down as little as possible. See how far you can read ahead.
3. Here is a cue and PTC. Re-write it so that it's no longer than 30 seconds. Record the script, then perform it, without memorizing it, by playing it back on headphones and speaking simultaneously. Repeat until it sounds natural and fluent.

> *Most smokers in Europe would sooner give up sex for a month than give up cigarettes. A new survey of 2000 smokers in six European countries also revealed that although the majority wanted to quit at New Year almost none would. ... reports.*

> *The research by the anti-smoking group 'Scape' emphasizes just how addictive nicotine is – particularly, it seems, amongst the Brits. Most thought that even bungee jumping or parachuting would be easier than kicking the habit. They'd sooner be celibate for a month than be without fags. The British topped the list here ... 80 per cent would sooner give up sex. In the Netherlands, Germany and France it was 70 per cent. In Belgium and Spain, opinion was almost equally divided as to which to do without. Even after a heart attack two-thirds of smokers resume the habit. And as for those New Year's resolutions ... forget it! While 62 per cent of smokers in six countries thought that this was the time to stop ... only 3 per cent were going to try it!*

4. Choose props and location for the above PTC and practise it without the prompt. Remember to keep it simple, especially the confusing statistics. You could even do this on the street without a video camera. Often the crew is out of view anyway with the reporter on a radio microphone. When you've done this one, write your own and practise it.

IN SHORT...

- Be familiar with your autocue script and follow it with your hard copies too for safety.
- Don't hurry. You choose the pace.

- Film scripts have vision details on the left, audio on the right.
- Write the cue first, giving the top lines to the anchor.
- Always make the words match the picture but don't repeat the obvious in the script. Aim for 'added value' information.
- Make your piece to camera active. Use props, walk, choose an appropriate location.
- Rehearse fearlessly, keep it simple and when in doubt, cut it out.
- If you really can't do it, have the grace to admit it and call it a day.

6 Presenting on television

Conjure up in your mind's eye a TV presenter. I expect he or she is sitting at a desk, beautifully coiffured, reading the news in a bright studio. In fact, most presentation work is done on the road in all weathers and is much less glamorous. Many presenters may never get into studio operations and even if they do it may form a very small part of their total output. So, on the grounds of doing the greatest good to the greatest number, we'll look at presenting on location first.

ON THE ROAD

A presenter's job varies dramatically depending whether you are fortunate enough to have a big crew handling all the different tasks or whether it's just you. News operations rely increasingly on Single Camera Units, known as SCUs, where you go on the road with a cameraman and no-one else. There's also a powerful move towards Video Journalists (VJs). VJs do absolutely everything themselves – shoot, edit and package the material. The BBC calls it Personal Digital Production. It's learned on a three-week residential course. By Spring 2003, 200 VJs were PDP trained and there'll be 200 more each year. (Laura Sheeter was the BBC's first completely bi-media PDP trainee; see Chapter 15.) The method makes news-gathering faster and cheaper but it puts massive pressure on the presenters and leaves them with little time to think about how to communicate the story well.

The film crew

These days, large crews are the exception rather than the rule. Outside broadcasts, dramas and documentaries may require a lot of manpower but in news, current affairs and features the name of the game is low numbers, low budget and fast turnaround. The following is a rundown of who might be with you although it could be any combination of these people.

The *camera operator* is responsible for the technical quality of the pictures and ensuring that the director gets the shots he or she wants. Camera operators usually shoot on videotape (there are a number of different acceptable professional formats) but it could conceivably be film. On occasions, when recording a special interview, perhaps with a Head of State, there may be two cameras each set up in different positions: one angled at you, the presenter, and the other at the interviewee. In this way cutting can be done simply by switching from one camera's footage to the other. If it's a single camera unit, sound will go directly into the camera without a sound mixer to adjust it. There may be an editing unit in the back of the car so that as soon as the material is gleaned it can be digitally cut and sent back via satellite link from the roadside.

The *sound technician* carries a portable mixer so that sound can be adjusted as it is recorded. This person is the expert in reducing external noise, using the right kind of microphone, advising where to record for best sound and getting the necessary sound effects so that it will all cut together smoothly in the editing suite. If, for example, you cut from your studio commentary to a roadside interview, there will be a sudden crash of noise. You will need a spare bit of traffic sound to come up gradually smoothing the transition.

The *lighting technician* looks after the lights, filters, spare bulbs, power cables, battery packs and reflectors (collapsible white or metallic material screens that can bounce what little light there may be onto the subject matter). He or she is a specialist in making the greyest day or gloomiest evening usable.

The *director* controls this technical team, ensuring that it achieves what the producer requires. This person visualizes shots to interpret the story. Often the director is also the producer – it's a very grey area.

The *producer* must, literally, produce the goods. The producer's job is to interpret the journalistic game plan which will have been agreed with the editor of the programme and ensure it's morally, ethically, legally and journalistically sound ... and within the budget!

The *researcher* has all the facts and figures, names and addresses, details of locations and screeds of phone numbers to make arrangements and changes while the team is on the road.

The *production assistant* (PA) is a real luxury these days on the road. The PA types up scripts, sorts out forms, budgets and crews, and does much of the organizational work to keep the crew moving. The PA might liaise with the director and producer over timings, costings and access. If you have a PA with you, he or she will also note 'continuity'. This means observing details like what clothes and jewellery the presenter was wearing, how they moved, which way they walked and so on, so that the next day's filming (and any retakes) will match.

The *presenter* is the other crucial member of the team! The presenter might be the kingpin, having researched and fixed the entire story, or may have had nothing to do with it (see Chapter 1). The reporter does not have to be on location all the time – it is even possible not to travel at all! The crew can collect the shots for the presenter to script back at base. Interviews can be conducted by the producer or researcher.

PRESENTING IN A TV STUDIO

Presenting involves a huge amount of multi-tasking. As you sit at a desk to host a show there are a million things to think about at the same time. What's the next item? How long until I must cut off this last interviewee? What is the gallery saying in my ear? What did the interviewee just say? What's the next question? Which camera is on now? Which camera should I look at next? How do I drop two items and carry on in the script? Do I look OK? Why haven't I got a glass of water? Who is the next guest? A storm of considerations. Preparation and prioritizing are essential. Get everything ready in good time. Get into a routine that will become second nature so that nothing gets forgotten. You may even find it useful to write out a checklist. It may sound over the top but once you are in the studio there's literally no going back.

The studio crew

It's helpful to understand what everyone else is doing and why. Try also to grasp what the technical processes are. If you know how long editing videotape takes, you will be less likely to get angry if a last-minute report has not been cut in time.

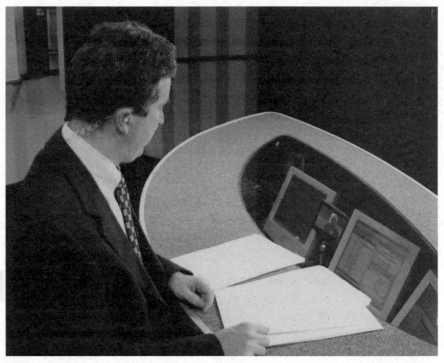

Figure 6.1
News presenter, David Golly, accesses running orders, VT, news wires and other information
through a glass-topped desk, unseen by the audience

Bob Ledwidge, who was for many years a presenter and reporter before
becoming a BBC editor, believes that getting a grip on the technicalities
is essential:

> *I think you have to get into a certain gear or frame of mind to pre-*
> *sent fluently – and I didn't get into this gear until I was well into my*
> *first job in local radio. Presenters need to be comfortable enough*
> *with their material and the whole paraphernalia of broadcasting to*
> *be able to enjoy what they're doing and be able to think one or two*
> *steps ahead. Then they can truly perform.*

News is probably the most demanding of areas when you are starting out.
You really do have to hit the ground running and it's no respecter of
novices or inexperience. Sometimes whoever is in the office, however new
to the job, may be the only person an editor can use for the Big One. News

presenter and reporter, Kirsty Lang, certainly remembers her first job that way:

> *My first 'proper job' was as a pool reporter on BBC Radio Four. Basically, it's like being a fireman. To mix metaphors, you sit on a taxi rank and get sent anywhere. It was an exciting time because there were a whole bunch of disasters. I'd just got the job and there was Piper Alpha (the explosion in the North Sea), then there was the Clapham rail crash, Lockerbie and then I did the plane crash on the M1 and then there was Hillsborough and I did the* Marchioness *riverboat tragedy. But it was slightly unsatisfying work because you'd have these periods of intense and emotionally distressing activity when you'd work like a dog and then you'd spend days sitting there doing nothing.*

The functions of the production team are hugely variable and are listed below. As with the location crew, it is possible to make programmes without many of them.

The *programme editor* is responsible for the final journalistic output and makes the ultimate decisions about the direction of the programme, its style and keeping it within budget. This is the person who hires and fires and to whom the complaints will go.

The *studio producer* is responsible for getting all the items on air, whether in recorded or live form. The producer controls the output from the gallery, ensures the timings are accurate and decides what will be dropped.

The *studio director* is responsible for the visual output, controlling the cameras, how the presenter is sitting and where the lights must be, as well as ensuring that graphics and inserts are used appropriately.

The *floor manager* ensures the programme runs smoothly from within the studio. A floor manager liaises with the presenter, guests and the gallery, counting down the final moments of videotape and cueing you in, fixing microphones, earpieces and talkback.

The *camera operator* shoots under the direction of the director. An operator will look for a good shot and 'offer' it to the director who may choose to accept it and go live through that lens. The director speaks to the cameras through headphones.

The *sound engineer* has to look after all the sound equipment and make sure it's providing the effect the director wants.

The *vision mixer* cuts to each camera as the director demands, effectively editing the vision content live on air.

GOING LIVE IN A STUDIO

A studio is said to be 'live' when cameras are 'turning' or recording. 'Live' in this sense does not necessarily mean that you are being transmitted to the public. You may be recording a programme for transmission (TX) later.

Clearly if you are in fact live (or recording as live which will also be without a break) there really are no second chances. You must get it right first time. This is when you have to be at your coolest even though you're at your most excited. As a result, things go wrong. The presenter's job is to cover for all glitches and failures, whoever's to blame. If you do it well you'll get no credit (except from the rest of the team) since no-one will even be aware there was a problem! If you do it badly you'll get masses of complaints and your boss may well begin to think of others who could do it better. Disasters happen to all of us. Bob Ledwidge may be a lofty executive now but an early horror story haunts him still:

> *I was presenting the BBC's* Look East *news programme from Norwich. The wrong take was run on a VT insert and there was nothing else lined up to play. They cut back to me having an argument with the gallery and then I had to ad lib with a co-presenter who 'froze'. It was a nightmare!*

Similarly, Lis Howell may have spent years in the trade and risen to be Senior Vice President of the cable and satellite group Flextech, but she stills recoils in agony when she remembers her live, on-air showdown with a mouse!

> *We were doing some Christmassy thing about a local animal sanctuary and they brought some animals in to the studio. It was all live at peak evening viewing time. This mouse got out of its cage and, what with the heat of the lights and all that, it bit me on the finger. I remember it hanging on with its teeth. And the immense desire to*

shout, 'Oh shit!' And you're thinking, 'Quick, quick, get this off me!'
It was terrible. As I shook my finger the mouse shook on the end and
you've got thousands of thoughts going through your head. I
thought, 'People are going to think I'm so cruel; I mustn't swear;
Oh my God the pain!; Will I need a tetanus jab?' It got into the
News of the World!

My own embarrassing moment came in front of millions on BBC World
television while I was presenting a live business report. All the numbers
from the money markets around the globe disappeared from the computer
screen in front of me just as I was about to read them out. The screen
behind me which should have had the figures projected on it, was blank.
No matter how many times I pressed my little magic button which should
have changed the graphics, nothing happened. My ad libbing was no match
for this! In the end, after what felt like an eternity, I had to admit defeat and
hand over to the programme anchor, the appropriately named Bob Friend,
who, to my eternal relief, smiled encouragingly and said, 'We all have
mornings like that sometimes, don't we, Janet?' It was later discovered that
other programmes had been playing about with the computer terminal and
forgotten to reset it correctly. It didn't save me from being hastily sidelined
as a business presenter! You really do have to be tough.

Step-by-step to transmission

As always, preparation is the one thing that will stand you in good stead
against all eventualities. CNBC's Nigel Roberts offers this reminder:

Make sure there's water on the desk or you'll get dry. Have a wee
beforehand and don't drink too much coffee or in a two-hour pro-
gramme you'll be going to the loo all the time ... or maybe it's just
me and my prostate!

Check that the order of your scripts and your running order match well
before the show and that the catchlines (or titles) of each item are the same
on both. It causes tremendous confusion in the studio when the director
says in your earpiece, 'We're dropping "Ships"' when on your script it's
called 'Boats'.

If there are any pages missing, ask where they are. Maybe it's a late report
and everyone is waiting for them or maybe the pages were, by mistake,
never put in your set.

Read through all cues. If time's a problem at the very least check the opening cues, so you know what's happening up to the first reasonable break you get which might be a taped report or a commercial break.

Know the names of the key people in the gallery so that you can speak to them swiftly. Most of the questions you need to ask will be addressed to the director and the studio producer.

Whatever you say will be heard by everyone, so be polite and very clear when talking to the gallery. Don't be afraid to ask about anything that's confusing to you. It's better to get it straightened out beforehand than to let it go wrong on air. From my own experience I know that it can be embarrassing to ask something when you asked the same question only a moment ago but you didn't listen to the answer. There's nothing shameful in this. Your brain is working at many different levels at once.

Beware of the unexpectedly live microphone. It might be a slip of the finger that's suddenly going to allow the nation to hear your asides. Consequently, never swear in a studio – the walls have ears!

Be of good humour and keep a brave, optimistic, confident attitude with your team. It's not just the public who need to know that the front person won't fall to bits! It really helps everyone if you can be relied on to keep calm, allow yourself to be produced and be told what to do.

Settle yourself comfortably and take the time to get your seat into the right position for you as well as for the camera shots.

Ensure your earpiece is secure. If you do a lot of studio presentation you will be expected to get an earpiece specially moulded to your own ear. Make sure it's your best ear … some people find one works better than the other. The cable sneaks behind your neck, is clipped to your clothing and then goes down your back. If you have a jacket the wire can run down inside it. At first it can feel cumbersome but try to ignore it and move naturally.

Make sure you have a drink of water to hand for yourself and for any guests that will be turning up.

Prioritizing is an art. Do only what you have time to do with ease before transmission. Don't force yourself through a huge list of reminders if you are going to end up rushing the checks. It'll defeat the object. For example, don't be embarrassed to pull out a mirror and check your face, smooth down your jacket, straighten your hair – if you have time. If you haven't, forget it. The programme content and arrangements are much

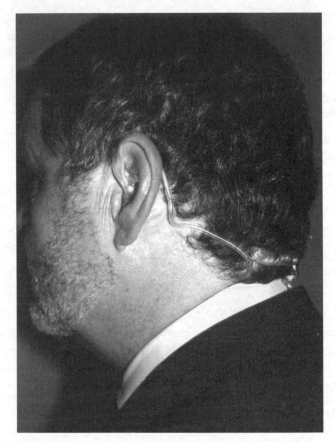

Figure 6.2
The earpiece is your lifeline to the gallery. If well-fitted, it is invisible to the viewer

more important. Don't fuss about things that are way down the running order unless you really must know about them now.

The gallery will want to check the level of your voice to adjust the microphones and they'll want to test the relevant cameras. There will be a few practise shots for later on when, perhaps, others are with you in the studio. For the most part, you can ignore all of that. It is only necessary that you sit there marking up scripts or practising the autocue while the director sorts out the studio arrangements around you.

Make sure you know the quickest way to the toilet, if there is a point in the programme when you are able to leave the studio. If you do rush off, don't use a lift – unless you absolutely have to. It has been known for presenters to get stuck in them!

The floor manager will tell you how long there is remaining before going live. Use this time to get calm and bury yourself in your intro music, taking your pace from it and preparing to immerse yourself in the show. With one minute left you'll get a series of silent hand cues ending with the index finger pointing directly at you. You're on!

Look directly at the relevant camera. Speak out confidently from the very start. It is astonishing how much of a pep you can give yourself by hearing your own voice coming out boldly.

Listen carefully to what you are asked to do during the programme. It's hard because, of course, you are speaking one set of lines and monitoring future instructions in your ear at the same time. An ability to do this calmly will raise your reputation hugely.

Make any interviewees feel at home when they arrive. If you can, speak to them and shake hands. Try to make this unnatural environment appear more normal. Even if you can't chat, at least smile at them. Warn them what the first question will be and tell them when they're going to be on. Explain briefly what's happening:

> *We're just seeing a report on lions in Africa. After that we'll go to the weather and then, when we come back I'll read the introduction to your item. We have a film about one and a half minutes long and then I'll be talking to you, OK? We'll probably start off with how endangered lions actually are. We've got about two minutes for the interview. Stand by.*

Satellite links are used regularly for domestic, not just foreign, broadcasts. You may be talking live to an interviewee on some hillside in Scotland, at a council building only a few hundred yards away, or on a ship at sea. Satellites leave a fractional delay between the end of your question and the interviewee hearing it. Likewise there is a delay between their speech and your hearing the answer. It causes that appalling moment of fear when you suspect the worst – the line's gone down! The delay can be anything between a second and a second and a half. That might appear to be nothing but it's quite enough for a presenter to jump in at the very moment when the answer begins to come. If you need to butt into an answer you must do so clearly and deliberately. Hesitancy results in messy sound and confusion.

When things go wrong, don't flap and don't blame. Concentrate on holding the fort at your end and obey the instructions from the gallery. If you have a better idea, put it swiftly and clearly. If it's thrown out, only remonstrate as much as is sensible in the circumstances, then do what you're told. The time for post mortems is later. A decent presenter should not be a puppet and must have ideas. But likewise, a good presenter must know when to put up and shut up.

When it's all over, collect your scripts and rubbish, log out of any computer you may have been using and clear out, remembering to detach your microphone before you move.

Thank everyone who helped you get the tone right. You don't want to sound pompous like Miss Piggy in the Muppets: 'Thank you for joining me in my little show here tonight!'

There is often a post-programme discussion. It usually doesn't last long. Everyone is tired and they can be 'high' after the stress of it all. It's not necessarily the best moment to discuss what went wrong. Nevertheless, if the faults aren't ironed out then, they may be forgotten and never resolved. Be very careful how you address the team to complain. Find out your facts first. Ask what happened. Explain what effect it had on you. They may not have thought about it the way you do from the hot seat. Be as objective as you can. If possible, forget that it was you who was made to look foolish on screen and develop the feeling for when it is worth persevering with a grievance and when it's wisest to let go rather than cause long-term upset for little benefit. These are difficult judgement calls. Sometimes you have to let everyone know you are not going to stand for an appalling level of incompetence. At other times it can be wisest to say your bit and let it go since you know that nothing can be done and all you'll do is make the rest of the team more disgruntled and unhappy. Of course, if this is the way of things, you may be thinking about changing jobs!

If you dared to consider everything that might go wrong you wouldn't go on. The wonderful thing is that 99 times out of 100 you do carry on, the programme does happen and the disasters are mostly forgotten by the public within hours – if, that is, they ever spotted them in the first place.

A VIEW FROM THE INSIDE: *POWER LUNCH...*
LIVE FROM CNBC EUROPE

Join me as a fly on the wall at the London studios of CNBC Europe, where they're about to do a two-hour live broadcast of business news and you'll get an idea of what really goes on, both in the studio and in the gallery.

Power Lunch is already underway. It starts at noon GMT. You have to make sure you don't look at the wrong clock and remember whether or not the UK is on British Summer Time. The anchor is Nigel Roberts. The transmission is world-wide. Whilst Nigel is sitting behind a vast unclut-tered desk with only a computer screen and keyboard for company, there is frantic activity amongst the team, out of view, in a darkened room adjoining the studio. Seven men and women are controlling the show in the gallery. They can't see Nigel in the flesh – there is no glass window. They view on monitors. Dozens of others are following the markets around the world, writing and updating news. They are at computers in a newsroom which incorporates the open-plan studio set. Eight cameras are available on the floor. A lighting technician is up a ladder sorting out cables. Two comms (communications) operators are beside the gallery in

Figure 6.3
CNBC anchor Nigel Roberts. A studio is a dauntingly large place on which to stamp your authority

a glass booth packed with a wall of monitors. They are bringing up out-side sources. You can see CNBC's Paris correspondent leaning idly against a desk waiting her turn to go live. She's reading copy and has a pen in her hand, oblivious of being watched in London.

The director is about to put up a new strap with someone's name and des-ignation on the televisions of the world. He previews it on one of the many studio monitors, groans and complains that the caption won't fit on the screen. Graphics operator: 'It looks bloody awful!' Studio producer: 'Whoops. Sorry. I didn't check it. I'll re-write.' She taps on a computer. Problem solved. Instantly she's back staring at the running order on the screen, checking timings.

Nigel is chatting away, apparently smiling in at the gallery through the glass of a large monitor, as if he could see them. In fact, of course, he's reading the autocue, ad libbing now and again. '... an interesting set of fig-ures to watch throughout the day. We'll be following that. Philip Middleton joins us now from Merrill Lynch ...'

He's into a complicated market analysis story about the company Amvescap. Middleton talks of 'high lack of visibility on next year's earn-ings with the stock', 'values based on stock trading of sixteen times board earnings', 'cross-border flows', 'pure additive volume'. The business terms bounce around. Nigel takes it in his stride interpreting the lingo to simplify and clarify. His interviewee talks fluently and his enthusiasm helps to keep even the non-business viewers on board for these short moments. Nigel is listening to instructions from the gallery as he asks a final question, checks the next item and looks impassive. The item ends. He looks at the wrong camera. The director barks, 'Camera 2'. In the gallery the countdown to the commercial break has begun. Two red digi-tal clocks are ticking away. One goes forward in real time, the other counts backwards showing the time left in the programme.

In the studio, the red lights of a digital clock showing hours, minutes and seconds glow above the autocue. Around the figures in the centre of the clock, a circle of seconds is lighting up, one by one, as the time runs out for Nigel to wind up. The music is now rolling softly. Nigel's still talking. Time's running out. In no hurry, he completes his 'after the break' trail. The shot changes. The wide reveals the presenter with a guest on either end of his studio desk. 'Shake' says the director into Roberts' ear. He turns and shakes each interviewee's hand in thanks. Immaculate timing. The music swells. The *Power Lunch* logo appears. The break happens right on time.

Figure 6.4
The anchor is used to ignoring newsroom activity right beside him

They are half way through the programme.

The countdown begins for the next segment. With only three seconds left to transmission, Nigel is chatting across the studio to a fellow presenter. There's a camera change. 'Camera 3', says the director. Nigel obeys and immediately launches into the trail for what's coming up. At the news control terminal in the gallery, the operator is feeding in video clips, graphics and sound bites, all of which the anchor is either talking into, over or out of.

Nigel hands over to the markets presenter who stands at the other end of the studio in front of a big board of risers and fallers. The figures are changing all the time because the London markets are open and there's worry about a big announcement on interest rates in Europe. The presenter is ignoring the autocue and ad libbing – too much. The gallery is jittery and tells him to wind up. He's not quick enough and they are over-running.

The programme is constructed in four half-hour chunks. Each item has a precise duration which is put into the electronic running order. The computer automatically adds it all up and shows, in the bottom left-hand corner, how far adrift they are in real time. With 20 minutes left in this section, they are 1'45" over. A minute after that, the screen is reading 1'53". Things are getting worse.

They go live to New York, then to Paris for a report on the Bourse. Block graphs, line graphs and statistics fly over the screen, twisting and rotating.

Nigel is rushing to get rid of the Paris line, trying to break into the seemingly unstoppable flow of the correspondent. It's become imperative to end her report because the gallery has just told him a different line to London is about to be lost and they must get to it before it goes down.

They are still over-running. The producer orders, 'No world news'. Drastic measures are needed. This has saved them 1'30". With nine minutes left in this segment, the producer has pulled them back to a 41-second over-run. Now there's hope. But the producer is not happy. She knows that the whole problem started way back at the beginning of the show when an interview went on too long. Everything has conspired against her since then. At the break, incredibly, the situation has got still worse. They are 1'15" over.

As the two minutes of commercials tick away, someone rushes to move Camera 1 on the studio floor. Two guests are hurried into position. They must sit quietly waiting for their turn later on. The anchor will continue as if they did not exist. The cameras won't show that they are there until the right shot is chosen from the gallery and, magically, they will be on TV.

The director queries with the producer which is which of the interviewees. He needs to know so that the correct captions can be put up. The producer speaks to Nigel, 'Just confirm, will you, that the chap on your left is the CEO from Whittards [the tea and coffee makers]. The other guy is the editor of *Jane's* [specialist publication on weaponry] for the Iraq discussion.'

Seconds from going live, Nigel replies: 'Actually, it's the other way round. Our friend from Whittards says he's quite good on tea or coffee but less good on weapons of mass destruction!'

As a VT runs, one guest is rushed out and replaced by another. Nigel picks up the lapel microphone lying across the desk and clips it to the new interviewee's lapel. Someone in the gallery says a round of coffee would be nice. 'We should get that guy from Whittards to sponsor us!' chimes in the cap gen operator (working the caption generator).

Nigel is settling the guest. Roy Ruddock of Halewood International is a financial commentator on the European economy. Nigel is asking him about his six-month-old baby: 'Are you getting any sleep?' 'No', comes the rueful reply. 'How do you change the rake on this chair?' Nigel leans over and fiddles with the seat. He must hurry now. Suddenly he sits up straight, puts his shoulders back and ignores the interviewee as if there was no such person. The film report ends. In the gallery they are preparing 'hot boards' – the graphics which will show the rise and fall of currencies and economies. Camera 1 is on Ruddock, Cameras 2 and 3 are on Nigel, Camera 4 is on another guest. Camera 7 offers another view and Camera 6 is standing by with the next contributor on an outside source.

The director suddenly shouts, 'Tell the newsroom to shut up!' The producer demands it instantly over a radio microphone. Everyone wired for sound can hear a sudden hissing sound as the staff in the newsroom whisper, 'Ssssh!'

The producer's got a new problem. The autocue is about to run out. An item which is due up has been put into the system so late that the cue isn't there. 'Ad lib to the next interview, please', she says. Already Nigel is at that point: 'So the Central Bank are meeting as we speak ... well, actually they're probably having a light lunch! After that they'll be discussing an ECB rates change ...' Suddenly everything's all right again. The script has gone in. The autocue is back up. Nigel is introducing the Frankfurt correspondent.

Rushing to the next break they're over again. There can be as many as twenty live interviews in a programme like this. Each item can and probably will alter the predicted running time. Nigel is told to cut script. He drops lines and hurries on.

More VT. More guests are brought in. Nigel speaks to the gallery, 'Can someone get water for our guests?' 'No' comes the gallery's laughing reply. He doesn't think it's funny. 'Water, please' he repeats, testily. Someone sprints in with water.

The breaker for the end of the ads is coming up. The producer moans, 'Oh no! She's going to be in the way!'. And sure enough, no matter which camera they choose, the silhouette of the girl who brought the water flashes across the frame as they go live.

The programme editor who has been watching from the newsroom suddenly arrives in the darkness of the gallery. 'Do we usually take a break

Figure 6.5
The director selects the shots of the interviewee on the left monitor and the presenter on the right. The smaller monitors to his left are the other available studio cameras and outside sources. Note the digital clocks, one showing real time and the other showing transmission time remaining

here?' 'Yes', replies the producer. 'Are you sure?' 'Yes.' 'Is that sensible?' 'Yes.' The editor withdraws. Everyone knows that whatever the problem is, it can't be discussed now. Post mortems are post-programme!

There are 9 minutes 43 seconds until the end of the show and they are 1 minute 56 seconds over. This is a real test. They can be a few seconds out either way during the programme but at the end they must be spot on. It's sold advertising and the American market. There's no question. Come hell or high water they must be out on time.

'That strap's wrong! Get rid of it!' yells the producer. Fortunately it was on a preview screen. It's changed instantly. No harm done.

Into the last minute and somehow they've managed to correct the situation. But someone's forgotten to prepare the 'Euro/dollar' hot board. The vital figures which are the top story of the business day are not ready. Nigel is ad libbing, hoping desperately that they'll arrive on the screen in time. He's watching the clock; 30 seconds of unscripted chat. Suddenly with 45 seconds left, the hot board arrives. Enough time to report the figures live. The countdown has begun. The clock runs down for the last time. The music rises. The camera pulls back. The *Power Lunch* logo fills the screen and turns to black.

EXERCISES

1. Record a live studio discussion programme, a holiday features show and a news bulletin. Compare the styles of presentation. Can you spot mistakes? Can you see the presenter reading the autocue? Does the ad libbing work?
2. Read any newspaper feature and then talk about it convincingly for two minutes. When you begin to run out of facts be sure you've got some ploys to keep you going. It's a long time!
3. Practise reading out loud with real emphasis and meaning. Any material will do. Try the back of a cereal packet, a page of a novel, a weather forecast, a poem.

IN SHORT...

Before going to the studio:

- Ensure you have the latest script and running order. If you haven't got either of these make sure the director knows about it.
- Take with you any notes you may need for live interviews. Ensure you've got the guests' names and designations right.
- Have a couple of pens with you. Sometimes a highlighter can be handy and a note pad.
- If you have your own earpiece make sure you take it.
- Remember your computer log-in and passwords.
- Put on your jacket and/or tie. You may have been working around the office in shirtsleeves.
- Look in the mirror and comb your hair.
- Go to the toilet. It may be a while before you can get there again! It's also a good place to get 30 seconds of quiet to order your thoughts.

In the studio:

- Settle yourself in your seat and adjust it for comfort. If it swivels (which it shouldn't because such chairs are a disaster for interviewees and interviewers alike) lock it off because, however well intentioned, you won't be able to prevent yourself from swinging in it.

- If you need a lapel microphone (one that is attached to your clothing), wait for the floor manager to put it in position for you. If you have to do it yourself, feed the wire up the inside of your shirt or blouse front and clip it to your tie or clothing about a third of the way down your chest. Alternatively, slip it up the inside of your jacket and clip it to your lapel. Put it where it can't rub against anything that will cause rustling.
- Put your earpiece on your best ear. The cable is looped round to the back of your neck and down inside your jacket or jumper.
- Make sure your script papers are in order and that everything you need, including your glass of water, is within easy reach.
- If there's time, start speaking your script. This is a chance to check that the autocue is operating. The gallery can 'take level' on your voice (i.e. adjust their controls for volume) while you're doing it.
- Log on to your computer and make sure it's working properly.
- If there are interviewees with you, help them to relax.
- Listen for instructions from the gallery but ignore commands being given to others.
- Be unflappable – even if you are quaking inside. It gives the entire team confidence. Don't fuss and interfere with the jobs of others. Concentrate on your own tasks.
- Keep the gallery informed. Whilst you want to keep out of the director's hair, you must maintain the information flow. Be precise and speedy but not curt.

7 Presenting on radio

It is the lot of radio broadcasters, as most will admit, constantly to be seen as inferior to television presenters. Sadly they often secretly believe it themselves and struggle desperately to get in front of a camera, regardless of their suitability. The two mediums, whilst requiring many of the same skills, also demand different abilities. Television is technically more complicated and, I believe, more stressful and cumbersome; it is certainly not true that because you have mastered it you can slip easily into radio. There is a closeness to the audience which makes the presenter,

Figure 7.1
Millions of listeners daily, yet still radio presenters have a lower profile. Georgina Bowman, presenter of *Newsbeat* on 1FM

potentially, much loved but also extremely vulnerable. Radio is not just TV without the pictures.

Jenni Mills, a Sony Award winner for her work in radio, has also built a career in TV, but while she has found herself to be a good presenter on radio she's far less comfortable in vision. Instead, her skill turns out to be direction:

They tackle subjects differently – radio can be more thoughtful, more ideas-led and requires a presenter to create pictures in the head of the listener. In TV the pictures are already there and it's the presenter's job to enhance and explain them. Radio is a very good medium for telling a retrospective story, whereas television is at its best when it's firmly in the present – things are happening now in front of your eyes and the story is unfolding in 'real time'. In television, your physical appearance comes into play much more – how you move, the expression on your face, whether you look stiff in front of the camera. As a TV director, I have to say that some people just look wrong in front of camera. Not everybody is photogenic – and that's not a matter of physical beauty, it's an indefinable thing which often bears little relation to how a person comes across in real life. I, for instance, look like a pale translucent blob on television. Bucket-loads of make-up were always required to turn my face into something that actually had a shape and I had to be very careful about what I wore – and that, of course, made me feel so unconfident that I wasn't able to relax and be myself. So while I would say I wasn't a bad radio presenter, I only just scraped through on TV. Ironically, now that I'm older, fatter and a great deal more wrinkly, I'd probably be a much better TV presenter than I was then because I'm much easier with who I am and don't care nearly so much about how I look – confidence works wonders!

CREATING A SOUND AND STYLE

Radio is a remarkably intimate medium. Every presenter says you should imagine your mum, partner or a friend and talk only to them. If there is a golden rule, this is it. But you need to do more than this.

A presenter either quite spontaneously, or else deliberately, will create a sound that will become a 'USP' (unique selling point) – something that marks you out from the rest. Since you can only be yourself this involves developing certain of your preferred characteristics. Maybe you are forthright by nature or maybe gentle and coaxing with people; these traits will form a style that 'brands' you. At the same time, when you're starting out it's as well to be able to adapt your sound so that you maximize your job opportunities and get heaps of experience.

Jenni Mills' early memories are, I suspect, typical:

> *My earliest ventures into presentation are best described as embarrassing! One of the first on-air jobs I had was presenting a weekly request show on BBC Radio Bristol. I was so nervous I had to write a script for every word, down to the time checks! It took weeks to separate me from my comfort-blanket script and persuade me to ad lib. Only then did I begin to communicate. The other huge mistake I made was talking* down *to the audience. I was in my early twenties. I knew that a BBC local radio audience was considerably older than I was, and wanted Jim Reeves when I preferred the Sex Pistols, but that's no reason to treat them as if they're senile! The problem was I didn't really know anyone who was much older than myself, apart from my mum, and I had no idea how to communicate with them. Again, it took a long time to realize that you can communicate with anybody if you think of them as being on the same level.*

AD LIBBING

Much of speech radio is unscripted. Being voluble by nature is not sufficient. Good chat requires general knowledge and an appreciation of your audience. There is a much greater risk on radio that you get carried away with a sense of your own importance and believe that anything you say must be interesting. Don't, as they say, go there! Research the facts then let your mind range widely around the subject. Make new and different connections, unusual observations. Listen to what your friends have to say. What's being discussed in the pub? Keep your feet on the ground.

Edwina Currie, who swapped a life in politics for a presenter's seat on BBC Radio Five Live, believes that this spontaneous aspect of radio is one of the things that really marks it out from television. Your senses must be very keen or you can land yourself in terrible trouble:

> *A radio audience listens carefully, so your choice of words is very important. The audience won't miss anything. My most memorable occasion in broadcasting was the night of the Omagh bombing in*

*1998. We commandeered the Belfast studio. It was three hours live
on air, mostly unscripted. The guests ranged from Sinn Fein to fami-
lies of the bereaved. It was awesome.*

Radio presenters often involve the audience to provide material. Terry
Wogan uses his listeners shamelessly for his Radio Two breakfast show,
to the extent that they have almost become part of his production team.
The style is fabulously successful.

Phone-ins, e-mailing and text messaging all allow you very personal contact with the listeners, bringing in ideas and entertainment, providing the
programme with a style and the station with a recognizable identity.

Of course there's quite a gulf between a music and a speech presenter –
here are some thoughts from some folk who ought to know!

Simon Mayo had been happy playing music on Radio One, although he
admits to sometimes becoming irritated by it. Then there were contract
negotiations and he chose the challenge of all speech Radio Five Live. It
was tough and he confesses the move wasn't without some problems –
like broadcasting on court cases:

*Having the mic open for three hours almost non-stop instead of a
total of twenty minutes between songs was a huge change. Nicky
Campbell took me out before I started on Five Live and told me that
it was all about using the right vocabulary. There are a few questions*

Figure 7.2
Old dogs, new tricks. Simon Bates, Kevin Greening, Simon Mayo and Richard Skinner made their names as
Radio One DJs. Also here, Steve Orchard, Director GWR Group (second left) and Phil Roberts, MD Music
and Artist Relations EMAP (far right)

that will fill six or seven minutes quite easily, such as 'What can you tell us?', 'What reaction has there been?', 'What has been the police reaction?' My advice for those coming in is to learn the trade and find out what you're good at.

Richard Skinner, now with Magic 102, believes producers are vital – but not necessarily the normal variety.

I fell into this by accident after a stint in hospital radio. I learnt as I went along. Even now I do appreciate 'coaching' but from outside the studio. Either a wife or best friend or a programme director – it doesn't matter. Everyone must have someone as their producer.

Kevin Greening, who has also shifted to Five Live, agrees. Despite his years in the profession, he sometimes records his show:

The day I listen back to a tape and am happy will be the day I have become a monster.

Simon Bates, too, is presenting all speech but he's committed to all radio – whether music or speech:

If you're not into radio you've got to be pretty dull. We know what we do doesn't really matter. We sometimes have a bad day but there is always the chance to do better tomorrow. You learn each day. Just one word of advice for those coming in to the job: be wary of who you take advice from. There are very few people in this industry who you work for when starting out, in whose interest it is for you to succeed. It's usually about their *careers, not yours.*

The former Head of Radio at the University of the West of England, Jonathan Hewat, who has himself been a presenter for twenty years, has this advice:

Successful, natural presentation styles are deeply founded in preparation, preparation, preparation. The other three great 'Ps' are practise, practise, practise. Whether it's news, continuity, sport or music presentation. If you can't get a go on hospital radio or a student station when you're starting up, then do it 'for real' in the privacy of your own home. And make it real. Keep to time – no stopping and no falling off air! Record it and play it back for analysis. Then, be honest with yourself. Also listen to others constantly and analyse.

RUNNING COMMENTARY

My first experience of doing an uninterrupted radio commentary was of a Royal visit to the refurbished real tennis courts at Hampton Court. It was a big occasion on BBC Radio London's schedule. In fact the 'action' was limited and could have been summed up in a 30-second voice piece *after* the event. But the job is to describe it, *as it happens*. You have to communicate the atmosphere and make the listeners feel they can *see* it all.

The bare facts looked something like this: large crowds, small school-children with flags, big black car arrives, diminutive lady in pale blue emerges, shakes hands with dignitaries and enters the building. Inside and out of view, she watches a game of tennis. She comes out some time later, waves again and leaves.

In the event, as so often happens, everything was late. The Queen was delayed in traffic. Unfortunately, I was live on air and had to talk for about fifteen minutes. I used every morsel of my research and ample numbers of children and dignitaries as interviewees. This is a good exercise in running commentary. Look at the Exercises at the end of this chapter to see how it's done and attempt it yourself. (For more about commentary, see Chapter 9.)

The whole thing is a study in lateral thinking. Make notes of people's names, historical events, anniversaries, articles you've read, things that you noticed earlier, comments made to you, other similar experiences you've had. It's better to have too much to say than to be left floundering.

Talking of floundering, tune in to this telling memory from LBC's Sandy Warr. It shows how very 'kick ball and scramble' unscripted radio can be at times. It's also a lesson in how persistent broadcasters are in the face of adversity!

> *Most comic was an outside broadcast covering the Boat Race on the Thames. We had left our radio car outside a pub at the finish line. The first problem came when my co-presenter locked the car with the keys inside and we missed our first contribution. I stood there desperately asking for anyone to break into the car just as a policewoman walked past! As we tried to force entry my co-presenter suddenly found a spare set of keys in his pocket! All went well until the race itself went past, followed by a huge flotilla of vessels and an enormous flood tide. Within minutes the river rose several metres and people got stranded on fence posts. I was live on*

air as the water began lapping round our car. I climbed onto the roof and pulled a few children up with me, all the while continuing a running commentary. Moments later we had to end transmission rather hurriedly as the water was threatening the electrics. The moment was immortalized in a Broadcast *magazine cartoon of a race commentator marvelling at how the light and dark blue boats had been beaten by a pale grey Cortina!*

KNOW THE LAW

Live radio is one of the most legally dangerous places to be. It's easy to stumble into one of the two main danger zones – a defamation or a contempt of court – whilst simply trying to be provocative. It's up to you to know what is libellous and what is simply fair comment, made honestly, on a matter of public interest. You don't want to be sued and you don't want to lose your job, but the real incentive to know your law is so that you can defend your right to ask difficult questions and get the answers the public have a right to hear. If you don't, you will always be bland and frightened.

Figure 7.3
Sandy Warr (safely on dry land!). When the person you're talking to is an unknown phone-in caller, you can only hope they won't defame someone before you can stop them

Raging self-censorship is the order of the day on radio and TV because reporters and editors are often ignorant. Politicians and others in public life frequently get much more training than presenters. That training involves how to frighten you off with phrases like '*sub judice*'. In fact the matters referred to as such are often not being dealt with by a genuine court of law and are therefore not out of bounds at all.

Contempt of court is one of the easiest rules to fall foul of. A contempt means that your words create a substantial risk of prejudicing a fair trial. It is very common for presenters to use the newspapers as topical talking points. But they frequently sail much too close to the wind where unresolved trials are concerned and where members of the public are being questioned by the police. A number of times in the recent past, judges have abandoned court cases because of ill-considered comments by journalists.

It is sometimes not at all clear whether a person is voluntarily helping the police, in which case you are free to comment, or whether that person has been charged, which means the proceedings are 'active' and therefore you can reveal only the bare facts. 'Active' proceedings means when the relevant *first steps* have been taken e.g. an arrest has been made or a warrant issued for an arrest. The trouble is, you often don't know the true picture. Technically, if someone is at the police station against his or her will that person is, in law, under arrest whether or not the proper procedures have been completed.

Guests sometimes have an alarming habit of defaming people on air. A defamation is a statement that tends to expose someone to hatred, ridicule or contempt, cause them to be shunned or avoided, lower them in the eyes of right-thinking members of society or disparage them in their business, trade or profession. There are defences if, for example, you can prove that it's true or that it was fair comment, honestly made, on a matter of public interest.

Phone-ins are a big worry. Some have a few seconds' delay on the output so that objectionable callers can be pulled off air. If you are embarking on a risky discussion, warn the interviewee of the limitations. If the interviewee does say something defamatory your station will be liable too since you broadcast the comments. Your only option is to mitigate the damage. Distance yourself from the allegation, correct it, attribute it, balance it but most of all end any attempts to return to it. You may be able to do enough to head off a writ. At the very least you will have demonstrated a responsible attitude which may impress the court when damages are being assessed.

Remember that the police can also be guilty of defamation or contempt. You mustn't feel safe just because the interviewee is someone in authority who ought to know better!

Your bible on legal matters must be *McNae's Essential Law for Journalists* (L. C. J. McNae, published by Butterworths Law). Make sure you get the very latest edition and keep updating it.

Be aware of your own company's code of conduct or set of production guidelines. It will contain advice on how you should behave in all sorts of moral and ethical dilemmas. Often it will be a great deal more stringent than the law of the land, for example in its policy on swearing or the use of children in interviews.

If you are in any doubt about such matters you must ask. Better to get it right than get a writ.

NEWS READING

Many newsreaders write their own stories. Others will be talking from someone else's script which can be surprisingly tricky. News presenter, Kirsty Lang, certainly thought so and sought help from Radio Four's Chief Announcer, Peter Donaldson (see Chapter 8):

> *When you are a reporter, because you're writing your own stuff, you connect with it in a way that you don't connect so much with something that's written by someone else. So I was just reading it out. What Peter said to me was that you had to visualize. If you are talking about two children burning to death in a house fire, you have to visualize two children burning to death in a house fire. My expression and intonations were all wrong because I was just reading out words.*

Sentence construction, the use of words, the logical progression of facts – all these things can be alien to your own style and sometimes you are forbidden to make any changes for legal reasons or because the presenter is not expected to interfere with the sub's work. Five Live's Richard Evans says:

> *Unlike many other jobs in radio and television, no-one teaches you how to be a presenter. People are generally thrown in at the deep end. The bottom line is that you have to be capable of being a 'gob*

*on a stick' – reading out what is put in front of you and making it
sound like it is your own – whatever you think of it.*

Always read your script out loud. It's the best way to test the sound of
it and ensure there's no repetition. Check all pronunciations. They'll
throw you if you don't practise and anyway it's insulting to get names
wrong. Read thoroughly or you may overlook a 'he' instead of 'she'
or that a conjunction has been omitted. You can be sure that when you read
it with the concentration of a live broadcast, you will read what is written –
and even if it's wrong! I once found myself fluffing halfway through the
first story on a Radio One news bulletin because I was reading precisely
what was in front of me … but three words had been left out. They were
words that I normally scribbled on the top of the script myself – my own
name! Because the words 'Janet Trewin reporting' weren't there, I
stopped. Incredibly I went back, said my name and then started again!
Adrenalin makes you do weird things.

Arrive at the studio with time to settle yourself. Walk. Running leaves you
breathless and your authority shattered. Put on the headphones and make
sure that you can hear 'cue programme' – that is, the sound of the output –
clearly. Do a level check by reading the first story exactly as you will do
on air so the volume of your voice matches the broadcast.

Spend the few moments you have practising the script. Check where you
can breathe. Mostly it's obvious, but just occasionally you may need to
make a mark to remind yourself.

The bulletin is punctuated by the pauses between stories. Don't rush. Try
to get the right tone for each one. You need your wits about you so you
don't start reading a funny story in a sonorous tone or *vice versa*.

WRITING FOR RADIO

I believe it is seldom a disadvantage to be without TV pictures. They can
be distracting. You have to allow time for them to be assimilated and that
means a simpler script. Without pictures your writing can afford to be
more demanding in its language and concepts. You will hear people say,
'That's a telly story', meaning the pictures will be great. It may be so but
I have never abandoned a story because it can't be done on radio. Always

think in sound when you are in radio. It may seem obvious but it's a habit to be learned.

The style must depend on who will be hearing it and when and how they will be listening to it. Are they quietly at home in the evening with few distractions or driving an HGV in a traffic jam during the day (a matter that TV doesn't have to deal with)? Is it a fast pop station for teenagers or Classic FM?

Voice pieces

As always, write the cue first and don't repeat those words in the opening story lines. I once complained to a student for doing this and he defended himself boldly saying he thought reporters were supposed to do that since you heard it all the time on the radio!

Make the cue striking, clear and concise, raising the questions that are answered in the piece. When the item is finished, re-read the cue and if the issues raised in it are not solved by the item then either the cue is wrong or you've gone off the point in the piece.

Keep an eye on timings. News copy stories can be anything from 10 seconds to 30 seconds long. Voice pieces may be only 20 seconds on a pop station but 30 or 40 seconds on a slower, all speech station. Again, the three-words-a-second rule applies.

Below are some examples showing how different styles can be. Note that the script is given a 'tag' or title. Every copy of this script and the recorded versions must be named in exactly the same way.

The first version is for a Radio Four-style bulletin (Figure 7.4).

And the same item prepared for a pop station (Figure 7.5).

Whilst the reporter's script will look like these figures, the studio presenter's script may well look like Figure 7.6. The presenter only needs the cue, the 'in words', 'out words' and the duration.

Note the other information. It's the 1600 Powernews Update. It's clear who wrote it. Radio scripts require much less technical information than TV scripts. Frankly, they can even be written by hand on the back of a fag packet – and often are!

E-COMMERCE   Speak

Cue:

A new report claims that e-commerce is not making the huge savings that companies were expecting. High Street banks are reversing their branch closure plans because customers dislike electronic business and prefer to talk to real people. Our financial reporter, Jo Speak reports:

The survey looked at 120 banks, insurers and asset managers and discovered that the headlong rush to online business was saving them only half the money they had thought it would. Customers want to discuss their affairs with people, not machines, and they get fed up with slow electronic response times. On average it takes eight hours to answer an e-mail. Already Europe's first Internet bank has closed and other banks, like Abbey National, are trying to make their branches more 'people friendly' by setting up coffee bars in them. Other companies too have been suffering the same effects. The Association of British Travel Agents admits that few people are buying online. Instead of the predicted 30%, only 2% of sales ore over the Web.

Figure 7.4
Script for a Radio Four style bulletin

E-BIZ   Speak

It seems that doing deals online is not the money-spinner everyone thought it was going to be. Customers don't trust it and get fed up with waiting for replies to e-mails … on average it takes eight hours for a response. Europe's first Internet bank has already gone down the tubes and high street banks are putting the brakes on their branch closure programmes. Abbey National's so worried they're setting up people-friendly coffee bars. Travel agents too admit e-biz is bad. Almost nobody wants to buy a holiday on line. They'd predicted it'd be 30% of sales. In fact it's just 2%.

Figure 7.5
Script prepared for a pop station

1600   POWERNEWS UPDATE   Speak

E-BIZ

E commerce is getting the elbow, according to a report just out. The study of banks and financial services says that the dash for e-biz is netting only half the savings they expected. Customers hate computers and prefer people. Jo Speak has this:

CUE IN: 'It seems that doing deals online …

CUE OUT: "… 30% of sales. In fact it's just 2%."

DUR: 20"

Figure 7.6
Studio presenter's script

TIPTREE.

CUE:

Come the hot, holiday times of summer, lives change. Bags are packed. There is travelling. Rules and concepts that are adhered to through the long, dark winter become inappropriate, our behaviour changes and often so do our friends.

Tiptree is a small place far out on the flat, unspoilt, coastal land of East Essex. It's mid-way between a village and a small town. BUT, in summer it becomes a veritable city, with an influx of people who come for only one thing — to pick the fruit in the orchards all around for Wilkin and Co., the famed Tiptree jam company. Janet Trewin has been to experience the extraordinary summer community that descends upon the fields of Tiptree from all over the world.

FX . BAND 1…
Leaves rustling, people's voices.

mix with

FX . DISC
Skylark.

dip and hold under

LINK ONE:

It's a green sea of strawberry plants. And bobbing in the waving leaves are scores of bright baseball caps. Beneath them in the shallows of the trenches are the pickers, sitting in the dirt, bent double, kneeling or cross-legged, fingers fishing for the scarlet fruit.

TAPE… BAND… 1
IN: 'WELL I'VE BEEN DOING IT FOR 34 YEARS…
OUT: '…THINKING OF OUR OLD AGE ISN'T IT EH?"
DUR: 1'11"

LINK TWO

We are not talking the odd day picking your own. Oh no. The ten million pound annual turnover of the Wilkin & Co, Tiptree jam company relies on these willing workers to harvest nigh on one thousand acres of fruit. They're here from June to October. That nice Mr Peter — that's the great grandson of the founder — provides the caravan park, you provide the elbow grease.

TAPE… BAND 2
IN: 'IT WAS STARTED BY MY…
OUT: '…PICK STRAWBERRIES.'
DUR: 33'

SEGUE

TAPE… BAND 3
IN: "IF I HAD A BUNCH…
OUT: "…DON'T NOTICE IT NOW"
DUR:15"

Figure 7.7
The opening of a ten-minute feature for BBC Radio Four

Features

The best radio features begin with something ear-catching – a sound effect, an astonishing piece of interview or music. Suppose you are presenting a story from a small town in France on a quiet Sunday. Consider recording bells tolling, the noise of feet on cobbled stones, distant conversations in French at street-side coffee tables. All this builds the atmosphere. The noise can be a fine backdrop to a voice piece or to two-way, as long as the mix is right. Don't allow the 'atmos' (atmosphere) to get too loud.

This atmos track is also handy to smooth off any sharp edits as you move from the interviews into your links in the same way as for TV (see Chapter 5). Always get a clean sound effects track to run underneath you. It only takes a moment; simply record the bells with no interviewee speaking for about a minute.

When writing your links don't repeat the words your interviewee has used. Keep your sentences short and lively. Avoid long words and be very specific about your grammar and use of language. A listener must understand what you are saying first time around. You can be conversational using contractions rather than 'do not' and 'will not'.

You must draw pictures in the mind. Describe what you see and relate it to the issue. This is a more subtle art than TV. There are many who attempt it in a clod-hopping way and it fails:

> *The birds singing merrily in this rural retreat seem to be the only characters who are happy since the news of the new development.*

It's tortuous and note 'news' and 'new' – not good scripting. How about ...

> *I'm just a few minutes from the M1 yet the noise here is not from traffic. A recent RSPB report said there were 30 species of bird in this area, so it's little wonder that there is fury at the news of the development.*

Incorporate the sound into the fact and make it a vital part of the evidence.

THE RADIO STUDIO

Radio studios are a great deal less technical than television studios – and are smaller. Often all that is required is a microphone and a table. Sound baffling on the walls and ceiling are *de riguer* in the best studios but you can manage without. Going underneath a table and putting coats over the top may be all you can do in the circumstances and you'd be surprised how effective it can be!

Many talk and music studios are 'self-op', meaning that you operate the microphones, phone lines, CDs and other outside sources. For bigger budget programmes, or ones where balancing the sound between guests is very important and too tricky for the presenter to do, there will be a studio and an operations room. The two are connected by a door and there's a large plate-glass window so that the production team can see the presenter. Visual contact can be important. It allows the producer to signal to the anchor. It also allows presenters to use the production team as an audience to bolster their performance.

Where you have a technical operator, the presenter simply sits at a large table with the interviewees around him/her. They each have a microphone on the table in front of them or hanging from the ceiling. The presenter wears headphones to hear instructions from the sound booth. The guests

Figure 7.8
A self-op radio news studio

need not wear cans but if they do they will be wired through another channel so they won't hear any of the backchat coming from the ops room.

Lights on the table and over the door, both inside and out, will come on when the studio is live.

Your scripts are in front of you, either hard copies or on a computer monitor. Needless to say a page is written on one side only.

If you are operating the studio yourself, the 'desk' in front of you comprises the microphone and an array of faders to control the other sources. There will be computer monitors and keyboards to update you regarding news wires or phone callers and e-mails. There are headphones, play-out systems, CDs and tapes. There are TV screens so you can keep abreast of other broadcasting, there's digital radio text scrolling and possibly a web cam. There may not be so much equipment as in a TV studio but in radio you must be able to work all of this yourself and still sound at ease.

ON THE ROAD

Radio presentation outside the studio is freedom itself compared with TV. Frequently there is only you and the recorder. This might be a digital player or a conventional professional cassette tape recorder. Editing can be done away from base on a computer and the finished product sent back using a portable satellite dish or phone. The small amount of equipment needed means you can get to all sorts of places that would be impossible for a film crew. Employers don't feel that you are so likely to upset the shop-floor workers, grieving parents aren't so embarrassed to show their feelings as they would be in front of a whole TV production team. You can establish a relationship with your interviewee much more quickly. Nor are you dependent on light or the weather, although high winds will boom on the microphone even if it's covered with a windshield.

Make the most of your opportunities when you are away from the studio environment. Search constantly for the places that will tell the story for you, even if they don't provide you with sound effects. You have to be there and see for yourself in order to relay it to others.

Sometimes silence itself is the effect that tells a story, like the hush of a mortuary. Too much noise can also tempt you to avoid the location but usually there are ways round it. Turn down the levels and work very

Figure 7.9
Radio broadcasters can get where others can't. Here's how to broadcast from a hang glider with a piggy-back training rig

close to your microphone or record a wild track and put your voice over it later.

When it comes to live location broadcasting, you almost always have to fly by the seat of your pants. The simplest things cause problems. Someone goes off to the loo and can't find their way back. A member of the public kicks out a vital lead that puts you off air. Good preparation and planning can save you from such nightmares. Sometimes, though, it just goes on being a nightmare! Due to a catalogue of disasters, Jenni Mills may be the only person ever to have apparently introduced a Radio Four programme with an expletive:

> *It was a live outside broadcast series in the 1980s called* Weekend, *on Radio Four. I and my co-presenter, the actress Helen Atkinson-Wood, were at the Chatsworth Horse Trials. The site was the show-ring itself but, because of the difficulties of getting the OB van close enough, the sound engineer was equipped with a backpack to beam the sound back to the van half-a-mile away, where the producer and an engineer would play in any pre-recorded tapes or music.*

Figure 7.10
OBs are fraught with danger…especially when there are this many people to mess up the equipment!

*Then the signal would go via a landline back to London. The pro-
ducer could communicate with us over talkback in our headphones
which were to be plugged into the soundman's backpack. So for the
broadcast Helen and I would be attached to him via a set of
unwieldy umbilical cords, like some sort of three-bodied Creature
from the Black Lagoon. An hour before transmission, Helen and
I set out from the OB van to the show ring to meet our interviewees,
carrying our scripts and a rather large clock on a pole. The
researcher was with us but the soundman was to follow a bit later
with the other paraphernalia. Twenty minutes to go and he
still hadn't turned up. We were a little uneasy but had no way of
communicating with the OB van, because he had all the gear. We
sent the researcher to run back half a mile and find out what was
happening. Luckily she was a fit girl – and about ten minutes or
so later panted back to say that he'd left the van ages ago but had
completely disappeared! Five minutes later the programme editor,*

looking a bit red in the face, panted up to say that the troops were out looking for him. Radio Four continuity had been warned there was a hitch and was standing by to fill until we found him and managed to get on air. All we could do was watch the minutes ticking by on the monster clock and listen to Radio Four's output on a tinny transistor, trying to look as if this happened every day so our interviewees (who were getting a bit fidgety) didn't realize there was anything terribly wrong. At two minutes past the hour, when we were due on air, we heard the news finish and the announcer back in London start desperately to fill, telling the listeners there was a 'technical hitch'. At this point, suddenly over the horizon there hove into view a pale and dishevelled soundman, staggering under the weight of his backpack. The programme secretary had found him passed out under a tree, having succumbed to a bout of food poisoning. He tottered towards us and started fumbling with microphones and headphones, at which point we all got into an almighty tangle of wires. I could hear the OB van shouting down the talkback link in my headphones that we were ready to go. London could cue over to us. The OB van was supposed to play in a bit of sig. music, before I welcomed listeners to the programme. But just at this vital moment the soundman got himself in a real muddle with all the bits of cable and started yanking my headphones off to try to get the 'knitting' sorted out – so I, clutching my microphone, yelled at him, 'Don't touch it!' It was precisely halfway through this phrase that the confused engineer back at the van opened the fader for my mic to go live on air. What the audience at home heard was the calm tones of Radio Four continuity '... and now we are able to join Jenni Mills live at Chatsworth', followed by an anguished squawk '... ch it!' from me, before the theme music. Thus I became the first Radio Four presenter (apparently) to say 'shit' live on air.

Faking it

It's always possible in radio to fake it. What the eye doesn't see the heart doesn't grieve over. There are sound effects recordings by the million, which you can use in moderation, but nothing is better than the real thing and if you haven't seen it for yourself how can you reliably tell others anything? Lying requires attention to detail. Pretending you are on the top floor of a 30-storey building when in fact you're on a blustery street corner won't work if the traffic noise or passing feet give the game away. Be sure your sins will find you out ... although sometimes they don't, as I can reveal by relating the tale of the BBC radio outside broadcast that never was.

Some years ago, whilst presenting *Going Places* on Radio Four, I had to transmit live from the newly completed Channel Tunnel rail terminus at Waterloo. The rain was pouring down and holes in the old station roof, under which the majority of our equipment was placed, meant that we were as wet in the building as out of it. With an hour to go, harassed technicians had still not managed to ensure all the connections. We had to decide whether to abort the programme. It had been in preparation for weeks and trailed for days. Many guests were turning up to be interviewed. We made what, in retrospect, seems a bizarre decision, which could only happen on radio. We would divert the guests back to our studio at Broadcasting House and do the entire show from there, but we would do it as if it was at Waterloo! Time was running out. We recorded only ten minutes of background noise at the station and rushed back. We put the sound effects on a loop of tape and set them going. Whenever the studio manager heard a station announcement involving train times he dipped the sound or I spoke more loudly. I changed all my scripts so that I never once *actually said* I was at Waterloo. Thus, out went 'Welcome to the brand new Waterloo. Gateway to Europe' and in came such things as, 'Waterloo was never more appropriately named. It's pouring down over London tonight but undaunted we preview the station that's about to become Britain's Gateway to Europe.' I did the entire half-hour standing up in the studio holding a hand microphone to allow me a better sense of liveness and excitement in my voice. Bewildered but appreciative guests all played along with this extraordinary performance. And no-one ever knew – until now!

A VIEW FROM THE INSIDE: CLAIRE BOLDERSON

Claire is a presenter of the *World Tonight* for BBC Radio Four and *Newshour* and *Agenda* for the BBC World Service.

I think 'presenting' is a particular skill, one that can be learned but one that is quite different from other broadcasting jobs. It took me a while to learn because nobody told me, I had to work it out myself. It's not like reporting at all. When you're the reporter you have to tell the story, you have to grab the attention of the audience and ram it home. Presenting requires getting *other people* to tell the story, teasing it out of them and at the same time gently filling in the gaps. It requires suppressing one's own knowledge and asking questions on behalf of the average person in the audience, while also maintaining some of your own character and personality.

In news programmes it also requires a vast general knowledge. That can be frustrating. I miss being a foreign correspondent in so much as then I had a story and I knew it inside out. Now I can converse at a dinner party about just about any subject – but not for much longer than about five minutes. Presenting news programmes requires range and versatility and the skill of being quick to study. It means reading everything, all the time. There's no down time. Holidays are nice but if you don't keep across the news when away, catching up is hell.

When it comes to dos and don'ts? Well, don't even try it if you're not an adrenalin junkie. You have to be able to keep calm when all about you is falling apart, to be able to keep your head when thrown a big story you know little about, live on air. Don't do it if you're not interested in the news – you will be found out!

Do do it if you are naturally inquisitive and stimulated by lively conversation and other people's ideas. Remember, it is *not* about what you know (a big mistake some people make); it's about what you can get out of others. Don't do it if you're a very private person who doesn't like to expose their feelings and flaws. You have to not really care that sometimes you'll open your mouth and anything might come out. You can't be so uptight that you don't give anything away because that will bore people stiff.

It helps to have a nice voice but that can be worked on. I had some very useful training for things like pace and tone that helped a lot.

One final thought. I've been a producer, a newsroom editor and a reporter for TV radio and newspapers, and of all the jobs I've done presenting is without a doubt the most difficult – and the best!

EXERCISES

1. The Queen is visiting the refurbished real tennis courts at Hampton Court. You are providing the commentary. What information will you use to construct your chat?

Here are some of the questions you should think about for preparation. Make your own list first without looking at these and compare them afterwards:

Why is she coming? What is she going to see? Who will greet her? What are the names and profiles of the dignitaries who will shake her hand? What is she wearing? What car is she in? Where has she come from? How much has the renovation cost? Who paid for it? How long did it take? Any interesting stories about the rebuilding work? Why rebuild? How many similar facilities are there in this country/the world? What's it like inside? What does the court look like? What is the terminology used in the game? Is there a National Association? If there's to be a demonstration match, who will play? How big a sport is real tennis today? What countries play it? What are the rules? Is it a professional or amateur sport? Where did it begin? How popular was it in the past? Any good stories about famous people or Kings and Queens who used to play it? Do any Royals play it today? Who will be able to use the new real tennis courts? Are there any youth groups bringing players through? Where do all the schoolchildren come from? What lessons are they missing to be here? What preparations have they made for the visit? Have they seen the Queen or any members of the Royal family before? Will they be presenting flowers or anything similar to the Queen? If so, who will do it and what is their profile? What are the children wearing? What are they carrying? How long have they been waiting there? What other onlookers have turned up? How long have they been there? How did they hear about the occasion? Has there been much talk about it on local TV and radio in the area? What is the level of security? Are there lots of police? Are they armed? How difficult is it to get a member of the Royal family, let alone the Queen, to visit anything? How far in advance do you have to apply? What engagements does she have afterwards? What will she be doing tomorrow? Where is the Duke of Edinburgh today? Why is he not coming along too? How many visits do they do together?

2. Below is a news story and voice-piece written in Radio Four style. It's 30 seconds long. Check the facts and then re-write it in a pop style of 20 seconds' duration.

NET DIVORCE

A new service allows you to end your marriage using the Internet. A firm of solicitors in Norfolk is pioneering the idea which has already run into controversy. Our home affairs correspondent Kim Talk reports:

The company based in Norwich is offering to arrange uncontested divorces using the net. The firm of solicitors has launched a website where you can start divorce proceedings from the privacy of your own home computer. Despite disapproval from a number of caring organizations and the church, the solicitors insist that currently 75 per cent of all divorces are in fact 'quickies' and are finalized in less than a year. They claim their service could reduce that by two months by limiting the amount of legal red tape endured by those using conventional methods.

Record yourself reading each version in the appropriate style with no fluffs and no mispronunciations. Time them to make sure you are being accurate. A possible pop version of Net Divorce is suggested below. How does it compare with your own?

POP style NET DIVORCE

Gone off your hubby? Perhaps you should log on and log him off! The latest thing in quickie divorces is a split over the net. Kim Talk reports:

The idea comes from a group of solicitors in Norwich who are offering the fastest marriage break-ups ever. You simply log on to their website and start a divorce from the comfort of you own laptop. The Church and some help groups are furious but the lawyers say that at the moment three-quarters of all divorces are uncontested and even then take a year to settle. But, they say, e-splits slash through red tape and can reduce that time by up to two months.

3. Listen to a sports event with running commentary. Note how often the commentator stops talking directly about the game and offers observations. Write down what extra information the presenter has supplied e.g. mentions of previous wins, newspaper stories, transfer fees, statistics etc. (see also Chapter 9).
4. Do an entertaining and informative running commentary about your journey to work as you travel.

II
Types of presentation

8 News and current affairs

News and current affairs has been an explosive growth area of broadcasting in the last decade. Radio and TV stations worldwide have discovered the public's insatiable appetite for watching global events unfolding in the living room. And yet, perhaps already, the ubiquity of news is breeding contempt. There are about 250 hours of news broadcasting on tap in multi-channel homes in the UK. An ITC study in 2002 showed that younger people, ethnic minorities and non-voters said it didn't relate to their lives. Instead, it's mainly the over-45s who are tuning in to news. The huge choice of viewing makes audiences, as the marketers would have it, more 'promiscuous' than ever. The advent of digital technology is breeding another swathe of channels. Companies are splitting their services so that they can provide dedicated news stations alongside their general output. All, of course, require that essential ingredient: a presenter.

Inevitably, as services expand, revenues (whether from licence fee, advertising or sponsorship) contract, which means changes in the nature of a presenter's life. There's less cash and less cachet. Thanks to multi-skilling, you may be the 'front man' but you'll also be the 'backroom boy'. You won't just read the news – you'll write it too. It means that you can't choose to be a news presenter – you'll probably have to be a newshound first and hope to get a break into presentation when you've cut your teeth in the field.

Here are two success stories from people who did just that. Both were news journalists but from different backgrounds – James Naughtie moved from newspapers to presenting radio news and Kirsty Lang came from radio reporting to presenting news on TV.

A VIEW FROM THE INSIDE: JAMES NAUGHTIE

Presentation was not what Jim Naughtie intended when he started in work. Clearly no-one else expected it either. He remembers going to a careers

139

interview at the end of his university course where he was advised to become a hospital administrator. 'When I said I wanted to be a journalist, and failing that something in publishing, they fell about laughing!'

However, when, many years later, he was asked to front BBC Radio Four's flagship daily news and current affairs programme *Today*, it was an offer he could not refuse.

James Naughtie was born in 1951 and did an English Degree at Aberdeen University followed by a one-year graduate print training course in Newcastle. In 1975 he took a job on the *Aberdeen Press and*

Figure 8.1
Today presenter Jim Naughtie

Journal, displaying ambitious tendencies so that, in 1976 he became (he believes) the only person ever to have covered an American political convention for the '*P and J*'. He has the distinction of having been turned down as a researcher on *Weekend World* in 1977 by a young producer, John Birt!* Instead, he became a reporter for the *Scotsman*. In 1984 he moved to the *Guardian* and in 1988 was asked to present BBC Radio Four's *World At One* weekday, live news show. He moved to *Today* in 1994.

Today is the nearest thing to a newspaper on the radio

I regard presenting on radio as a kind of natural development from print for me. I loved my newspaper days. Writing front page leads for the *Guardian* from Westminster is a dream for anyone. But time moves on and, frankly, if someone says to you, 'Would you like to present the *World at One*', you jump at it, don't you? I had done a bit on the radio and I'd been interviewed as an expert a few times on the *Today* programme and that's how they spotted me, I suppose.

It's real journalism. *The World at One* and *Today* are the nearest things in broadcasting to writing for a newspaper. You're writing a front page every day. I had the chance to develop interviewing skills which was a great challenge. It was sad to leave the *Guardian* but it was a terrific challenge.

There is power but don't think about it

No you don't 'get a buzz' from the power. If you thought about it like that you'd be too concerned with status and performance rather than doing the job. It would be foolish to say you are not aware that there are consequences to what you say and I'm actually more conscious of that – the obligations and the pressure – than of the 'here am I sitting pontificating'.

I'm a radio man

One of the good things about sitting in a radio studio is that, after a while, it's quite easy to forget you're there. Of course, you can't forget it completely

*Sir John Birt, Director General of the BBC 1992–2000

and start effing and blinding but you've got to be natural and spontaneous. The great thing about radio is its intimacy, the direct collusion with the listeners, so that they can be walking about the house, brushing their teeth, walking the dog, getting the kids off to school and the radio follows them about. I enjoy the craft of radio. I'm not saying that TV doesn't have enormous strengths but there is something about the directness of radio. You can communicate with the listener without pictures intervening. A good documentary or radio package, even an interview, is a wonderfully potent journalistic form. It's marvellous how we've managed, in this country, to maintain the quality of speech radio.

I learnt how to do it as I did it!

I did some dummy *World at One*s but I had no formal training of any kind. Nobody put me on a presentation course. The best advice anyone gave me was to imagine you are talking to one person who is sitting in the corner of the studio. That is absolutely the best thing to remember. Editors and producers are advising you the whole time but it's something you learn as you do the job. Some say it's good to do a presentation course, others say it wouldn't make a blind bit of difference. I think I'm in the latter category but there's no formula.

Nerves? I don't have them!

You get the odd flutter, but I'm not of a nervous disposition! I don't do anything much to prepare myself physically. No exercises or deep breathing to calm my voice, nothing like that. I just get on with the job.

I'm a news junkie

To keep on top you need to know what's going on. It is a perpetual topping up of the tank and it's vital. I'm up with what the Tories are saying and what Blair's saying. I know what Kennedy's thinking. I'm up with what's happening in the United States. I know what's going on in Europe. You've got to be across all that. Not in vast detail every hour of the day and night but you've got to be able, with very little effort, to put a new 'top' on a story. I'm slightly embarrassed about how little television I watch but then that's partly because I have to get up so early in the morning. I slog through all the papers in the office or at home. Of the journals and periodicals, I read *The Statesman, The Spectator, The Week* and *The Economist*. As far as broadcast news and current affairs is concerned, I watch and listen to everything and follow the wires. I am a news junkie. You depend on people in the office for briefing for the big interviews. You need a top-up from them about the key facts and most recent events you're going to have to address.

My working day

I wake up at 0305. I read the papers in the car on the way to the office. I'm there by 0400. As soon as I get in I look through the running order, talk to the overnight producers and see what's to be done and then immediately start to write. Most of the cues have to be written from scratch. Those that go with pre-recorded packages simply have to be tweaked to my style. I have to do about nine or ten live interviews each morning. There isn't time on a show like *Today* to discuss massive strategies for interviews with the producers, as you would if you were doing a set piece interview. Of course, if the interview is with a big politician you'll spend more time considering it than you would if you were chatting to a train driver about losing his sandwiches! The programme runs from 0600 until 0900. I leave the studio quite a bit during those three hours. The best opportunities come during newscasts and weather forecasts. There's a post mortem afterwards which is about twenty minutes. Then we sit with everyone who's been on and talk to the new shift starting the next day's programme. This allows us to keep in touch with the office itself. But three hours is a very long time on the air and actually you have to get out. You need to clear your head.

My most memorable moment was 'kebabing' Neil Kinnock

It was 1988. It was an absurd little episode, yet the row became infamous. It was a *cause célèbre* of its day. He was in the radio car for a pre-recorded interview after an NEC meeting. I was in the *World at One* studio. He got very angry at my questioning and exploded, saying, 'I'm not going to be bloody kebabed by you.' The interview was stopped. It wasn't broadcast in full because he'd unleashed a torrent against me. They ran the cut interview but it became clear that there'd been a row. Then the tape was leaked by someone out of the back door of the BBC. It became a huge 'BBC versus Labour leader' row. These things happen. It was simply that the chemistry went wrong for a few minutes. The funny thing was that it didn't bother *me* for more than a minute and a half. It was no big deal. It went wrong for a moment and that was that. Yet I had to live with it for a long time, mostly because of the response from others. The *Daily Mail* were camped outside my house. You have to be prepared for that kind of stuff if you're in this position and you have to be able to cope with it.

Don't be a presenter. Be something else first

My advice is not to think about being a presenter. To be a presenter you've got to be someone who's got an all round journalistic feel. You cannot be a bimbo, male or female, who just wants to turn up and be the star turn and hope to do it properly. You just can't. It doesn't work like that. You've got to be either a good reporter or a producer with a flair for on-air broadcasting. It springs from the real guts of the job which is reportage. I mean you could train a monkey to ask questions of the Prime Minister that were implanted in its brain, but it wouldn't be a good interview. You need a little bit of feel and touch, and you need to know when to pass the ball, when to dribble and when to put in a rough tackle.

Beware the onset of 'unproducibility'!

No presenter is beyond regular production and if you begin to think that you are then you're in real difficulty. It's crucial to be able to listen to what others advise. It's also one of the really important things about being a senior producer or an editor that you can develop relationships with your presenters that allow you to produce in this way. The producer must be listening the whole time and be willing to say, 'Have you noticed that you've developed a habit of doing X, Y, Z?' or, 'Let's go about it this way and let's develop this kind of aspect.' You've got to have an editor who is a candid friend and will tell you what you least want to hear. If you're a presenter it's desperately important never to feel that you don't need that. Presenters are very bad at recording themselves and going home and listening to the tape. If you ask them they'll tell you they do but that's complete rubbish! They don't.

A good presenter has the X-factor

I think there's an X-factor. I don't know what it is. Is it charisma? There's got to be something that 'clicks'. Clicks with an audience, with a style of programme, with a production team. Partly it's just sounding natural and convincing. Editors have got to believe that they know what this X-factor is when they hear it, but they don't always. There is no identikit of a presenter. You may have a correspondent who's been very good, who writes well, who's got a decent voice but you could stick them on the air and they may be no good. I can think of all sorts of people who, on paper, have got it all but it just doesn't work.

Words of warning

Don't get pompous and don't get lazy. By lazy, I mean not thinking through the answers to questions. Starting to believe that the questions are more important than the answers. The answers are more important than the questions. Stay fresh. Quit when you stop enjoying it.

A VIEW FROM THE INSIDE: KIRSTY LANG

Kirsty Lang is, if you like, a reluctant presenter. She's done her time on the front line as 'a fireman', that is a general reporter ready to be sent to any story, anywhere. She made foreign reporting her forte and fell into presentation on Channel 4 almost by mistake. She's typical of the modern breed of news presenter with a strong journalistic background to bring weight and authority to the newscast. She's currently the news anchor for *World News* on the digital station, BBC4 and BBC World.

She was born in 1962, has a degree in International Relations from the London School of Economics and in 1984 did a postgraduate diploma in journalism at City University in London. In 1986 she did the prestigious BBC News Trainee Scheme and began news reporting for BBC Radio Four. 1n 1991 she became the BBC's bi-media correspondent in Paris, did two years for *Newsnight* and in 1995 became the *Sunday Times* Paris correspondent. The presenting started with *Channel 4 News* in 1998.

Figure 8.2
Presenter Kirsty Lang

I went into presentation for childcare reasons!

I wasn't that bothered about telly, ever. It was journalism I wanted to do. I wasn't wanting to be a presenter particularly. You could say I went into presentation for childcare reasons because in 1998 I was in France reporting for the *Sunday Times*. I'd been there about three years and I like to move on after that time or I get bored. I'd had a baby there and I wanted to come home again. Then, *Channel 4 News* phoned me up to ask me to be a roving Europe correspondent and I said it sounded really lovely but I'd just had a baby so 'No'. But they rang back a couple of weeks later and said, 'How would it be if you did 50 per cent reporting in Europe and the rest co-presenting the newsbelt with Jon Snow?' It was unexpected but sounded perfect. I had thought it might be a good thing to do 'later on'. A lot of correspondents think like that because there will come a time when you're fed up with being on the road.

It's harder than I thought

I underestimated how difficult presenting was and at first it really didn't go very well. I had thought it would be a doddle – just reading an autocue. And I think *they* thought, 'Well, she's done loads of live television, it'll be easy for her.' It was true that I had done lots of live stuff as an interviewer in a reporting role and also as an interviewee in an 'expert' role in Paris. But the switch to presenting was not easy. I was pretty bad to start with. I stumbled a lot. I spoke too fast. I looked uncomfortable. They had given me no training at all which, with hindsight, was bad. In the end the really key piece of advice somebody gave me was to watch myself back. Get the tapes and see where you are going wrong. You do learn from that. Finally, Channel 4 paid for me to have some news reading lessons with Peter Donaldson, the Chief Announcer on Radio Four. We had just two hours and it was fantastic. When you are a reporter, because you're writing your own stuff, you connect with it in a way that you don't with something that's written by someone else. So I was just reading it out. What Peter said to me was that you had to visualize. If you are talking about two children burning to death in a house fire, you have to visualize two children burning to death in a house fire. My expression and intonations were all wrong because I was just reading out words. Then, as I started to relax, I started to use techniques I had always used as a reporter when I was doing a piece to camera. Before I started, I would think about someone I really liked, loved or fancied! Now I just think of my son. Back then I used to think of various men I was in love with! I would visualize them before I looked at the camera so that I would have a warm, friendly look on my face. It means that I'm talking to just one person whom I like and want to communicate with.

You need training

You've got to have training and you've got to have a decent broadcasting voice. It's not about just reading a bunch of words. I'm a bit old-fashioned about this but I would say that for news reading you've got to have gone out and done your time in the field. You've got to understand what news is about. Most newsreaders these days have been reporters.

You need to be aware of all sorts of mannerisms and things that you should change or overcome or mellow a bit. I don't get nervous any more and I don't do the deep breathing stuff. But I do have a tendency to fluff ... but then I have a tendency to fluff my words in real life anyway! So I need to speak more slowly than I normally would. I have a big problem with hand gesticulation. Television exaggerates your every movement and the business of having to sit still is really difficult. One useful tip I found worked brilliantly out in the field, particularly when I had to do eight hours of live broadcasting from New York for 9.11, was to hold a clipboard. My hands were firmly clasped around it, out of shot. Otherwise I clasp my hands together or hold a piece of paper, maybe my script. I also have an unfortunate habit when I'm interviewing someone of jabbing a pen at them. I have to be really careful about that because it looks quite aggressive when you review it on the tape.

I used to think looking good didn't matter

I think at the beginning I underestimated how important appearances were because I'd been on the road for ages and I thought I looked fine. But of course, it's totally different. Out in the field you can look a bit windswept and scruffy and the audience doesn't mind. When I first arrived at Channel 4 I thought, 'Why can't I just wear a nice jumper to read the news?' But no. They are actually quite conservative. They want you to wear a jacket. I'm not a jacket person although they are useful for carrying battery packs and hiding cables.

When we had the first focus groups for Channel 4 (and there were lots of them), I had endless people saying, 'Yeah, I really like that girl, but her fringe annoys me' or, 'I don't like the fact that she doesn't always brush her hair.' Of course I *had* brushed my hair but I quickly realized that the reason why all news presenters have short hair is because it's impossible to keep it neat – you'd have to go to the hairdresser every day. I changed my wardrobe. My life as a TV presenter means I now have cupboards filled with jackets that I would not otherwise be seen dead in!

My presenting day

I get up at about seven and listen to the *Today* programme on the radio whilst watching TV with the sound off. We have to switch endlessly between *News 24* and various cartoons that my small son wants to watch. I zap on the hour so that I can see what pictures are coming in that I might have to be playing with later on. I drop my son off at school and then have a cup of coffee reading the *Herald Tribune*, the *Guardian* and the *FT*. These papers are good for their foreign news and my show is about world news. Before, at Channel 4, I would read the *Daily Mail* and the *Guardian* i.e. a popular one and a broadsheet, before going in. I walk to Television Centre. It takes me about twenty minutes and I do my phone calls on the way. At some point in the day, sometimes first thing, I have my hair washed and blow dried by the BBC hairdressers.

I log on immediately when I get to the office so that I can read the wires. I have a chat with the editor about what's happening that day. On this programme you have to write all the scripts yourself and the headlines too. Everything. So it's quite hard work. The idea is to stamp the presenter's authority on the programme. It's intended to be a vehicle for the presenter and they hope that this will give it more 'attitude' than you would normally get on the BBC. We have a small team – only about five or six people, including the editor. We have an informal programme meeting in the morning. We usually have one featurey kind of piece from somewhere in the world which will probably run last in the programme but I look at it first because it's in first and because things will get hotter later. If I've got an interview with some world leader, the editor will want a 'set-up' piece, a kind of backgrounder that will run before the interview to put it into a context. I'll have some help to put that together because I don't have time to do it all. If someone else has written it, I must change the script and then voice it up.

We have another programme meeting at about three in the afternoon to discuss the headlines. That one's quite fun actually because, as at Channel 4, we always have a snappy caption on the screen behind the news presenter. So we all turn ourselves into *Sun* headline writers for a bit. I then have to write five or six headlines. This is a real art. I use a thesaurus now more than I ever did before! I have to do a trail at 1630. So at 1600 I go to make-up for half an hour. I record the trail, then go back to the office. More writing. Then there are briefings for interviews. I might have three or even four to do. The interviews have to be very structured otherwise you won't get the key points in, so we discuss what the first question should be, what they are likely to say and what I should ask next.

The other thing we do is what we call the 'illustrated two-way', with a correspondent. That has to be carefully choreographed because you'll have the correspondent in Washington talking into a clip of George Bush and then talking into a clip of someone at the UN, for instance. So I chat with the editor and the correspondent on a conference call beforehand to decide precisely how it's to be done. For example, after the clip of Bush I have to come back with a question and then the correspondent will answer and go into another clip.

Before transmission I get my make-up touched up which only takes five minutes. We go into the studio at about 1930 and pre-record the heads [headlines]. We rehearse a bit and go on air at 2030.

When it's all over we have a post mortem, but it only lasts about two minutes ... unless there's a disaster.

It's a fickle business

Even once you've got all the necessary skills, it's a very subjective thing as to whether you'll stay in work. This is an incredibly fickle business. We've all seen good presenters go by the wayside because senior management don't like them. You must have confidence in yourself. In my career I've had bosses who just didn't like me and I've thought, 'Right. Get out of here!' When you are an on-screen presenter you are more vulnerable than most. You mustn't take it personally. Be prepared to go and re-invent yourself elsewhere. Sometimes it's a changing programme style and you have to be prepared to adapt to that or go.

9 Sport

In the last decade or so sport has moved up the broadcasting agenda with the same speed as business news. Once it was nothing more than a Saturday afternoon round-up on TV and an, 'and finally, the cricket score at the Oval is ...'. Nowadays sport itself is big bucks and professional and the broadcasting of it has necessarily moved in the same direction. With dedicated 24-hour sport channels, there are many opportunities here for presenters. Some may now get in through reporting on sports programmes. Others come from news and, increasingly, others are hired from the football pitch or running track where they were themselves performers.

As with most broadcasting, the wider your knowledge the more work you can expect. Thus being expert at darts or crown bowls alone will be very valuable when the world championships are happening but will not provide you with year-round work. Sue Barker is a great example of how a career in sports presentation can be expanded to include just about anything.

Increasingly sport is news, so it's important to appreciate the broader agenda. Controversies about cricket tours, football violence and horserace fixing mean that you cannot live in a sporting vacuum. With or without a journalistic background, sports presenters find themselves having to display an unexpected objectivity. It can be hard to report with detachment since the personalities involved may be those they know well and who do favours by supplying dressing-room interviews, tit-bits, team info and exclusives regularly. It helps to read the sports pages and the news pages to keep informed.

Covering sport necessarily requires a great deal of live work which means, in that most appropriate of phrases, kick ball and scramble! Much of what you say will be improvised. Scripts may be scribbled on pieces of paper and not neatly typed into computers. Similarly, the information you receive may be mouthed at you or signed by a producer doing a poor impression of a tic-tac man!

There will be lots of running commentary (see Chapter 7). This is particularly the preserve of the radio presenter. Do your homework. The obvious facts are top of the list: names and profiles of players, teams, standings in league tables or competitions, attendances, prize money, world rankings and so on. You need a basic understanding of the rules and governing bodies of the sport. If there are areas you don't know, get the answer quickly, don't try to bury the issue. Often the listeners will be able to help out with e-mails and texts. You only have to ask!

Some sports, like tennis, defy all attempts at a really satisfactory blow-by-blow account. In a fast-moving match, it is impossible for a mouth to keep pace with the ball. This is when you develop techniques of keeping listeners informed of the state of play without going through every single stroke. In football, too, there is a balance between naming each player passing the ball and more general observations about the flow of play. By contrast, cricket requires a great deal of background knowledge and observation whilst waiting for the high point of the action. A commentator will be noticing everything around the ground; the changing position of the fielders, a player limping or the disconsolate body language of the batsman.

Remember too that a sport is about more than just the rules. Draw a picture for the listener about the occasion itself. What's the weather like? What can you see from the commentary box? What do the stadium and the pitch look like? What is the mood?

Keep part of your mind aware of the pace and style of your commentary. You want to have light and shade, conveying the excitement but slowing down on occasion to take stock, otherwise it will sound manic.

Needless to say, you must not let your allegiances get in the way of fair reporting. It's not usually acceptable to say 'we' or 'our team', even if referring to the national side. Admit your preferences if you like but be scrupulously unbiased thereafter. Keep a sense of humour at all times. Sport should be fun. Look for the amusing angles and mention those too. People at home are excited and hopeful of a win for their team or player. They are in high spirits and so should you be.

Outside broadcasts are a way of life. They happen in all winds and weathers, and in all manner of uncomfortable locations. Working on an OB means you will not have the normal equipment with the same capabilities that you have at the studio. If you're on the road and things begin to go wrong, you have to grin and bear it and use your ingenuity to get round the problems without letting on to the audience that you're close to going off air!

Know the lie of the land on an OB. Where are the toilets? How do you get to the entrance and how long does it take to get there and back? Where are the teams' changing rooms? Do you need passes?

You must have everything to hand, including your research material, lap top, paper, pens and highlighters. A pocket radio and earpiece is valuable for checking output while you're away from the microphone.

Clothes for sports presenters must, above all, be sensible. No high heels for a day at the races. If you have to climb a vertical ladder to get to the commentator's eyrie, it's wisest not to be wearing a silk skirt or a kilt! Always prepare for wet weather on the sunniest day. Even radio presenters don't want to appear like drowned rats when interviewing celebrities! What's more, radio presenters often find themselves in front of TV cameras in this bi-media world.

A VIEW FROM THE INSIDE: JOHN INVERDALE

One of the UK's top sporting presenters is John Inverdale. He's widely respected, both in the business and by audiences, for his affability, relaxed style and critical analysis. His career spans twenty years, beginning in news and broadening into sports presentation and chat shows.

John was born in 1957. He graduated from Southampton University in 1979 with an Honours degree in history. He has always been a keen sportsman – particularly in rugby and tennis. His career started as a journalist in news at BBC Radio Lincolnshire in 1982. In a decade he worked through all types of reporting for radio, including for the flagship *Today* programme on BBC Radio Four, but real fame came with his arrival as a news/sport presenter on BBC Radio Five Live. He was Sony Radio Broadcaster of the Year in 1997.

Know the sport you're talking about ... but you don't have to like it

I think you need to know an awful lot about each of the sports you deal with but you don't have to like them ... mostly I do, but you can effect an

Figure 9.1
Sports presenter John Inverdale

interest in things even if they bore you rigid. Enthusiasm is hugely important. If you aren't enthusiastic the audience will be saying, 'If this guy's
not keen on it, why the hell should I be?' You can turn your hand to anything. I suppose I could do Formula One racing, for example, but I would
find it rather boring.

If I'm about to do an interview on a sport about which I know nothing, I
find out. I read newspapers and cuttings. I phone someone up who knows
about it and say to them, 'OK, tell me ten things I need to know about
archery.' You have access to the rulebooks of the sport but you don't really
need to go into detail like that. If you had to do a *documentary* about

archery (and that's a sport I know nothing about) you'd have to know everything. But the most you're likely to have to do is a four-minute interview which would involve about six questions at most ... so just don't say something dumb!

It's also about whether you've got a reasonably good memory. It's like mugging up for an exam. You can cram the night before and then forget it all afterwards! I retain some of it – probably the most important stuff. The rest probably wasn't that important anyway. And, of course, the great thing about interviewing is that element of bluff. The moment that you toss in some piece of information that's quite obtuse but relevant to someone you're interviewing, they'll think, 'Goodness! This guy knows his stuff!' A little bit of 'fact-dropping' can get you an awful long way!

You should have journalistic skills – but I would say that, wouldn't I?

On my passport, I call myself a broadcast journalist, not 'sports presenter'. These days news is sport and sport is news. Sport is on the front pages, not just the back pages, so an understanding of the journalistic requirements of the job is very important. You can't present horseracing and not have a journalistic base so that if anything controversial happens you can ask the right questions from a broader perspective and have relevance to those who are not keen fans. If you are a sportsperson first and then become a broadcaster, there's a danger that you won't be so objective. Your first allegiance will be to former colleagues in the sport rather than the audience that you're broadcasting to. Of course, it depends a lot on the output you want to achieve. If you want coverage that incorporates the good and the bad, something that will be reliable, entertaining and authoritative, then that's what you have to aim at. What you don't want is the moment a thorny issue comes up a presenter shying away from it. But it depends very much on the people. Take Steve Cram. I think he's absolutely outstanding. He's not got a journalistic background but when a hard question has to be asked he'll do it because he understands that there is a bigger picture. His sport, athletics, comes under a wide public scrutiny and it actually does the sport no good at all if you're seen to be avoiding the issues that confront it. Also, Steve Cram hadn't been competing for a decade. Often the problem is when you get people straight off the football pitch and they have to be interviewing people who they had been playing with only two weeks before. On the other hand, the ex-sportsmen and women who go into presenting can often get things from interviewees that ordinary sports journalists can't get because there's that mutual trust and understanding born from having played together or competed against each other. It's a balancing act.

I don't get nervous

Sometimes, when it's a major event, you think, 'There are millions of them out there. Don't b...r this up!' But once you start it's like when a match starts: the moment you've kicked the first ball, you just get on with it. Once you've said 'good morning' or 'good evening', then it's just another programme.

I like both TV and radio

When I was growing up in the Far East [in Singapore and Malaysia], we didn't have a telly and the World Service was the be all and end all. Radio was a constant companion. It's always been my mate. I think that's the difference between the two mediums. A radio is a friend. People on the radio become your friends. I don't think that's ever the case on television. You don't have so much control on TV. On radio it's just you and the microphone so you can say whatever you want and there's that warmth and immediacy. On TV there are directors and producers and if you start going off on a tangent it throws the whole thing into disarray. It's the team that inhibits you on TV, yet it's also the team that's one of the best things about it and I enjoy being a team player.

I cried after Hillsborough

Presenting *Sport on 2* on the day of the Hillsborough disaster was my most memorable broadcast. At five to three we were all gung-ho on FA Cup semi-final day, excited by what lay in store. Just fifteen minutes later, at ten past three, we were staring at a major tragedy. It required everyone involved to change their approach completely. We became news reporters and presenters in a split-second. I cried when we came off air, not because we had had a pretty tough afternoon of it but because of the enormity of what had occurred, the nature of those involved and because it made most other Saturday afternoons appear utterly trivial in comparison.

There isn't a typical working day

Last week, I had two contrasting successive days. A new TV sports show I presented received just one paragraph in the paper, with a viewer saying my shirt made me look like his grandad. A radio show I did, which included a long interview about the prospect of war with Iraq, prompted a huge response from the public saying what a brilliant interview it had been. All of which just goes to show that you shouldn't take any of it too seriously. One day sun, next day rain. The whole business is inherently transitory. You can't even wrap your fish and chips in it. But we're very lucky to be doing it because it is enormous fun and the idea that I get to go to the Olympic Games, and someone pays me to do it, I still find bizarre.

Watch out!

Don't ever believe that you, as the presenter, are the most important thing on the programme. You're not. You're the conduit through which and by which the programme works or doesn't work.

Don't ask a question where you *suspect* you know the answer but you don't. The likelihood is that you'll say something stupid. Be certain that what you know is certain.

Know everything and know nothing

The key skill of being a presenter is to know everything and to know nothing. If the programme you are presenting is detailed and specialized, be detailed and specialized. If it's a general kind of programme, the likelihood is that most people listening will be as ignorant of the subject as you are, so be ignorant because that way no knowledge is assumed and you get the most out of the interview. The crucial thing is knowing who you are broadcasting to. If it's a specialist programme on basketball it's no good affecting the 'I don't know what's going on here' approach because the audience are going to think, 'Hang on a minute. You shouldn't be doing the programme in the first place if you don't know about it.' In those circumstances you have to know everything. But if you're broadcasting on a general programme, whether it's news or sport, and the subject happens to be basketball, that's when, even though you *do* know everything, you ask questions that imply ignorance since 90 per cent of your audience will know nothing about it.

My advice

Listen to anyone who hears the programme and take on board their views. Those are the opinions that count, not those of people in the broadcasting hierarchy to whom you probably pay too much account.

Prepare properly. Listen to interviewees and respond to their answers. Be yourself. No more, no less. My first attempts at broadcasting were ham-fisted. Aren't everyone's? I was trying to be Kid Jensen, young and hip, because that's what I thought was required, when in fact I should have been Brian Redhead – well, OK perhaps not quite, but at least if you have in your mind's eye how you appear when you're having a conversation in the pub, that's how you ought to sound when you're broadcasting. If you're confident in what you are and who you are then you can be like that from the word go. If you have a natural insecurity about you or are nervous then you'll start affecting mannerisms that are detrimental to your presentational style.

10 Lifestyle and features

Lifestyle and features are often seen as the 'softer' end of the market ... but don't you believe it. Here we are talking hours of daytime television and radio involving profiles, magazine and consumer programmes. They require every bit as much journalism, no less effort and, sometimes, considerably more ingenuity than plain news. Heart-wrenching, televised agony columns in front of live audiences, fashion makeovers, DIY re-builds, cooking, history, pet shows and gardening programmes – these are the bedrock of the broadcasting day. Increasingly, headhunters want celebrities to front them. And if they can't be famous then, at least let them be specialists who can be made famous. This has happened to countless presenters who've found themselves thrust into the spotlight. TV chef, Brian Turner, is one of them.

In common with presenters from more conventional broadcasting backgrounds, there is little, if any, training forthcoming. Such experts impress talent-spotters initially because of their knowledge and personality, but whether that transfers to TV or radio is a gamble. The fame that such shows can bring is another unknown quantity. Even if it all turns out well, there will be a time when the producers decide that everyone's had enough of you. That's when you're glad you kept the day job!

A VIEW FROM THE INSIDE: BRIAN TURNER

Brian Turner has become one of TV's celebrity chefs. It is not a title he likes. He's 56 and has never been anything other than a chef. He worked for his Dad at his transport café in Leeds from the age of 8. In the 1970s he was rated amongst the top five classically trained chefs. Now he has a string of restaurants in London and Birmingham. His TV career began when he was approached by *Food and Drink* on BBC2 to

Figure 10.1
Chef and presenter, Brian Turner

cook with Antony Worrall Thompson on a battleship, returning from the Gulf. Celebrity chefs were almost unheard of but that was about to change.

There was an appetite for food on the telly. It was nothing to do with me!

We did two eight-minute slots for BBC2 cooking in the galley on HMS *Birmingham* which took us four days in the most horrendous seas you've ever seen. I nearly died. I was ill every five minutes. Of the 360 sailors on board, 120 of them never got out of their bunks for all that time! Then the editor of *This Morning*, Richard and Judy's show, saw it and thought it would be fun to do something similar. So she got the two of us and Marguerite Patten to do a celebration meal for their 999th show. We were good and it was great and they wanted more. I never looked for this. I was just happy to be doing it.

I had done some teaching but gave it up because I missed the restaurant

TV wasn't so far removed from what I'd been doing. First, it was a subject I knew a lot about and enjoyed but, second, I'd always wanted to be a teacher and in 1973 I did 15 months teaching mature students at a technical college. The communication of the skill was really good but I missed the roar of the crowd, the smell of the greasepaint of a real restaurant. So I went back to cooking and for seven or eight years I did *This Morning* on Mondays and Fridays, and then other opportunities just opened up. Probably a quarter of my time is given to TV and 75 per cent to working within the restaurant businesses and charities.

I enjoy the camera and the atmosphere. It's about communicating an enthusiasm rather than teaching. The time is too short to teach. It's my intention that people go and cook the dish. If anyone goes away saying, 'That looked fantastic, I can almost smell it. I'm sure I could do that', then I've achieved. The greatest accolade anyone can offer is when someone says, 'You know, I've tried your Yorkshire Pudding recipe and it works every time!'

I talk to Aunty Betty

I had no training whatsoever in presentation. I was taught by people around me. They said: (a) you need to talk to your Aunty Betty at home. You know that she's behind that camera and you're telling your Aunty Betty whom you love and adore, '… this is how you do it'; and (b) when you're doing public demonstrations, look for a friendly face, which is, again, your Aunty Betty. Eventually you'll build up confidence to speak to unfriendly faces. I've also learned to do the opening lines near the back end when you've warmed up, got more confidence and you're being yourself.

I'm not a presenter; I'm just me being me

Most of the TV I've done has been live, ad lib TV. One lady said to me recently, 'You know the thing I like about you is, whenever I meet you, you're just the same as you are on the telly.' For me, I don't see it as presenting in a different medium. It's just me being me and doing what I do. Not every chef can do it. There is no such thing as a TV chef in my opinion although we are developing them. I don't like to advocate that. People say to me, 'I want my son to be a TV chef.' That's nonsense! First be a chef. Learn your subject matter and if you have the personality and presentation skills the next step might be that. I am actually a professional chef who cooks on TV occasionally. There's a spectrum of those that can entertain and those that can cook and in the middle there are very few who can do both well. Glyn Christian, a friend of mine, presented well but I don't think he could cook to save his life. Anton Mosiman, who's a great cook, has very few presentation skills, he's so bland.

I don't use scripts

Directors do give you scripts sometimes. But I can't learn scripts. I've never been an actor or a thespian. I'm a cook who can talk a bit and the minute you try to give me lines it sounds false. They say, 'It doesn't sound quite right.' And I say, 'Of course it doesn't. These are *your* words not mine! Tell me what you want me to say and I will say it as *I* would say it.' My attitude towards the TV crew is, if someone is paid to direct, someone else to produce and I'm paid to present then that's what I should stick to. I'll offer advice if I'm asked otherwise I'll keep out of it.

I get very nervous

I get very nervous and like to go to the loo and then I pace up and down. On *Ready, Steady, Cook* with Fern [Britton] I used to have a corridor where she and I used to just walk up and down, talking. When we did it live in Birmingham they had classical music so we used to sing at the tops of our voices whilst marching backwards and forwards waiting for someone to say, 'You're on now.' Once you're on, most of the fears disappear.

The cooking can go wrong but I can live with it

We do what we call choreography. We 'dance' through a recipe. Even the taped shows are recorded as live. So we have a run through with a home economics person helping, saying, 'Next it's this and then we move to this ...' I move from left to right, therefore camera right to left, and my cameraman can feel when I'm going to stop whisking and start speaking. We don't do it like Delia, who, I believe, does every dish six times and records it, so that when they do the cutting and editing there are no blips anywhere. I can live with blips because if it starts to go wrong you say, 'Ah, that's not what I wanted. Now let me show you how I'm going to get out of this.' Then you get back on track again.

I don't diet; I breathe in!

I don't worry about my appearance for TV although I do check my weight occasionally and people in the office will say to me, 'Turner, you must do something about your tummy!' Well, I can't really, so I breathe in! What you see is what you get. The great thing about being a cook is, of course, that you should never trust a thin cook. Therefore, I'm my own best advert.

There's a new breed of TV chef ... but I wouldn't employ one

There are competitions all the time to find TV chefs. So for young people their ambition is to be discovered. When they've finished a working day, what do they do? They sign autographs! When *I've* finished, I come back to the restaurant and work there. These kids are keen and know a bit about cooking but if you asked me whether I'd employ them in my restaurant, 'No.' It's a double-edged sword in many ways, because although TV cooking has taught young people that the food industry could be a business to be in, unfortunately it's also taught them they could be stars. I want to bang the drum of the professional chef who knows his stuff inside out. If he discovers he's got communication skills, he can tell people what he knows. But if you've only been in the industry for two or three years you can't know that much.

TV? I prefer restaurants

I'm not famous. People recognize my voice rather than my face. I'm quite lucky because Jamie's [Jamie Oliver] a scruffbag, Worrall Thompson's short and fat, Rhodes has got spiky hair and Ainsley's tall, black and bald. I'm an average-sized fellow. I've not got those special things that people recognize instantly. I enjoy TV and love it to death. It's probably saved my life financially. But given the choice, I prefer restaurants.

My advice is be the tops in your trade

Know your subject matter; you need to be able to speak with authority. Be the tops. Then take a sideways jump and you may go far. Television is fashion and fashion by definition could be here today and gone tomorrow. I work in an industry that will always be here. Everyone will eat every day, please God, and as long as that continues we'll always have a future.

TV chefs are on the way out...maybe!

Television is a nice little bubble to get involved in but it can burst just as easily as it starts. I think the TV chef thing has reached a plateau. It's not going to grow much more. But then I'm the one who predicted that *Ready, Steady, Cook* could only last about twenty shows because there's only so much you can do with a breast of chicken and we're still recording 2000 shows on.

11 Music

Being a disc jockey, whether it be of pop of any variety or classical music, is perhaps one of the most personality-based radio presentation jobs. In this milieu you can become a legend and last a lifetime, as long as you remain versatile and in touch with your audience. Live radio of this kind is a privilege and a joy. Those who do it can often use their fame to access all sorts of other areas of creative work like personal appearances, TV presentation, advertising, after dinner speaking, newspaper columns, training and consultancies. However, it is also one of those areas that is fraught with the worst in-built dangers. The symptoms are an inflated ego, an over-anxious fixation with audience figures, stress and vulnerability to management whims. It's like most things where the rewards are great, the stakes are high and the drop is swift.

Clearly the music is the main reason for the audience switching on but your character is a surprisingly close second. Recent research by the Radio Academy called *Presenters – Who Needs 'em?* makes fascinating reading. They interviewed the management teams in five radio stations – Heart, GWR, Kiss, 1FM and BBC Radio Two. They also conducted 756 interviews with listeners aged between 15 and 45. Interestingly, they did not speak to the presenters themselves. So here is a chance to see what is expected of you if this is the career choice you've made.

1. Presenters are here to stay! Eighty-one per cent of listeners like to have a presenter. What a relief. The industry perceives presenters as making radio different from playing a CD. They entertain the listener, they offer information about travel and events, and they offer a means for interactivity with the audience. They also bring knowledge about the music played and are often regarded as experts in their field. Thus it is that if a DJ plays new or unusual music the audience will stick with it because they are trusted. This is good news for the music industry because it helps to get new music played.

2. Music is the main reason for people listening to music stations. This may seem obvious but it's worth remembering because if this is so, the mere power of your personality won't be able to overcome the wrong kind of music for the kind of audience you're targeting. Let that be a warning! Presenters are, though, a close second to the music in importance.

3. Of all the things that matter about presenters, it's their entertainment ability which is most significant, their personality comes second. Amongst employers, presenters are also seen as reinforcing the person-

The type of music played	8.3
The presenter	7.41
The balance between music and talking	7.02
The presence of information other than news e.g. weather and traffic	6.14
The frequency of the news	5.56
The opportunity for listeners to get involved e.g. phone-ins	4.78
It's local	4.78
Having interviews with celebrities	4.03
Whether there are any adverts	3.21

Figure 11.1
What matters most in music radio? Respondents rated the relative importance of nine aspects of music radio using a scale of 0–10, where 0 is 'not very important at all' and 10 is 'very important'. The table shows the average scores achieved for each factor (Source: Radio Academy.)

Entertainment and humour	44%
Personality/character	22%
Provide information about songs	17%
Interesting/provide variety	16%
Break up the music	15%
Provide information on bands/concerts/celebrity gossip	9%
Good/lively atmosphere	7%
Interaction/involve the listener	4%
News and traffic information	3%
Provide general information	3%
Waffle/talk too much	3%
Make you feel like there is someone with you	2%
Annoying/nuisance	1%

Figure 11.2
What do presenters add to music radio? Mostly entertainment and humour. Interestingly, more people want this jollity in the morning. In the evening, audiences are slightly less concerned with that but expect a greater knowledge of the music being played (Source: Radio Academy.)

ality of the station and its branding. 1FM called them 'almost like mini-brands'. They can be used to lead marketing and publicity. Kiss believes that this will continue in the future:

One thing we have found, which is interesting, is that personality radio has come back in a big way. Radio has evolved through a lot of research where it has been 'keep speech to a minimum, hone the links down so they are very defined' ... This was a reaction to very long links that had gone before which made no sense and then the radio stations came along and the links were very tight. But the actual personalities were pretty devoid of personality ... and that became pretty soul-destroying. I think the market has moved back to saying 'we need more personality' ... because people get bored.

A VIEW FROM THE INSIDE: LEONA GRAHAM

The Radio Academy research showed that Kiss believes that increasing numbers of female presenters with 'something to say' will emerge. They aren't the only ones. The trend has been slow but is now easily discernible.

Figure 11.3
DJ Leona Graham

To say that Leona is the product of this 'female-friendly' attitude is not entirely accurate. People like her are the cause of it. She's got onto a network station thanks to constant and determined battering on the male-operated door. She's 31, was born in Birmingham and did a four year BA (Qualified Teacher Status) in drama and biology. She freely admits she had no intention of teaching but wanted the university experience. She fell into DJing by chance and then positively bombarded prospective employers with CVs and demo tapes in an operation that could only be likened to a military campaign. It paid off. After a series of positions, she got the job she most wanted – a rock show – and is now a DJ on Virgin Radio.

I went to Uni to do drama and biology but on day one I found I wanted to be a DJ!

I was looking round Warwick Uni with my Dad. We walked into the Students' Union building and the student station was doing an OB in the foyer. Nobody was taking much notice of them but for me it was like a bolt of lightning. I said, 'That's it. That's what I want to do.' I was into rock music but this had never occurred to me before. I had wanted to be an actress but was put off because of the 'luvvies' but when I went to the radio station they seemed normal people – just like me. At school I'd been one of those irritating folk who rush in saying, 'My God! Have you heard this song?' Then I would provide a tape player and make them listen to it! In the late 1980s, everyone was into Radio One chart pop but I was passionate about Bon Jovi and Deep Purple. I wanted to play these great songs to others. Having an opportunity to do it on the radio was the solution. If I ever had anyone in my car I had a special compilation tape made up of all the latest songs so that I could subject my passengers to great music. Within a year I was the President of the Rock Music Society at Warwick. I got a show immediately on W-963, also known less glamorously, as University Radio Warwick – the Thursday night *Rock Show*. Two hours live. I chose all the records from my own collection.

Presenting news improved my style

Everyone said I had a great voice so they gave me this half-hour, daily, live news programme on W-963. I had no experience as a journalist but I had producers who put it together. I was told what to do and what to say. I played out pre-recorded features and linked them. That made me a stronger presenter. Learning to be tight and work under pressure. It's very different presenting speech. On the *Rock Show* I had been talking from the heart about my favourite songs. Now I was presenting stuff that I knew less about but having to sound as if I knew lots. It required more skill. During the summer of my final year they put big speakers up outside so all those sitting on the grass could hear me and it was the first time I actually felt like I was broadcasting to a large group of people. I could see them out of the window. That was a great experience. I recorded those shows and made a ten-minute demo tape.

I was so keen to get a job I sent a demo tape to a pirate radio station

When I left Uni in 1993 I went on the dole and made getting the job I wanted my full time occupation. It took eighteen months. I sent my demo tape to every radio station in the country – both BBC and ILR. There were about 40. Then I did follow-up phone calls and sent more tapes. It was a constant barrage of stuff. I spent my life buying jiffy bags and audiocassettes. I was so keen that I even phoned up a pirate radio station I thought was good and sent them a demo tape. They were pretty shocked because you don't send demos to illegal outfits! They were very interested but get this, it was a soul, R'n'B, black music station and here was I, a 22-year-old, white, ex-student rocker. Couldn't have been further away! But they took me on. I did the weekend breakfast show from 6 until 10 in the morning. It was brilliant! I just totally got into the music. I didn't want to sound like a fool so I went out and bought all the magazines that were related to that genre of music. I was absolutely religious about the way I prepared. I had an A4 scrapbook labelled 'A–Z' and filled it with articles about artists. So when I was on air I'd think, 'Oh, I'm playing Aaliyah. What do I know about her? She's got a new tour starting in January. This is her latest single.' So it looked as if I knew what I was talking about. And in the end I *did* because I'd done so much research and by then I really enjoyed the music. Now I was making up compilations of *soul* and boring all my friends with that!

When I got into a black station I was told I sounded too white!

I became involved in a consortium to get the licence for a new station in Birmingham. Despite being up against immense competition, we won. It was called Choice FM Birmingham, aimed at black listeners. But then I wasn't put on the air because the boss thought I sounded 'too white'! Yet radio is the one place where it doesn't matter what you look like. Previously on the pirate station, people would phone up and ask me what part of Jamaica my parents came from! As long as you fit the station sound, your colour and background don't matter. Needless to say, I won them over in the end!

You may not like the music but never let on

It helps if you like the music you play. To do that you have to find out about it, then you can probably appreciate any type of music. There's one exception in my book and that's manufactured pop. I never got into it. But if you don't like it don't let on. You've absolutely got to be versatile. To get where I am today, on a national radio station, you've got to be supportive of the music style of that station. There's a whole department dedicated to programming the music and they don't want DJs messing it up.

What type of DJ do you want to be?

There are three types of DJ. There are the personality DJs, who are usually on at breakfast time and get the big audiences. There are the format DJs, who drive the station through the day without getting in the way of the music itself too much. Then lastly there are the specialist DJs. These are the experts. They needn't come through the conventional ranks in radio. They can be pulled out of clubs. Because they're specialists they can perhaps be forgiven for a lack of sophistication sometimes in their style of presentation. What they're hired for is their consummate knowledge. I have experience of all three types. And I liked being a rock specialist best. Young DJs might want to choose which path to go down but in reality you must work hard at all three if you want the best job opportunities.

A specialist show gets a specialist audience and they know what they want

On the Virgin *Classic Rock Show* I was talking to a bunch of people who, just like me, adore their rock. I had more fan mail than ever before. They were inspired to go up to their lofts and dig out their old vinyls. Some said they stopped going out on Saturday night so they could listen. One guy went out to his shed every single Saturday evening to tune in because his wife didn't like rock. We dubbed him 'Eddie the Shed'. I was constantly getting e-mails from young rock fans who had just bought new guitars and were loving it because I played Led Zeppelin, Jimi Hendrix, Rolling Stones, The Who and Bon Jovi. This audience is really dedicated. They are not casual listeners. It's a date in their diary. They tune in specifically for their fix of you and the music. It's a great responsibility. You are talking to people who know. You can't afford to be wrong. They identify with you so personally. It's almost like you are their leader.

Daily DJs are 'doing the business'

A format DJ will receive less adulation because those shows are about playing the station sound and you are there to 'do the business' of the station. You promote the image. You provide the information and all of that is almost more important than your personal whims. In this situation you are representing the core values of the station. It's disciplined and highly produced. You don't get this show to chat about yourself.

Breakfast show DJs are hired for their personality

This is what a lot of young DJs aspire to. It's much more speech based. You're talking about light-hearted issues of the day. Sideways views of things. The unusual. Odd observations. Perceptions. Some people, like Chris Evans, seem to be born with the personality of a breakfast show host, but for the vast majority, you train yourself to be a good format presenter, build up your experience and confidence and develop your personality. If you're given the chance at a morning show, it's your opportunity to find out whether you can do it or not ... you may find that it is just not for you.

Local radio is often the starting point; it's also the backbone of the radio world

Local radio is competing with much richer, national stations. Why would anyone listen to a local station? The answer is that the DJs talk about things relative to your area. In Brighton, on Surf, it was easy. There was so much happening. During the day I might be walking on the sea front and see this ridiculous sculpture that cost a huge amount of money but looks like a donut. It's great material. Make a note of it 'cos you're bound to forget it if you don't. You come on air and you say, 'What do you think of that sculpture?' You must be careful. You don't want to run down the area. You want to be celebrating it. But you can have a bit of a joke. I had a travel *boy* (as opposed to a travel girl) and I would send him out with a microphone to get views from people on the street.

If something good's going on in the area you want to be supporting it. In Brighton they had the South Downs and the beach, for example. So you could incorporate that whole feel. 'It's a lovely day. I'll be heading down to the beach later.' Any chance to mention these things. Work at it. Get your local paper and check out what the places and events are.

Most people live in an area because they want to and they're proud of it. If you're a DJ, the chances are you've not been brought up there and you don't know the first thing about it. You can't let them know that. You've got to do your research. In Brighton, one of the issues was about whether to allow the rotting West Pier to collapse into the sea or whether to spend money to renovate it. I did a sponsored swim around the West Pier. When I was doing the *Breakfast Show*, I started a thing called 'Pee for Free'. It was a bit of a joke but it had a serious edge because Brighton had started to close all the free public toilets. You want a bit of attitude.

You have to make sure you don't end up talking about yourself. Having a co-presenter is good sometimes. They can take the mickey out of you and bring you back to earth. 'Are you actually going to talk about something other than yourself?' A good programme controller will haul you in after the programme if you've not been doing it right.

I can do the show even when I'm in tears and no-one would know

I can do my show however awful I feel, whatever the personal crisis. It's necessary. Over the years I've got it down to a fine art. At one station I did a show where I was crying during the records and then opening the microphone and sounding completely fine. That happened because I was doing overnights constantly, for almost no money and I was so tired all the time.

Incidentally, young aspiring DJs have to accept that the only place they're going to start is on the night shift and you just have to get used to the disrupted sleep patterns. I found that really difficult.

I sent out so many demo tapes it was like a production line

All through my early jobs, even though I was happy in them, I kept up the demo tape distribution. I did it constantly. It has to be a consistent process. Radio stations change hands every five minutes. Every time you hear of a different programme controller going to a station, get them a tape that arrives with them on their first day. I had sent a tape to Capital who wanted a co-presenter for Chris Tarrant. I got an audition and was in the top five but didn't get the job, then I got a call from Power FM in Portsmouth who are part of Capital. They'd heard the tape and wanted me to be a co-presenter on their breakfast show. So once again perseverance paid off. But I was still sending out tapes. It was a never-ending process.

I had a chart on my wall of radio stations. It was like a production line. Getting the CV and the covering letter done, getting the tapes done, doing the covers so the tapes would look nice, finding who to send it to. I'd have a tick sheet and every night I'd do another hit and tick it off. It was a lot of work. I even used to buy those tapes that you could take apart by unscrewing them. I'd stick my name and phone number on the *inside* of the tape so that they could never peel it off. In those days I didn't have a computer so making the presentation look decent was a nightmare. When I was at Choice FM I used to sneak into the computer room in the middle of the night by crawling on my hands and knees in pitch darkness so that I wouldn't be seen by the CCTV camera watching the room! These days you want to be sending out CDs or mini discs. Keep your ear to the ground about what's going on in the business. I heard about a new licence bid for a radio station in Brighton. I was on their case before they'd even sent in the application! I sent CVs and tapes to all the relevant groups who were applying, saying 'Would you be interested in me?' Then on the day the winning group was announced I phoned up their Chairman and said, 'My name's Leona Graham and I want to be a DJ on your station.' He said, 'Send a tape.' I said, 'I already have!' He found it in that day's mail! Then I just hassled them. I really wanted to be broadcasting in Brighton because that station was young, funky, dancey and cool. It paid off again.

I got the *Breakfast Show* on Surf and, at last, all by myself. I had left University in 1993 and started on Surf in March 1998. That's how long it had taken me.

When job hunting, it may not be the size of the audience that matters

I heard about the digital stations starting up and went in that direction because, even though digi radios were scarce, the stations were good quality and national. I got a job on Core doing 3 until 7 in the afternoon. The general audience was probably tiny but all the decision-makers in radio had access to these stations so it was a shop window for me. I hoped they might scan the dial and catch me by accident. And that's what happened with Virgin where I started in April 2000.

Women DJs used to be quite rare

Even now, there are more men than women in the business. I'm the only female DJ on Virgin. The change is slow. For example, Radio One has a female breakfast presenter followed by a female mid-morning show presenter. A few years ago nobody would ever have had two women on back-to-back. Women have to sound as strong and as confident as a guy. Virgin can put me on in the daytime and know that I can carry off a competition and give away £10,000 or a teddy bear and sound as confident as a male presenter.

Audience figures are a science

Don't get fixated with audiences. Let the other departments do their job and you do yours. The temptation is to start interfering. Really, they've got it all covered. When it comes to play lists, let the music department deal with it and when it's audiences let the programme controller deal with that. If you're a format DJ the audience figures will be more about the structure of the show than you yourself. On *Breakfast Time*, though, the audience figures are vital because you set up the figures for the whole day. They peak at around 8 am and decline during the day. There's more pressure here because it will be sudden death if it goes wrong.

I hated listening back to my own voice but you must

Practise. Listen to other DJs. I used to say, 'Why do they sound so hot and I don't?' Painful as it may seem you have to record yourself. I hated it. But I forced myself to do it and think, 'Ah, that's why!' You've got to sound confident, like you love what you're promoting. 'Tight' is a word we use in the industry which, especially for a format jock, means not sloppy, not waffling and slick.

Get a foot in the door

Be enthusiastic. Be helpful. Volunteer to do things. Make yourself indispensable, even if it's something boring like cataloguing the music. You could become an integral part of the station. Don't be afraid to work in the middle of the night. Don't complain in the building. If you must, save it for the privacy of your own home. Nobody wants moaners. There are a lot of other people who would happily do it.

12 Children's programmes

This is yet another growth area with whole networks dedicated to younger audiences. A number of broadcasting students I have taught have revealed the desire to become a presenter on a wonderfully chaotic Saturday morning youth TV show or on *Top of the Pops*. But beware! To the uninitiated, it may seem that presenting for a children's audience is a good place to start before graduating to the high-energy, peak-time viewing, pop slots. However, you will be amazed at the demands placed upon you and the potential career problems you will encounter.

You cannot be a children's presenter if you do not have your heart in it. Those involved in children's programming understand how discriminating and demanding their audience is. Young, they may be but children won't be satisfied with half-hearted performances or patronising tones. For this reason, the powers that be are seeking a very particular type of person.

In the commercial world, children and young people are a formidable section of the purchasing public. They, with their pester power and pocket money, and the parents, seeking to keep abreast of all the latest fads, are a multi-million pound advertising target. Broadcasting bosses intend to keep it that way. So those presenting have a heavy responsibility.

There is a substantial difference between presenting for pre-school age groups and presenting for those of primary school age. The former requires a degree of unabashed, merry nuttiness that may make even the most ambitious presenter quail with embarrassment! The BBC now admits that a slightly older, more mature figure may be better to front the toddlers' programmes.

There are very few programmes made for teenagers. This is simply because these viewers and listeners are actually enjoying adult shows like soaps. It's felt that there is little of a specialist nature that needs or can be done for this age range.

A VIEW FROM THE INSIDE: PAUL SMITH

Paul Smith is an Executive Producer and Head of On-Air for the BBC's successful digital network CBBC. He's spent two decades working in this field, producing shows, spotting and nurturing presenters. He's 43 and did a degree in microbiology and genetics at University College London before deciding to work at LBC radio! He did journalism courses at the London College of Printing. His BBC career started in 1979 as a studio manager where he used to cut the 'ums' out of Robin Day's interviews. 'You could actually shorten a three-minute interview by 30 seconds!' He worked his way through TV presentation to specialize in children's shows, like *Going Live* on Saturday mornings. He developed the 'wrap around' concept of children's presentation which transformed into CBBC. The technique enables items of varying lengths and genres to be transmitted seamlessly by using a presenter to change the mood. Paul Smith worked on this with Philip Schofield in the much celebrated 'broom cupboard' which was a small continuity studio, plastered with paintings and birthday cards. He also created another star, Schofield's

Figure 12.1
Head of CBBC On-Air, Paul Smith

sidekick, a small furry puppet called Gordon the Gofer, who we can now reveal was none other than Paul Smith himself!

He was closely involved with the BBC's *Making It* search-for-a-star competition launched in the spring of 2002 by BBC Talent to discover a young anchor for CBBC. It became yet another of the very public star-making shows. Paul Smith has his doubts about this type of recruitment, but from the thousands of wannabes 19-year-old unknown Maddy Stevens from Eastbourne emerged. She picked up what anybody would give their eye teeth for – a twelve-month contract to present children's TV. Paul Smith is her boss. It may be an extraordinary way to get a job but it serves to show how any way in is worth a try!

When talent-spotting I'm looking for warmth and intelligence

When it comes to children's presentation, there has to be an extra level of warmth. There must be a genuine 'accessibility'. You must be able to relax on screen. Ironically, you may be young at heart and in fact, but you must be mature in temperament. You have to be a team player. Bright and quick. By bright, I mean intelligent. Nobody will make it if they can't find their way out of a paper bag! I'm looking for someone who is enthusiastic and who has taken some steps to understand what a presenter does. They must be natural and able to communicate ideas. One of the questions I always ask people is, 'What do you think the job of a presenter is?' The people who don't last very long in my office are the ones who say, 'It's presenting myself in the best possible way', which is a very common answer. That is actually *not* what the job is. The job is to communicate the ideas of the producers. The clue is in the title.

I also want somebody who can bring something extra. For example, it's great if somebody knows a lot about sport or has some hobby that makes them a more interesting person. There are an awful lot of people who don't have anything like that. You can put them on TV but they are not going to get anywhere because they have nothing to say; they've got no experience to fall back on. Admittedly, many of the people I see are young but that shouldn't stop them having other talents. If you're interested in the world, interested in people, then you will have been doing stuff since you were at school. I'm not asking for intellectual Goliaths! Perhaps you've built your own website. This may never get used by us but it just shows that you have got something else to say. One of our presenters here is a Black Belt in Tae Kwondo. We've not had cause to use it yet, but when you talk to him about it he's got a lot to say and you can see this person has the potential to pick up other things as well. Developing talent can be exciting but the process is terribly long. It takes a lot of practise to be a good presenter.

How I found Zoë Ball

The Saturday morning show had been collecting tapes of people who wanted to be presenters and after they'd made their selections I took all the tapes away to see if there was anybody interesting who I wanted. The person who stood out was Zoë. I had no idea that she was Johnny Ball's daughter until about a year later. There was just something really natural and warm about her. That was clear from the show tape. So we got her in and thought, 'Yes, this is a good idea.' Zoë is a character. She is also a bit of an exception to my usual rules. She is somebody (and she'll admit this herself) who can't get to work on time. She's quite all over the place; something I normally wouldn't stand for. She's the sort of person you feel you could walk up to in the street and talk to. I think these are pretty basic requirements for all presenters.

The talent competition is flawed

My views on this are a bit controversial. The BBC wanted to show it was reaching out to the audience, so it devised the competition *Making It*. It encouraged wannabes around the country to come forward for auditions. I was one of the judges. The finalists went into a show and were voted for by the public. I have grave reservations about whether this is the way to find good presenters. Don't get me wrong; Maddy Stevens, who eventually won through, will be fine. She's fun and we'll have a good presenter there. But I think the whole way these open auditions work leads to many of the wrong people coming forward. Even amongst the ten finalists we had people who had never thought of becoming a TV presenter before the open auditions. People just go along for the hell of it, thinking, 'Maybe I could be a star.' It's a problem for me because I want people who actually have a hunger to do this. This isn't the best way to find people. I suspect that it's really more of a high-profile PR thing than it is an effective way of developing talent.

There are 'stars' and there are presenters

One of my big things is trying to take on people who can be themselves. By and large, I would hope that most presenters are like that. But there are different sorts of presenter. Take Jim Davidson. I would argue that, in my definition, he is not a presenter. He is a light entertainment personality who presents. He started his career as an entertainer, not as a presenter. Similarly, Cilla Black is not a presenter. She started her career as a singer and entertainer. At the end of the day, these people are playing a part. I'm more interested in developing people who are playing themselves.

Being a children's presenter can be embarrassing

Children's presenters have to immerse themselves in children's lives and therefore the problem that comes up on screen is that they can be seen as being a bit 'soft'. It can be very embarrassing for them. There's a loss of face and they end up not being able to perform the way they must to do the job well. There is a big distinction between presenting for children and for teenagers. A lot of presenters in their early twenties don't realize that when we talk about 'children's' programmes, we mean it. We mean kids under twelve. When it comes to CBeebies for pre-school children we've changed our policy somewhat. We've started to bring in older presenters because they often have more of an ability to perform to the required standard. A lot of the presenters on CBBC would not be suitable for preschool. We used to mix them all up but now we've separated it. With 'youth' presenters, you're looking for someone with a lot more of an 'edge'. Interestingly, Zoë springs to mind again, also Sarah Cox, Chris Evans and Johnny Vaughan.

Ad libbing is a must

Memory is very important although it's not necessary to learn lines like an actor. I tend to give people bullet points and they construct a script around that. They have to know what the important points are and they ad lib around them. That's why people who've done journalism can be very useful because they are able to pick out the significant bits and make sure they are related along with the fun and nonsense. They also need a good memory to remember people's names and what is going on. Learning to read autocue is a skill that is quite easily taught. I suppose you could say that knowing how to read, and read well, is fairly vital, too! The other problem that we face is that people must have good grasp of the language. They must be able to handle grammar and vocabulary. We can get a lot of grief, particularly where children are concerned, if the presenters use the wrong words. This is all part of your communications skills. The other things they need to practise are how to stand, the pace at which you say things and the order of delivery if it's not scripted. Pausing in the right places sounds obvious but it's an art. It seems strange but, sometimes, presenters don't remember that they're on television so people can see them and you may not need to say anything. You can just look at the camera. The best person that I've worked with who used the camera like that was Philip Schofield. He would just stop talking and look at the camera in a certain way and you knew exactly what he meant. You shouldn't be frightened about leaving a pause or creating a silence.

Learning to interview is key

Doing interviews is a really important skill which takes a hell of a lot of practise. I think people like Michael Parkinson would say he's still learning how to do it. If you talk to my presenters, the very young ones will say, 'Oh yes, I can interview', whereas the older ones will say, 'Oh my God. I still don't know how to do it.' It's tough to get the right stuff out of people and ask the right questions in the right order. There's only one way to improve – with practise and they effectively practise on air. We put a 'framework' around people so that they aren't given things they can't cope with. One of the most important things is casting. You do have to cast even presenters; it's not just an acting thing. Some people are better interviewing than others, so you get them to do that.

It's not about fame

Most of the people who I take on don't get the fame thing until later! Inevitably people do get flattered by their own celebrity and are quite impressed by it sometimes. We try to keep people's feet on the ground by involving them in the day-to-day operation. By and large, what I *don't* do with my presenters is, I *don't* get them to come in five minutes before they're on air, put them in a dressing room and then put them in the studio. I expect them to be in the office earlier on, working with the production team. They have to build relationships with the team otherwise it won't work. I just don't believe in treating people like stars. They should be treated as if they are doing a job of work because that is what it is. Having said that, there are some more glamorous bits because of TV. They occasionally have to be sent to have their hair done, buy some clothes or something, which is not like a normal job.

You have to tell presenters what you think of them

I am honest with my presenters ... and they know that. Just a moment ago, I spoke to one of my presenters and told him I didn't think he was very good on a particular programme. I'm not here to massage their egos. If they're not good they need to know. Of course, people are used to me so they take it reasonably well. Sometimes it upsets people. The worst scenario is, as happens occasionally, when somebody hasn't been very good even although they've worked quite hard. Then it turns out that it's not their fault and, understandably, they get upset. Normally, though, they know if they haven't put any effort into it and they realize they've been rumbled!

The shelf-life of a children's presenter is very short

I've had presenters as young as 16, although normally we're talking about 21-year-olds. By the time they are getting to their late twenties they are beginning to reach their sell-by date! That's when they normally have to begin to think about where to go next. I'd say the shelf-life of a children's presenter is probably only about five years ... and that's an optimistic estimate.

It's hard work

I'm sorry to sound old-fashioned here but, no matter how young you are, I'm looking for someone who's got a bit of a work ethic. It's really imperative that you are where you're supposed to be on time and ready to go. Television is expensive. We've got whole teams of people standing by and we can't be kept waiting. Strangely enough, the one exception to that was

Zoë because she had a tendency to be late for everything! It became something we had to cope with. It wasn't because she was being deliberately lazy; she was just like that. There comes a point, sometimes, where even a person like me just has to accept the inevitable! You just have to accept that if you want the best out of this person you will have to put up with such foibles. But normally, I expect people to be here and to be up for it and interested because, if they're not, why are they here? Most people will shape up because they don't want to lose that opportunity by messing around.

Being a children's presenter can be a dead end

This is the really difficult thing. What do they do next? I hate to say it but, unfortunately, it often takes a scandal like Richard Bacon (the *Blue Peter* presenter linked in the tabloids to drug taking) to move them on to another level. That's a great shame really. It shouldn't be like that. Partly they get typecast. I suspect that's because TV producers can be lazy and see people in a context and won't look beyond it. They'll just employ a person because they've seen them on Channel 4 which is hardly a good enough reason! The traditional routes out of children's presentation have been via the Saturday morning shows but they aren't what they were. When I was working on *Going Live* we were getting five or six million viewers. These days the Saturday morning shows are lucky to get a million. You find that people end up doing reports on *Holiday* and they're fast on their way to the shopping channel. That's why it's very useful if people have other skills because sometimes you can pick up something and explore new avenues. Simon Thomas on *Blue Peter* is very interested in sport so you could see a time when he becomes a sports presenter. I've got a person here who is interested in technology. She could be a *Tomorrow's World*-type presenter or end up working on the Discovery Channel. The big problem is that it's just not obvious what happens to them next. A lot of them have realized this and made sure that they are able to do other things behind the scenes. I've got one presenter who can Avid edit and direct films. Andy Peters did this as well. He doesn't have a career as a presenter any more but has a career behind the camera.

13 International business programmes

Such is the world today that almost anyone presenting on TV or radio can expect to have an international audience. Even programmes made initially for home consumption are frequently sold overseas – and not just to English-speaking countries. International broadcasting is very big business so companies have foreign outposts and network centres all over the place.

English may be the international language of broadcasting but it is still worth learning languages. Foreign correspondents are expected to know or to learn a new tongue. Speaking constantly through interpreters is obstructive, time-consuming, expensive and, frankly, dangerous. Many are the times that reporters have thought they could rely on a translator only to discover that questions have been interpreted badly or the answers given have been 'rephrased' in an 'acceptable' way due to pressures of the ruling establishment.

For the most part, your nationality and skin colour will not be particularly relevant. Wherever you go in the world you will see presenters of Asian, Indian, African, European and American appearance presenting to any or all of those continents.

You must have a genuine understanding of the political, cultural and social differences of the country you're broadcasting to. Simple things like what you wear can be important. Mostly international business attire is the accepted dress but in Moslem countries female broadcasters may offend if they show their legs. Beards may be unacceptable – even for Western broadcasting organizations (as you will discover in what CNBC's Nigel Roberts has to say).

International time zones don't just mean that you have to re-tune your body clock, they have a dramatic effect on broadcasting itself. Obviously, a news event in Hong Kong at 8 pm would hit lunchtime news shows in the UK and early morning ones in New York. Thus the morning rush-hour terrorist attack on the Twin Towers in 2001 was seen live by millions literally from one side of the word to the other.

The reverberations of 24-hour global broadcasting can be huge in politics and economics the world over. Nowhere, perhaps, is this more apparent than in the fast expanding area of live business newscasting. Like it or not, it is one of the most internationally influential areas of broadcasting.

A VIEW FROM THE INSIDE: NIGEL ROBERTS

Nigel Roberts was born in 1953, got an economics degree and became a high-flying BBC News trainee. He's done just about every form of reporting and presentation in his time ... including fronting a tremendously successful ITV children's show which involved much jelly-throwing and slapstick! After all, the same rules apply – don't patronise, be enthusiastic, know your target audience and appreciate what appeals to them. Having reported and presented for the BBC, Central TV and Channel 4 News, he now presents a two-hour live business news show on CNBC Europe.

You've got to know what you're talking about

It's the breadth of the things we do that's actually difficult. I mean it really is smart television because you've got to know what you're talking about. You're covering a lot of bases – the fixed-income markets, debts, bond markets, equities, currency markets, macro-economics and you've got to look at the geopolitics as well. My job is great because what I do is ask vaguely intelligent questions to very clever people and then bask in their reflected glory! I like business. I'm interested in it. I've been reporting and working in this area for years. I've got an Economics degree which is useful in as much as it allows you to see how things *don't* work! A degree may not be required by your employer but you must have a reasonable amount of understanding. Another of our presenters here used to work for the *Wall Street Journal* so he obviously knows what's going on. You can actually learn it on the job ... but there is a lot to learn.

Figure 13.1
CNBC anchor Nigel Roberts

What my day is like

I get up at seven and trawl through the papers before I get in. If I'm not cycling in, I'll read stuff on the train. I would listen to the radio on the way if there was any point but, unfortunately, because it's so home-based it tells you nothing about the global scene. I think the BBC is useless in this respect. It's completely lost the plot. The international nature of the audience and the subject matter means that I must gather knowledge widely. I read the *Wall Street Journal* and the *FT* daily. Also the foreign papers which you can get from their websites.

I get in to the London studios at about ten and check what's happening. My two-hour live show will involve maybe twenty live interviews so I have to be well prepared. I research the stories, look at the wires, look at the companies concerned, look at Companies House results, read the accounts, the balance sheets and work out for myself what is going on. So obviously you have to be able to decipher that kind of material. My show, *Market Wrap*, goes out at 1600 GMT. I continue the background work all the way up to the TX [transmission]. You read the papers, talking to people in the markets. You're doing the journalistic job. Most of the presenters do all this themselves. We have got some back-up to produce research notes if necessary. We've got a huge database with stuff on companies so you can find things out from that. If you've got a couple of dozen interviews you have to be meticulous. So within the running order I write notes for each one, so I've got it as an aide memoire when I get to it in the programme.

It's a bit like sports presenters in a way. You've got to know your history and how the game works. There's the pre-game show with *Squawk Box* which sets up the day. After that you've got *Market Watch*, then *Power Lunch* at mid-day as events are unfolding. Then in the late afternoon, I do the post-game analysis on *Market Wrap*.

You have to make connections across the world

Ours is not just a national focus like the BBC has in their business news which is just the FTSE 100 and a few other quick mentions of other stock markets. We have to make connections with the global markets and if you do that it actually makes sense. CNBC Asia, CNBC Europe and CNBC US have the same sort of programmes which set up the economic issues for the day, follow them through and report on them for the world throughout a 24-hour period. For example, it's 1410 in the UK now. That's BST. That means it's 0910 in the US and the market there is about to open, so everything we say here now is going to have an effect on trading there. Asia is eight hours ahead. It's gone ten o'clock in the evening, so they are just wrapping up the market and looking to the US to see what's going to happen. The American equity market is obviously the most important to be aware of in a working day, but don't forget currencies and bonds are being traded all the time. So there are people trading out of hours in their own region because they're trading with someone in another market which is in the full throes of a trading day. For a presenter in a live business news setting, the fact that you're working on an internationally screened show is not only significant because of the time differences. You have to remember that we are covering global markets regardless of time zones and you have to make the connections between all these events no matter what time of the day you are doing it. For example, we're in the UK. We're not within the Euro zone. But what the European Central Bank does is important. In the same way when Greenspan is talking, that's going to be important because the US is the biggest economy which in turn will affect the Euro zone and everyone else. So you have to take the wider view.

The audience is incredibly diverse

It's a mixed audience because on the one hand you've got a core constituency of financial professionals, of senior executives and on the other hand you've got smaller investors and people with tangential interest. A lot of people watch in their office. This is very much news that you can use but there is an audience of people who aren't in the City [of London], who are not professionals, and there are those who *are* professionals who may not necessarily understand the intricacies of covered warrants because they are in a different part of the market. In television, you've got to aim for instant intelligibility and if the audience suddenly goes, 'Hold on. I don't know what the hell he's talking about', you've lost them. The trick is to keep it simple but without losing the facts or over-simplifying. After all, you must remain authoritative.

Being live and global can be scary

There are very few places where they're pumping out the amount of air time that we pump out every day and, even more significantly, it's live. A lot of it is improvised. There is a structure there but within that it's flexible because you've got to be reacting to news as it happens. Very often on CNBC we are breaking stories ourselves. This is important because you see the effects of that. For example, we have a Chief Executive Officer on. We ask a question and he doesn't answer it well and you can see the stocks are going down. Or perhaps he announces a share buy-back and the stocks will go up. It's kind of scary sometimes. The effects are instantaneous and dramatic … almost like remote control. The difference is that we're right in it, creating it, not just reporting. We're talking to the decision-makers, we're telling the news and adding the interpretation to it.

Doing interviews

Some presenters have the questions they must ask written on the autocue. I don't. I work out my own interviews. I don't write out the questions, just the key issues. Then you have an area to work within rather than a set of sentences to spit out! The thing I bang on about is 'structured spontaneity'. You've got a structure there but you can be spontaneous, you can work your way round it. Often people will say, 'What's your first question going to be?' and I'll say, 'Well, actually, I don't know!' It sounds a bit quixotic but as you go into it something springs to mind so you might just fling it at them.

Tips for presenters

If you are doing live stuff, you need to be able to juggle lots of balls at once. And if you are doing international stuff, you must be able to see the bigger picture. Don't be too focused or too technical or things will go right over their heads. Fortunately the international language of business is English, so it's easy enough to talk the right language although sometimes you have to make qualifications to statements. You can't say simply the 'Chancellor' in a British economic story because to the Germans watching that would be a reference to a Head of Government. You have to be specific and say 'Chancellor of the Exchequer'.

At all costs avoid what I call 'lip-gloss poisoning', by which I mean the idea that all presentation is about is looking good and reading the autocue nicely. You've got to be engaged. If your brain isn't engaged with what you're saying and you're simply reading and performing, it will show in your eyes.

Have water close by you because you do get dry. Have a wee before hand. Don't drink too much coffee before a two-hour programme or you'll be going to the loo all the time! If you've done a good programme and it's been really exciting then you tend to be bouncing around. You are a bit wired and you have to take the time to come down. I frequently cycle to work about six miles, so going home again afterwards means the exercise brings me down to earth.

Training to be a presenter is c—!

A lot of people who train for presenting get the idea that they've got to consider body language, that you've got to declaim and get your voice pitch right. My personal view is: that's bollocks! It is complete and utter crap! There's a ridiculous debate about Andrew Marr's ears and whether he waves his arms about. Marr [the BBC's political editor] has got one of the finest minds in British journalism. He's a joy to watch because he engages, he knows what he's talking about and he's giving you some insight. It doesn't matter a toss if he waves his hands about. That's what he does!

I have never done voice training, elocution lessons or deep-breathing exercises. Once they actually wired me up for an item we were doing about stress. They monitored my blood pressure and heart rate and the weird thing is that when we went live, my readings all went down! But then maybe I'm just a sick and twisted individual. I get focused on what I'm doing and that makes you calmer.

I remember when I was at the BBC they had a stylist who came round and tried to work out what all the colours were for the presenters and decide whether you were Autumn, Winter, Spring or Summer. They said to me that I was an Autumn person. I said, 'So what colour suits should I wear?' and they said, 'Blue, grey and brown'. Funny that! Those are about the only colours that they do suits in!

And then there's the beard. I must be one of the few presenters who has a beard, apart from one of CNN's Whitehouse correspondents and Keith Graves on Sky. When the Americans first took me on there was great debate about it. They thought it might be seen as shifty or untrustworthy. They said, 'Oh he's got a beard!'; 'Well, maybe it's a European thing'; 'Oh hey, that's OK then'. Beardism is rampant. When I was at the BBC I was asked to shave it off. They said to me, 'We're worried because you look a bit too real.' As if somehow, because you're presenting you're supposed to look unreal! This is me! I actually look better with a beard. I like to think I've got this job because of the quality of what's in my mind, not what's on my chin. Thankfully CNBC don't mind. What I say is, when you are presenting you are adopting a persona. You're not playing a role because if you're an actor you should be doing that and probably making more money out of doing it, if you can play a role convincingly. You adopt a persona which is appropriate for the social context in which you find yourself. Everybody does this all the time. It's no different on television. It's a slightly alien area with the lights, the cameras, someone talking in your earpiece, but you should let it happen naturally. It should still be you.

14 Travel news

Radio is searching harder than ever for new services to provide 'added value' to listeners. RDS signals and digital technology mean that travel reporting has become an essential part of the output. It has also acted as a springboard for many presenters – those on Five Live are personalities in their own right. It may seem a lowly job to start with but it requires all sorts of journalistic skills – as any other reporting does – and it gets you into a newsroom! A good travel presenter shines out and stands a decent chance of moving into other areas.

Presentation here requires that you structure your scripts logically for a traveller to know immediately that what's coming relates to them. It's a real lesson in how to have consideration for your audience. Resist the temptation to ring the changes in your script and make each travel story chatty and entertaining for other listeners who are not affected. You have a job to do. There is only one chance for a stressed-out driver to hear this news. Don't try being a personality or a joker at their expense.

What do you think about this piece of travel news?

> *The emergency services are having a very difficult time clearing up the wreckage from an overturned lorry which has caused all lanes in each direction to be blocked on the M1 in Yorkshire. It's at the Dodworth turn off. Police have been working at the site all morning.*

It's lousy. By the time you've got to the information that alerts drivers to where it's happening, you've already gone past the details they'll need to hear. Worse still, there's no mention of the junction number and, whilst there's a colourful line about what a hard morning's work the police have been suffering, there's no indication of how long the disruption will continue or how to avoid it. Keep it simple and direct:

> *On the M1 in Yorkshire, the emergency services are clearing up the*
> *wreckage from an overturned lorry ... [this gives listeners plenty of*
> *time to prick up their ears and wait for the crucial details they need*
> *to know] ... which has left all lanes in each direction blocked. It's at*
> *junction 37. That's the Dodworth slip road and the police think the*
> *motorway will remain closed in both directions for at least another*
> *hour. Southbound traffic is being diverted off at junction 38 just*
> *north of Barnsley; northbound traffic is leaving the motorway at*
> *junction 36. There are already long tailbacks.*

Notice also that the script has deliberately mentioned twice, in different ways, that *all* the lanes are closed, so that those who didn't hear that before the mention of junction 37 will know how serious the disruption is when it's said again.

Travel news is not just about traffic jams and pile-ups. It can be part of the radio station's main news coverage on fires, demonstrations, security alerts, bad weather and air crashes. It can bolster the sense of belonging to a station e.g. *Five Live Match Day Travel* which links the commentaries on the football games with the station's service to the listeners trying to get to the grounds. It even cunningly encourages the direct involvement of the listeners by asking them to phone in with information.

The most vital elements about travel news are that it is accurate and up to date; if not, the entire operation is undermined.

Sometimes the injects come from small studios in AA, RAC or police buildings around the country. There's a table, a mic and cans. At the other extreme they can be more adventurous, as with Capital Radio's *Eye in the Sky* – the station's own helicopter viewing the jams in London from on high. However, thanks to the relative simplicity of radio technology, travel presenters can work from their desk with nothing more than a mic, headphones, computers and telephones. Andy McColl does just that.

A VIEW FROM THE INSIDE: ANDY McCOLL

Travel presenter, Andy McColl, is a broadcast journalist on the 24-hour rolling news station LBC 1152 am and DAB. His job is to coordinate live

Figure 14.1
The busy hum of the newsroom provides the right background effects for Andy McColl's traffic reports. He is close to all necessary sources, enabling him to get the information out swiftly

pieces from reporters and bikers on the roads, from police, air, sea and rail service providers, and from press officers during major events. Sometimes he'll do interviews too. He must compile the information into a 60-second package six times an hour, linking in to programming with the flick of a switch from his bunker in the main newsroom.

It's not just travel news – it's news

The beauty of rolling news is that a travel story can often make the headlines, especially during industrial action or with a spate of serious incidents on the rail network. Being a travel news correspondent, I'm often first with the news of major incidents involving public transport.

We also have to deal with demonstrations and incidents of public unrest. The 2002 May Day protests turned quite nasty in the evening with clashes between protesters and police in Soho. That night I was recording two-way reports from our Motorbike Reporter, Simon Rahemtulla, on both the traffic disruption and the violent scenes.

One of the most bizarre stories I've ever covered was the closure of the M3 in Surrey – not because of an accident or roadworks. The trouble was caused by a cow that had wandered onto the Hampshire-bound lanes from a nearby field. The tip-off came from ITN VJ [video journalist] Chris Ship who couldn't believe his own eyes when he spotted the bovine wandering around on the tarmac. You have to get the balance right – it sounds comical but it caused miles of tailbacks right onto the M25.

The tragedy of September 11 required massive travel coverage

The whole shift seemed just like a plot to a Hollywood movie. When I first took a glimpse at the ITN news channel at 1355, I thought it was a film or a mock-up of a fire at the World Trade Centre. The caption then flashed up: 'Plane crashes into World Trade Centre, New York.'

I was based in the Travel Centre at the Trafficmaster HQ in Bedfordshire, miles away from the ITN Radio base in central London. My first reaction was to phone the newsroom in the capital to find out the angle we would be taking for the headlines at 1400. I was on at 1401. The deadline was tight and I needed info fast. I called the British Airports Authority at Heathrow for advice about flights from the UK to the States. I went with that as the top line in my 1401 bulletin to run alongside the open-ended news coverage. As the hours passed, the phones were jammed with calls from airport press officers advising me of flights being diverted, American airspace being closed and then a no-fly zone being declared over the City of London.

Different stations like different presentation styles

Previously, when I was the Broadcast Information Officer at AA Roadwatch at their London Control Centre, I soon realized that different clients liked the information given in different ways. The BBC local stations liked bulletins delivered with authority with a bit of banter once the main report was done. The commercial stations were more relaxed with their presentation style. However, during a major incident it was often straight on air with the story, a bit of background into the incident, a recap and then lock out.

However you do it, one thing's for sure, it's got to be right.

I was hooked on radio from childhood

I remember as a child in the early 1980s listening to Essex Radio in the evening to a bloke called Timbo (*aka* Tim Lloyd). His irreverent style and the ability to make me laugh had me coming back for more. When he moved to Radio Mercury in Crawley, I went to no end of trouble trying to erect an aerial in my parents' loft so I could get even the fuzziest of signals!

Later, as a teenager, I developed a more serious liking for speech radio and discovered LBC Radio. I was instantly hooked on a weekend show called *Through the Night*. I was captivated by the way the broadcasters could communicate with the callers.

I was determined to get in. I started in hospital broadcasting at the tender age of twelve, nearly two decades ago. I remember my first programme very well. It was a one-hour Sunday afternoon request show. I was so nervous, my knees where knocking together about an hour before starting. In fact, when I went on air it felt very natural to be talking in a room. One of my mentors at the time told me, 'Remember you're addressing one person. You're in a one-to-one with the listener and nobody else.' I felt quite comfortable with that, as I've always been more at ease talking to people in small groups. I worked unpaid for the *Dartford Times* and finally got a chance to present a breakfast show on an RSL (Restricted Service Licence) in Medway. Then I bombarded Metro networks and RTM Radio with tapes which paid off – I ended up working for both!

Getting on

I can't stress enough – get loads of practical hands-on experience. That's how I managed to claw my way to where I am now. When I've been recruiting new freelancers, I often find potential staff have excellent academic grades but no practical know-how. Having both will give you the edge.

Practise your voice skills by reading out loud into the mirror. It sounds daft but it's worth it.

Record yourself speaking. Get used to hearing your voice and learn how to pitch it. Use it as a tool. It's going to be your trademark. You'll be surprised at how fast you speak, so record and then speak deliberately more slowly than before. It usually sounds much clearer.

If you have a regional accent, don't ever be told you need to lose it. I was once told that by a Broadcast Assistant at a Local BBC radio station. I think her words were, 'If you're going to work in the south you'll have to get rid of that appalling Scottish accent.' Charming! You may need to tone it down but don't lose it completely.

Make sure you enunciate and breathe in the right places. Listen to a number of different voices on both BBC and Commercial radio news. You'll become very aware of the various styles broadcasters have.

One of the most vital skills of presentation is to be interested in the message you're trying to deliver. Be, or at least sound, well informed on the subject you're talking about. There's nothing worse than listening to an anchor or presenter who sounds as if they don't give a damn.

III
Starting out

15　How to get in and get on

There have never been more opportunities in the field of presentation. Broadcasting output is increasing almost daily; local commercial multiplexes are allowing yet more digital channels to spring up. Someone's got to be there to keep the station on the air ... it could be you. There are as many different ways to get into the business as there are people trying to do it. Luck is involved to some extent but I'm a firm believer that you mostly make your own luck. There is nothing that will beat hard work, dedication and enthusiasm.

WHAT ARE THEY LOOKING FOR?

Prospective employers usually are hunting for someone with 'what it takes'. This usually means the relevant knowledge, experience, looks, sound, availability and an agreement over contract money. Inevitably, at a time when the most popular courses in higher education are media-related, there are many candidates who will have all these assets and a lot of them will have youth on their side.

Academic qualifications are not compulsory when breaking into this field but they can be helpful. So many people are now applying for each post that editors have a full-time job simply compiling a shortlist. Anything you've done may be relevant and in many cases those vital words 'postgraduate diploma in broadcast journalism' or 'degree in media studies' can be the thing that will tip the balance in your favour, initially at least.

Talent spotting is not an easy skill. Employers may detect ability, but is it the right kind of ability for the particular job on offer and can they provide the right back-up to extend and nurture that talent? Lis Howell's experience in the independent TV sector, both as a presenter herself and later in top management, is typical:

I've made some terrible mistakes myself, thinking I could make a silk purse of a sow's ear. There are some times that you just can't do it. You think this person's got great potential but it withers on the vine. Several times I employed people as reporters but in the end the presentation side of it defeated them. They didn't want to stand in front of a camera. Sometimes they thought they did want to stand in front of a camera but they just weren't any good. I mean some people can't communicate. Or they look wrong. There is no way of knowing for sure what will happen. Remember too that producers and editors have a hidden agenda. You go in and do a brilliant audition or a fantastic pilot or whatever. They're sitting there thinking what this programme really needs is a Welsh person with one leg who can relate to the disabled group that we've got listening in Croydon. On the other hand, I've had lots of successes. For example, Ross Kelly and Penny Smith are a couple of my choices. Penny's a presenter on GMTV and does a show on Classic FM now. But I took her on from being in the press office at Central Television. A friend of mine said, 'Have you ever met Penny Smith? She's looking to get into TV. She might be quite good.' But there were hundreds of people applying for the vacancy I was filling. He told her to apply and I gave her a job on screen at Border TV. I thought she had tremendous wit ... but also I was looking for a fair-haired English presenter because I had a dark Scot!

Another of those indefinable but highly prized qualities, not mentioned in the job spec, is 'attitude'. All things being equal, the one who gets the job will be the one who has confidence in his or her own abilities and, crucially, awareness of any shortcomings. It is the one who has a sense of how much he or she *doesn't* know and a desire to continue learning. It is the one who is ready to muck in and make the tea but not be unfairly used or abused. Someone who is modest but without false modesty. Someone with a sense of humour and diplomacy. You need to know when to laugh, albeit half-heartedly, at a camera operator's rather poor-taste joke when you're out on the road and when to make it clear that the repartee is inappropriate ... but you need to know how to say what you think is necessary without breaking the team apart. Needless to say, your ability to work with a team will be one of the attributes they will be trying to assess (see Chapter 3).

Figure 15.1
Things can get heated in the gallery. Can you handle it?

SHOW REELS

Most employers find show reels a help, but only if they are short. Be brutal with your editing. Use only 30 or 40 seconds of each item you have available and make the show reel or demo-disc appropriate to the job you are applying for. If it's a newsreader's post there's not much point in showing how you can fall into a bowl of jelly for charity at some student event. Make the quality as good as you can and label it clearly with your contact numbers and e-mail address on the tape or disc so that if the outer sleeve gets lost the information is still to hand. Don't expect to get it back. It may get thrown out as soon as it's opened or it may reside on a shelf for months until it's needed. Package it with a good CV. Director and broadcaster Jenni Mills has a few words of warning:

> *Personally, I think many of the privately-run presentation courses – the sort that promise to turn you into a presenter with a show reel over a weekend – are a total waste of time. If you want to spend a lot of money having a bit of fun in a studio and getting a taste for what it's like in front of a camera they're fine, but I would seriously question how many successful presenters have come from that route. As for show reels – they're useful once you have some experience under your belt but most languish unviewed on producers' shelves. Beware of people who offer to make you one for a large sum of money. If a director is seriously interested in you they will ask to meet you and if they think you have potential they will screen test you themselves.*

WRITING YOUR CV AND JOB APPLICATION

Make sure you spell *curriculum vitae* correctly! This is not said flippantly. All too often impressive CVs are entirely undermined by poor spelling and bad grammar. Remember that presenters and reporters will have to read scripts and, more significantly, to write them. It's no great advertisement for your superlative presentational powers if you simply can't use the English language!

Look closely at that job description. Frequently, presenters' jobs have remarkably few demands specified so, if there are none or they are sketchy, phone up and get more details. Armed with this information, go back to your CV and consider carefully how to match up your skills with what they want.

Constructing a CV is something of an art form. The dictionary definition of it is: 'A short resumé of one's educational background and career.' This is what it must be in every respect – with the emphasis on 'short'. Tailor your CV for the particular job. All your formal educational achievements come first with dates. Then come the extras – languages, driving licence, computer skills etc. Hobbies are definitely relevant (see Paul Smith's view, in Chapter 12) and how you present them depends on the type of job. For example, suppose you are an ace horse rider. This would normally be the kind of detail that goes in the 'hobbies and interests' section at the end of the CV to show that you have a life outside of broadcasting.

However, it may be truly relevant if the job is the anchor of a leisure programme, in which case it should be given more prominence, along with your interest in other sports and your all-round fitness. Suppose that a news editor is looking for a local early evening news presenter/reporter, is it relevant now? Well, it might turn out to be much more than a sentence about your hobbies at the end of the document if you can point out that over the years you have cantered around the entire county meeting the inhabitants and chatting to them, giving you a unique insight into the locality.

If you have had broadcasting experience then, of course, you will mention it but be honest with yourself about the relevance. A DJ on hospital radio could be more significant than a disc librarian. Needless to say, if you overplay you own abilities you may get onto a shortlist only to be shot down in flames in an interview and it may well blacken your reputation in the future.

Don't worry that you can't allude to paid work. Any experience counts. It doesn't matter that you did it only for a short time if you honestly feel you learnt something from it. Frequently, the significance of such episodes is not that you did the work but that you got it in the first place. Anyone who has fired off dozens of letters to production companies, knocked on doors (literally) and turned up in offices unasked, is clearly determined and is able to achieve in spite of hardship and rejection (see Leona Graham's view, Chapter 11).

DOING A JOB INTERVIEW

There is only one way to succeed and that is to be prepared. I'll say it again: BE PREPARED. Having been on both sides of interview boards and having taught broadcasting students, it is clear that the desire for the job alongside the general panic of the moment can make even the most rational people take their eyes off the ball. Presenter and reporter Kirsty Lang may be a well-known face on TV now, but back at the start she freely admits that she was ill prepared during her first attempts to get in. She applied to the BBC News Trainee scheme three times over three years before she finally made it:

I think there's a technique to these applications and the first time I hadn't taken any advice about filling out the form. It was incredibly competitive. They would take something like only twelve people a year and about 2000 people would apply. Even although I knew this, I still hadn't prepared properly. You have to know what buttons to press. So take advice from others about how to fill in forms and what kind of things they'll ask and how you should answer. I think the second time it was incredibly close but I just didn't quite make it. The third time, I think they just recognized me and said, 'God, it's her again! Better give that woman a job!'

Read the job description and your job application thoroughly again and ensure that it is still accurate. Vacancies can take weeks to fill and your circumstances may have changed. You may also have learnt new information about the job that changes your suitability for the position, either for the better or for the worse. Be honest with yourself and work out what you are going to say if they challenge you on this point.

Do your homework about the programme you are to be involved with. Don't be so insulting as to attend an interview without having listened to the output or watched the show on TV. You must know everything you reasonably can about it, including the names of key personnel. I have had people excuse themselves by saying they couldn't listen to the output because they were in the wrong part of the country. In which case, I ask myself, how can they possibly know that this is the kind of show for them? It's simple enough to get friends to record transmissions or simply to phone up the company to ask for some ROTs (Recordings of Transmissions). The worst they can do is say that you'll have to pay for them!

Getting a job in broadcasting is tremendously competitive and initiative shows. Ask to come in and watch the programme. Get permission to hang around for a couple of days. This way you can discover whether you could genuinely do it and whether you like the people and the set up. It also has the advantage of making your face one that is known come the day of the interview. Now you can speak with genuine understanding about the programme.

Think about the content, style and format of the programme. It is inevitable that you will be asked why you want to work on it. Have you got a good answer? You need to be able to discuss the type of material used on the programme, the way they package items and the editorial stance, amongst other things. It won't wash if you simply pour out flattery. Every programme has weak points and the editor knows it. If you can't see them, perhaps you are not such a clever candidate.

Be honest about the bad bits. It's likely you'll be asked what you dislike most about the show or what you think doesn't work. Sometimes an interviewer will say, 'Did you hear this morning's programme?' You, obviously, will reply that you did and may then find yourself fending off questions about the shouting match interview with the government minister. What went wrong? Who was to blame? Was the anchor (alongside whom you'll be working) too aggressive? Was the research poor, so that the stated facts were wrong? Was it actually a jolly good listen and nothing to worry about at all? Would you have done the interview like that? You would be wise to think hard about such issues before you walk into the lion's den.

CONTACTS, CONTACTS, CONTACTS

Nurture contacts and make use of them. This is the kind of business where the intensity of the shared work experience can put you on first-name terms within seconds. The people that you met during one short work experience week while you were in the sixth form at school can be approached and reminded of your last meeting years later when you are in a position to seek a job. What's more, presenters' posts are frequently not advertised in the normal way. If you want to be a temporary stand-in you must get the tip-off from contacts that regular anchors are going on holiday. A student of mine at City University had to interview one of the BBC's correspondents. In no time he had asked what would be the chances of trailing the job for a day or two, just so that he could see how it was done. A bold move but the response was, 'Of course. Give me a ring.' He did and got an invaluable insight into working at the coalface.

A broadcaster cannot live without a contacts book that's bursting at the seams. (And, incidentally, make sure you have a copy of it somewhere. I, like many other journalists, have had my contacts books stolen and have never been able to recover entirely from the loss.) Journalism students, particularly those on practical courses, are encouraged to use every contact they have come across and those of their parents and friends too. It is not that you are trying to get something for nothing. After all, you won't last long if you can't do the business. You can regard it as using personal influence if you like but if you want to get in it's worth a try. In my own case there were no friends who knew anyone, no family connections and no colleagues with influence. I simply offered to do work, for nothing if necessary. I did not think of it as 'gaining experience'. I did it because I was addicted. I tried everything, learned lots and built up those contacts for myself. Thousands of others have done the same, so don't feel excluded if you are not from a Dimbleby-esque dynasty. You can still get there!

Your contacts may also be helpful in suggesting sideways steps in your career that you may not have thought of. Presenter/reporter Kirsty Lang had done a degree at the London School of Economics but it wasn't enough to get her onto the highly competitive BBC News Trainee Scheme. In the end she began a desperate hunt for any kind of journalistic work. This proved exactly the right thing to do because those she met and what she learned from them undoubtedly got her onto the BBC scheme at the third time of asking.

> *After getting turned down for the Trainee Scheme, I just applied for every job anywhere. I took a lowly, very short-term contract as a researcher updating royal obituaries for Radio Four. There was a very nice lady who ran the Department and I said to her that I really wanted to work in news. She said, 'Oh, I've got a friend who works in Bush House [BBC World Service] in the current affairs department. I think she could do with a bright thing like you!' So I got a six-month contract working in current affairs at Bush. This was really my territory because I'd done International Relations at LSE and that's what I was interested in – foreign news. I could have just stayed there. But I mentioned to my boss that I had applied for the BBC Trainee Scheme and been unsuccessful and he said I should try again because now I could do it as an internal applicant. He said I could stay at Bush forever but at least the trainee scheme would teach me TV as well as radio. So I went on and did that even though it meant a considerable pay cut because by that time I was working as an assistant producer.*

STARTING OUT

When you start out on the broadcasting road, success can seem so close and so attainable but, in an Alice-Through-The-Looking-Glass kind of way, the more you learn about the business, the further away you seem from your goal. However, you would be surprised at how quickly you can move on once you're in the broadcasting environment. Everything adds to your armoury of skills and develops your confidence.

If you are doing a reputable broadcasting course, say a postgraduate one, and you have a decent amount of talent and determination, it may only take you two or three years to get into a seriously 'moving' position. Some students have gone into network programmes immediately, but this is a rarity. My experience of lecturing on the postgraduate diploma at City University is that almost everyone gets a job somewhere in the business within months of leaving.

A VIEW FROM THE INSIDE: ANDREW BAILEY

Andrew Bailey is Head of News, Virgin Radio. He got into the station as a breakfast news presenter just three years after finishing his diploma in broadcast journalism. News presentation involves the preparation of national bulletins every 30 minutes from 6 am until 10 am and after that on the hour until 1 pm. The station goes out nationally on 1215 AM, Sky Digital or at www.virginradio.co.uk. Its audience is 20–44 year-olds who like, as he puts it, 'REAL music – no pop allowed!'

Andrew did a BA Hons degree in Music and English Literature at Middlesex University. In 1998 he started the postgraduate diploma in broadcast journalism at City University in London and did work experience at

Figure 15.2
News presenter Andrew Bailey

Radio City in Liverpool, BBC News and at *London Tonight*, the independent TV news programme for the capital. This was followed by some freelancing at Piccadilly Key 103 in Manchester and Rock FM in Preston. You can see how every small job builds up that impressive CV! After the diploma he became the drive-time news presenter/reporter at Radio City. Then it was two years as the morning news editor at Century FM/Capital Gold and Digital News Network in Manchester, during which time he collected a couple of awards – Radio City's Newcomer of the Year 1999 and NTL Commercial Radio News Team of the Year in 2000.

With that invaluable regional broadcasting under his belt he arrived at Virgin, which is nationwide, digital and in London, which certainly boosts job prospects.

Describe what you thought broadcasting was all about when you first started

This is so hard because I think you lose all sense of being 'wide-eyed' about the industry after a relatively short time working in it. I thought working in broadcasting was probably *very* showbiz and also *very* hard work. I remember a tutor at City University telling me on my first day on the course that I'd never have a lunch break again. I laughed smugly to myself at her melodramatics … but she was absolutely right! When do you ever get the chance to leave a busy newsroom for an hour to eat? If you're hungry, eat at your desk between bulletins! I'm now one of those terrible hacks who uses the phrase, 'Lunch – what's lunch?'

I thought broadcasting paid more than it does!

And I thought presentation was the ultimate 'place' to be. Who would want to be a reporter whom nobody knew? Better to be the voice everyone wakes up to. Well, to a certain extent that's where I've ended up, but having spent time as a reporter as well, I understand just how satisfying it can be to get a story, chase it and package it up to go on air. I guess I miss that.

What was your first bit of presentation like?

My first bulletin was terrifying. I honestly felt as if I was going to die. I was sitting in the news studio at Radio City in Liverpool, rigid with fear. I still get nervous when I hear Britney Spears' *Baby One More Time*, as that was the song played into my first bulletin. I managed to get through it without too many problems – although I had to breathe deeply to control my voice. When I finished though, I was hooked. The adrenalin rush was addictive. The hardest task was really in preparation. In a commercial station like Radio City, the newsreader also edits the bulletins. Choosing stories and running orders when you are a rookie is terribly daunting and it took me a while to know what was a story and what was chaff.

Was there anything that you were not prepared for?

See above! What surprised me really was the attitude many commercial stations have towards news. I've made my career in commercial radio as it's where my style fits best but if I hear the phrase, 'News is a drain not a gain' one more time I may consider applying to Auntie Beeb! Here at Virgin they love news but I know throughout the industry many commercial stations dislike news because it breaks up their pop songs and ads. So sad…

What do you believe are the vital skills for good presentation?

To be unflappable when chaos reigns. It's so important to keep calm and not sound panicked when running orders and stories are changing around you whilst you are on air. It is also vital that you know your stories, particularly if you work with a presenter who will question you about them after the bulletin. And you must be confident with your material and station style – if not, it will sound awful.

What are your words of warning to others?

Never, ever, *ever* – no matter how late you are – run to read a news bulletin. I did it once and will never make that mistake again. I could barely read two words. It sounded terrible and I was thoroughly ashamed. Also, never eat just before a bulletin. Your mouth will be full of saliva and I defy you to get through a read without a huge gulp. Oh, and always leave your mobile outside the studio. I heard one local newsreader presenting a story about a rape when her phone began ringing. For the next few seconds all you could hear was her battling on whilst the *Dambusters* theme blared out in the background. Shameful.

What's the most memorable piece of presentation you were involved in?

There are loads. Reading the 7 pm news on Radio City in Liverpool when the presenter and his producer switched all the lights off mid-bulletin just for a laugh. I struggled to read by the light of the travel monitor until they turned that off as well. I finally had to abandon the bulletin and explain who had turned the lights off. My editor was listening and was on the phone in seconds. The presenter had his ear severely bent!

During a reporting trip to Pristina in Kosovo I remember entering the house of an Albanian family and not being able to believe how filthy it was. I was trying to describe the scene into my mic but the soldiers told me to cover my mouth because the air was so fetid it was dangerous. They ordered me not to touch anything. When I met the family, their youngest child was clearly very ill. The interpreters said he was riddled with cancer and looked close to death – pallid and deformed. All the soldiers could do was to give him their own personal allocation of paracetamol to help the pain. It was one of the most distressing things I've ever seen and I was glad I'd been told to put my mic away as I wouldn't have known what to say. Another image from that trip was seeing children and dogs, side by side, scouring the roadside rubbish tips looking for food. The dogs were better at it. The experience brought everything into perspective.

What advice would you give to new recruits?

Enrol on a decent postgrad broadcast journo course. It's the best way in and will guarantee you good contacts through work experiences and alumni networks. Honestly, it's worth the money.

Beg for work experiences and then work hard when you're on them. That's how I got my job at Radio City. Get some voice training if its not included in your course. You should *live* the news. Watch, listen, read and digest it every day.

A VIEW FROM THE INSIDE: LAURA SHEETER

Laura Sheeter, broadcast journalist at BBC Radio Northampton, is the BBC's first completely bi-media Personal Digital Production journalist.

Figure 15.3
Presenter, reporter, director, editor and sound recordist Laura Sheeter in Khazakhstan!

She shoots on video, edits on Avid and transfers soundtrack for radio. Her news stories are already being transmitted on BBC news. She graduated from Bristol University with a BSc Hons in Geography in 1999. She'd already done student radio and was hooked. After work experience in HTV and BBC Three Counties Radio, she did a postgraduate Diploma of Broadcast Journalism at City University, London and immediately got the broadcast journalist job. Within months she took a brief sabbatical to make a training film for VSO in Russia and Kazakhstan. On the strength of this she became one of the BBC's first fully trained video journalists.

Describe what you thought broadcasting was all about when you first started

I think I just liked the sound of my own voice. My mum has just found a tape of me, aged about 8 years old, saying, 'And now for the nine o'clock news with Nicholas Witchell and Sue Lawley … I'm sorry, Nicholas Witchell and Sue Lawley can't be here now … so it's the news with me, Laura Sheeter.' It's just not healthy! I suspect, as a child, I thought it was about sounding serious. When I started out in broadcasting it came as quite a shock to find how many people work behind the scenes and how much work's done in production.

What was your first bit of presentation like?

My first TV reporting experience was a two-way about a trial I was covering for Radio Northampton. It was being held at Birmingham Crown Court, so I had to drive to Pebble Mill – through the middle of Birmingham in rush hour – to get there in time to do a pre-recorded piece from the newsroom camera. The hardest thing about it wasn't, as I'd thought it would be, cutting my answers short as I knew the story very well by then. It was simply the organizational aspects of writing and filing a voice piece for the radio news, driving to Pebble Mill, doing a live radio two-way and then running across the newsroom to do the telly two-way – all in the space of half an hour. Oh, and then to try to look unflustered …

One of my earliest radio reporting experiences at Radio Northampton was being sent out to cover a multiple car crash caused by thick fog on one of the major routes through the county. I parked on a bridge over the road and could barely see beyond the end of my nose, let alone the accident. Then the presenter's first question was, 'What can you see?' Having always been wedded to scripts, it was a shock to have to expand on 'nothing' for a couple of minutes.

Was there anything that you were not prepared for?

I didn't expect that 'filler' bits would be so important – news teasers, ins and outs – all the things you take for granted because they sound slick.

What do you believe are the vital skills for good presentation?

For live reporting without a script, the most important thing is to be clear and simple. If you lose track of what you've said no-one will understand you. For news reading your voice is far more important. You have to engage in the story. I hate nothing more than hearing news being read by someone who sounds like they don't care. I don't mind stumbles but monotonous delivery is inexcusable. In either job you need to be unflappable. If something happens, you can't panic and dry up. Keep calm and stay on top of things.

What are your words of warning to others?

Beware of technology and have a piece of paper to back you up!

When reporting – the less you write down the more likely you are to think about what you're saying. And, if you're like me, *slow down* – you're talking faster than you think.

What advice would you give to new recruits?

Watch telly and listen to the radio so you can find out what you like the sound or the look of. Practise is the key. Go and try it wherever you can; student radio, hospital radio, bedroom-at-home radio! Despite my chaotic experiences of student journalism, they were more useful than expected.

What are your innermost thoughts about the whole business of presenting?

What does disturb me is the number of people who've suggested I try telly because I've got the right look – rather than because they've heard any of my work as a reporter.

16 Sexism, ageism, racism and disability

All of the above may make it more difficult to get a job. It shouldn't, but let's be realistic. Sadly, there probably isn't a presenter alive who doesn't feel that he or she has suffered from one of them. Frequently it is prejudice of such a subtle kind that even the person guilty of it is unaware of it. Networks can always defend themselves by claiming the on-air performers are there because they are 'the best person for the job' and it's 'what the public wants'.

The antipathy to offering jobs to these groups is often simply down to lack of imagination or ignorance. The bosses see the *problems* instead of adopting a 'can do' mentality.

Attitudes in this fashion-led industry are confused and constantly changing, as demonstrated by the fears of one of the new generation of talent. Laura Sheeter, a broadcast journalist, has been in the industry for only two years:

> *The one concern I've had in applying for jobs is whether or not I'll appear to be too young. There seems to be more tolerance of young-sounding men than women. As far as colour is concerned, I know one black colleague of mine has had to change radio stations in order to get into 'mainstream' local radio programmes rather than working solely on a show for the black community.*

Jonathan Hewat, formerly Head of Broadcasting at the University of the West of England and himself a radio presenter, says:

> *Sex, age, race and disability shouldn't make a difference but that won't guarantee it doesn't matter to the good folk you are applying*

to. In some instances a 'disadvantage' may be an 'advantage' – for niche broadcasting especially. My advice: turn any implied disadvantage to your benefit but not accompanied by even a hint of a 'chip'. One applicant for my postgrad journalism diploma was called 'Julia Caesar'. She was certainly granted an interview! She went on to work for HTV West.

SEXISM

Once it was all women who were being discriminated against. Now there are heaps of women in certain areas, like presentation, to the exclusion of men, but they often have to be good-looking, *young* women. So, ironically, the aggrieved group has become even larger. It includes a large proportion of women *and all men!*

In an entirely unscientific test, I recently checked sixteen international news channels at 8 am in Hong Kong. It was a peak morning period in East Asia, early evening in the Americas and late night in Europe. Only six were using male anchors. Those using men were CBS evening news, two Japanese stations, a Spanish channel, a German network and Sky from London. It was noticeable that three CCTV channels (China TV), so different in their outlook and style in so many other ways, used young, glamorous women who would not look out of place on any Western set.

If you speak to those on the inside there is a tired acceptance that women get in more quickly if they're pretty and get kicked out more quickly when they get wrinkly. Everyone says it's bad and claims it's a phenomenon wrought by others and one that is changing. Awareness of the problem is one thing. Eradicating it is another. For now, it is a fact that all presenters must live with. When you go for a job, look as good as you can and be prepared with arguments as to why you are so supremely qualified that issues of sex become irrelevant. Broadcasting lecturer, Jan Haworth, has this view:

The advice I give to women who want presentation is to be good at something else. It may be hard enough to get the first job but getting a second one is very hard, partly because of the age barrier and because women of child-bearing age have a disadvantage. If you're very young you are not seen as a mother-to-be and likewise

Figure 16.1
Jobs for the girls? Women are wanted in the front line worldwide

if you're over 45. So there are twenty years in the middle when you need to be able to offer more than just a good voice. You should have good journalistic skills, a specialism, something like that. I've been a company director and I know what it costs for women to go off to have children when, as an employer, you have to keep the job open and pay, not just for them, but for the replacement and for child care and flexible return-to-work arrangements. I did all that willingly because I believe in it but I do see how much it costs. A small independent company particularly will find it difficult. If they have a choice between a person who will be having a baby next week and one who won't, they'll choose the one who won't! Funnily enough, I had the opposite situation recently. A male student got a job at the BBC and within two weeks had to ask for statutory paternity leave. He thought he ought to just go sick rather than admit to the birth of the baby. I said no since we've fought for so long for these rights. They hadn't asked at the interview whether his partner was pregnant. He'd told them these two weeks were already arranged as holiday...he just hadn't said why but they hadn't asked. Anyway, he got the leave, he's still in his job and the baby's doing fine!

AGEISM

Broadcasting is a profession full of young talent but there is a place for older entrants. Having discovered Harry Enfield and long since lost him to television, BBC Radio Four happened upon his father who now does radio talks. In local radio there are many openings for those who have the time and for whom the wages are not so vital! As always, it's a springboard to other things or it's a great place to stay if career moves are not so urgent.

May Marshall became a book reviewer, quite by chance, on Moray Firth Radio in Scotland at the age of 62. She had gone in volunteering to help when the station was founded. She suddenly found herself being interviewed on air about books. She was asked back the next week and the next and the next. She soon had her own slot and her studio became a vital venue for all authors and publishers on tours. She later took on presentation of a weekly classical music and opera show and, twenty years

Figure 16.2
May Marshall's career as a poet, columnist, author and critic blossomed at 62 when she became a presenter on MFR

on, she is a key literary influence across the North of Scotland:

> *I had to learn the skills of presentation like anyone would. The key to my success is that I know the subject I'm talking about. No-one gives me favours because of my age. In fact, I don't think anyone knows how terribly old I am now! They just think, 'poor old thing, she's in her seventies'. And who am I to disabuse them? [She's now 82.] Others who had previously been interviewed to help on the station had said they had time on their hands and were bored. I said, I have no time and am never bored. The manager wanted me.*

For older women there is, according to veteran presenter Sue MacGregor, a great physical advantage:

> *Women in radio are ageless. The voice doesn't change until you are possibly well into your eighties and not always then. We are more ageist on television than even America. I rejected TV over the years because I was more relaxed on radio and not anxious to cross over. I now do some television, mostly* News 24, *which is seen all over the world.*

Inevitably there is hostility to older people too in prime time shows. One of the most outspoken critics of ageism has been TV news presenter, Peter Sissons, who in September 2002, at the age of 60, announced he was standing down as anchor of the BBC's *Ten O'Clock News*:

> *The BBC does have one or two blind spots and its biggest blind spot is its tendency to ageism. I've been to many leaving parties for people who've turned 50 and they're at the height of their powers and they're out. Some really gifted people who've cost hundreds of thousands of pounds to bring to that state of being so good. I think it's very sad.*

The Corporation responded by stating, defensively:

> *... in true BBC tradition we're always looking to find the best of new talent.*

When, in September 2002, the BBC announced their revamped news line-up, the wrinklies were indeed gone and in their place were the fresh-faced Huw Edwards (aged 38), the highly competent Fiona Bruce (also 38) and, in the prime time early evening slot, Sophie Raworth (aged 34).

However, some research suggests that the drive for younger presenters, at least in news, may not be what audiences want. A survey by the Independent Television Commission and Help the Aged (*The Numbers Game*) revealed that only 5 per cent of viewers considered that being 'physically attractive' was an important quality. The two key features were 'knowledgeable' (99 per cent) and 'professional' (98 per cent). When it came to a league table of favourite presenters of news, Sir Trevor Macdonald (aged 62) came top, followed by Michael Buerk (aged 56).

RACISM

It is law that all employers operate equal opportunities programmes. The broadcasters are working hard at overcoming prejudice and have all sorts of committees and working parties. There are more ethnic minorities than ever on screen and the hunt for others continues. There are new opportunities on specialist cable, satellite and restricted licence radio stations, although it can be hard to break into mainstream programming. My own experience has been that editors are, albeit haphazardly and off the record, operating a system of positive discrimination in favour of minorities.

Figure 16.3
Wesley Kerr – one of the first black faces regularly seen on BBC TV news and current affairs

More than one executive has asked me to recommend a black candidate out of a class of students who are looking for jobs.

BBC presenter and reporter, Wesley Kerr, has been in broadcast journalism for twenty years as a presenter and correspondent for the BBC. Conceived in Jamaica but brought up in London, he went to Cambridge and became one of only two people ever known to be simultaneously offered places on two different high-flying BBC training schemes. He joined *Panorama* at the incredibly young age of 21:

> *I was an accomplished producer and was directing films on national programmes in my early twenties. For me there was no colour bar ... until you got in. There was no problem getting in because how many black people with scholarships to Winchester and Cambridge were there in the late seventies? But whether they made the most of the opportunities they had open to them in hiring me is questionable. No, I think the BBC was a profoundly racist,*

sexist, homophobic organization in the early eighties. As to my own treatment in my career, it's invidious to complain. I think there was a big glass ceiling for women in the BBC and I think that's largely gone. I think there is a big glass ceiling for blacks. I think they love to have black and Asian faces, pretty ones, presenting with posh-ish accents, but they don't actually like to give blacks responsibility over the airtime. Even today, there are no black people in senior editorial positions in, say, news and current affairs. But there are lots of black faces reading the autocue.

Of course, the BBC defends itself stoutly against any suggestion of racism. Quite the opposite, in common with other broadcasters, they proclaim a growing commitment to an increased racial mix. At least as far as on-air talent is concerned there is noticeable change. It may take longer for the change to permeate upwards.

DISABILITY

Technological advances now make it possible for disabled people to achieve in what might appear the most improbable areas of broadcasting. Frequently it is only the employer's own narrow-mindededness that limits the possibilities. Entrenched attitudes have resulted in compulsion. The final elements of the Disability Discrimination Act will become law from October 2004. Amongst other things, it insists on new levels of accessibility to buildings for both employees and visitors.

There follow two views from the front line from those who are in the thick of it right now.

A VIEW FROM THE INSIDE: PETER WHITE

Peter White, the BBC's first Disability Affairs Correspondent, is the first blind person ever to report on mainstream network television news: 'I've always thought that was the real breakthrough. My dad, who died a few years ago, would have been proudest of this achievement.' Peter is 55, a presenter of Radio Four's *You and Yours* and much else besides. He's been blind since birth due to non-development of the optic nerve. He wanted to be a broadcaster from the age of four. Instead he was advised to

223

Figure 16.4
Peter White had to wait twelve years before being given the chance to present live

take up law: 'There are quite a lot of blind lawyers around. People used to say to me, "You're argumentative, so you ought to make a good lawyer."' He started a law degree at Southampton University, before realizing it was a mistake. He spent a year as a community service volunteer in York amongst 'people who were rebels. These were people I felt more comfortable with.' There followed another attempt at a degree – this time Social Sciences at Kent. Whilst there, he heard that a BBC local radio station was opening in Southampton, his home ground. On a whim, he hitch-hiked there and presented himself. He was 21.

Getting in

I didn't make an appointment, didn't say I was blind, just turned up in reception at Radio Solent with a white stick. They said, 'Go away. Didn't you see the crowds outside?' – which, of course, I hadn't! – 'They all want to be Tony Blackburn.' I tried to explain I wanted to do serious broadcasting but they didn't take much interest although they took my phone number. I was preparing to hitch-hike back to Kent when I got a call from a producer. When he said he was doing the blind programme my heart hit my boots. It was the last thing I wanted to do. But I had the sense to realize that you had to get in any way you could. So, on the promise of 'I'll teach you how to use a tape recorder if you do a bit of freelancing', I left university. I was earning a puny £5 a week! Local radio was full of people like that. I wasn't presenting the programme at first but I did quite soon. I was good. I had the voice and the temperament for it.

Discrimination?

Solent were exemplary. It was partly because they could see potential. The producers were not patronising. I got sent back to do my first interview again because the levels were too low. That was great! The second producer I had was even more of a slave-driver. He used to cut my tape to ribbons and say, 'That's no good.'

I started selling things to the *Today* programme, *Woman's Hour*, the *John Dunn Show* [Radio Two] and so on. But what opened the doors in the end was *In Touch*, the Radio Four programme for blind people, the ethos of which was that it should be done by blind people. But blind people who could actually deliver were a bit thin on the ground! It was true then and it's true now. Again, I didn't want to do 'disability stuff' but I needed to get into network.

I think the worst piece of discrimination was not presenting live stuff for twelve years. I should have been doing it within six months because this is what I'm good at. It was fear on the part of management and me not being pushy enough. They lacked imagination. They couldn't visualize how it could be done.

Suddenly it occurred to someone that I could present the live two-hour morning current affairs programme for Solent. It was 1983. I'd been doing presentation but always pre-recorded and packaged. That first time I was very nervous. There was so much riding on it. I was self-opping and I had to wait for a break point in the sig tune that you had to hit. And I missed it! I just froze. Couldn't open the bloody microphone ... for five seconds. It felt like five years. And then it just freed up. I still get the dream!

After that, I did *Same Difference* for Channel 4 and *Link* on Central TV. It was all disability-specific but it taught me techniques, PTCs, writing for telly – all the things I didn't know. Then I was offered the disability correspondent's job which hadn't existed. I've got a feeling that they thought they ought to have one and because I was an experienced broadcaster they got me. And this finally got me into mainstream news.

How do you do TV?

I went in thinking: 'It's going to be really hard and the people in telly news are going to be bastards! They're so competitive.' It wasn't like that at all. Everyone, almost without exception, has been happy for me to be doing it. In PTCs I say to them, 'Don't make any allowances. If the eye line is wrong, say so. Tell me anything you think I ought to know.' You must not expect any favours. I'm trying to do the job as well as I can. My eyes wander because of the eye condition. But, with advice, I can put my eyes in the right place I'm told to although they may not stay there. No-one's ever said to me that it's an issue … even on the two main evening bulletins. People have asked David Blunkett to get dark glasses but no-one in the Beeb has asked me to do that and I would refuse if they did because it would serve no purpose but to disguise something real about yourself.

For presenting in a studio, I need a Braille script. I produce that myself. I have paper in front of me like any other presenter. It can be a bit tricky if you're doing live breaking news but actually most of those really sudden stories are ad libbed anyway. I've done live news presentation in an attenuated form … on local radio, where you have a bit of music and can quickly write a cue. I've done cues where the producer is speaking it into my headphones and I'm speaking it simultaneously on air. If a producer is trying to give you a story while you're on the air, there are even machines that can convert ordinary print to Braille but no-one has successfully used them in studios … yet.

I can't read autocue. You have to read a Braille script. But I've done that on TV South and it works well. I don't have to look down and, after all, sighted newscasters have a script in front of them too.

I am not doing so much on TV as on radio. It's just pressure of my radio work. I don't think anyone has said, 'Oh we don't want that blind git on telly'! In fact, when I go to TV news with a story they usually say, 'Why don't you come more often. We'd like to use you more.' I don't feel any sense of discrimination there.

How does a blind reporter get to the story fast?

This was the biggest problem at the start. I couldn't get taxis because I couldn't dare to be more expensive than other people. I dreamed up ploys to get round it. Southampton was a TV centre as well, so I used to go to the morning television meeting which took place an hour before the radio meeting. They'd decide what stories they were covering because TV had to get on the road more quickly. I'd whip back to the radio meeting, suggest the same and, because I'd made friends with all the cameramen, I would get a lift in the crew car. It's as much a problem today as it was then.

How do you keep track of fast-moving news?

In the old days I couldn't read the wires. That's why I concentrated on feature material using my own contacts, which was better than relying on wires anyway because an editor wants a story no-one else has got.

Nowadays, you get speech software. You can get a package through 'Access To Work' which is the Department of Employment. They assess you and put up the money. The radio station doesn't have to pay. The equipment I have now allows me to read e-mails and wires. It has a voice that speaks to me and I can vary the speed of it so I can listen fast. You can get into cuttings services and use the Net. It's not that quick though and there can be a problem with compatibility. You need a lot of patience and stickability but there are now people who work in news and use this all the time.

How do you do research?

The sheer bulk of information is the difficult thing. So much of the job depends on reading. You have to prioritize and make compromises. Of course, sighted people do this too. Blind people have to make extra arrangements which always takes time. Suppose you're doing something about a celebrity and you want to read a biography of them. Even if you're a Braillist, only about one in a hundred published books are published in Braille. You'll have to get it read to you. Everything has to be thought through in a different way. It's demanding enough for a sighted person. If you're blind, there are all the logistics on top. You have to be highly motivated.

Trailblazer?

I do feel that I am a trailblazer. Most people who have got in have come to me at some time or other. They start thinking, 'How am I going to find the toilet?' It's a pretty low starting point! You just have to blow all that away. It's quite handy to say, 'Peter White does TV news and *You and Yours* which is live presentation and as scary as it gets.' I'm there and I'm visible. That helps.

On radio there is no problem about public acceptance. On TV we don't know until someone does presentation in a very high-profile position. I did it on *South Today*. We got a reasonably big audience and there was no backlash. One woman wrote in and said, why didn't I get my teeth fixed? The only other comments they got were from people congratulating the station on doing it at all.

Why aren't there more blind people in the business?

One of the main reasons is they don't come out of school literate. They don't read Braille fast enough. Fewer people seem to be able to do it now than in times gone by. We've got lots of reporters who have got all the personal skills and can learn the technical skills but they can't read which means they can't present and even find it hard to do a feature.

The other advice is the same as for anyone. Do a degree and do the journalism course. You've got enough disadvantages so get as many advantages as you can.

Your attitude

You have to have the mind-set that they don't owe you any favours. It's right to press for equality, for good equipment, but this is a competitive industry. Of course I would urge people who are appointing not to have preconceived ideas but, for every one sighted person who gets into news on TV, there are about another 100 who would like to. So it's no good coming in saying, 'You ought to do this for me because you ought to have more disabled people working for TV and radio.' I hear too many people saying that who actually aren't any good. Go to interviews with ideas ... the same as anyone else. You need to bring things to the party.

You need a lot of self-confidence. I don't buy the argument that what disabled people do has to be better. That isn't fair. You should go in thinking, 'I can be *as good*.'

Getting on

It's the biggest problem. If you are good, don't allow yourself to get stuck. Don't sit there waiting for the next thing to happen because it may not. You have to push.

Sometimes the personal and technical support isn't there. Within the BBC, trying to get the speech software put on the computers is a real grind. Just as you've got it, they update the system so it won't work. It drives you mad. You have to find alternative ways to do things. You get people to read stuff to you. All blind people ask favours of others to help them survive. But you underestimate the amount *all people* ask favours of each other. Grovel a bit and be as personable as you can.

The thing about blindness is that you can often do the top half-dozen jobs where there are others to run about for you (like presenting). It's the lower jobs where you have to do everything for yourself that can prove tricky. So my advice is, 'In at the top!'

A VIEW FROM THE INSIDE: HELEN SMITH

So you want to know whether you can get into journalism with physical disabilities? Try this ... work as a TV news journalist despite having had all four limbs amputated. Nothing need be impossible. Helen Smith is 28 years old and has been working as a news reporter at Anglia TV in Norwich for two years. Having graduated from Bath University with a degree in molecular biology, she contracted meningococcal septicaemia at the age of 22 and had to have all four limbs amputated – both legs above the knee, her left hand at the wrist and her right arm below the elbow. She uses a wheelchair and four artificial limbs which she has been instrumental in designing, not content with the four 'table legs' she was originally given. In fact it was campaigning on this issue that brought her to Anglia's notice. She was living in their patch [Cambridge] and they asked her to front a series of films about key disability issues. They were so impressed they offered her a traineeship and, thanks to an imaginative and doughty

Figure 16.5
In 2000 Helen Smith was the joint winner, with model Heather Mills, of the Cosmopolitan Secret
Woman of Achievement Award. Anglia TV was so impressed, they gave her a job

news editor, Surrey Beddows, and a management team eager to find ways
to make it work, the company literally opened doors for her. They created
access where there was none and worked at overcoming what must be
regarded as excessively complicated – but not insuperable – problems.
Other employers would do well to take note.

Doing a PTC

I can stand up to do a PTC but what I can't do is walk and talk because
it's so much concentrating just to walk. PTCs are quite hard because I'm

Figure 16.6
Despite the amputation of all four limbs, Helen can appear like any other presenter

always trying to find something more inventive. You can't always have me just static talking to the camera. So I use props and I discuss with the camera operator how they can get movement in the shot so that it's the *camera* that makes the moves.

I can't be bashful because the cameraman has to put the microphone down the front of my blouse!

Writing scripts

Effectively I'm a two-finger typist – just like other journos! I use a typing stick and a special mouse.

Interviewing

Sometimes people can't believe that I could be the reporter. I have an assistant who helps me in and out of the car and stuff, and they think *they're* the journalist and wonder, 'Who's this girl that's come along in a chair to watch?' But they always respond normally after the surprise. It can be beneficial. People who've had a health problem or an injury are more forthcoming. They tell me everything. I can't imagine they'd do that with anyone else.

Looking good

I can't even pluck my own eyebrows, so someone has to come in to do that. I have to keep slim even though I'm in a wheelchair, so I do a lot of swimming and I'm training for a marathon race. I've had to fight to get decent limbs. With orange table legs I couldn't begin to feel normal!

Getting to stories

I always ask people whether their property is wheelchair accessible before I arrive, yet they still don't seem to understand. I've had to get out of my chair and climb up a spiral staircase on my bottom to interview someone, yet when I'd phoned them beforehand they'd said, 'Oh yes, you can get into my house, no problem!' A lot of the stories I do are hospitals and companies so it can be OK. It limits my stories but then other reporters also get taken off a job to do something else sometimes, so it's just one of those things.

Although I can turn my stories round in a day, I prefer to do feature pieces that I can plan in advance because I have to organize transport, carers, access etc.

Getting round the studios

At base, they've had to make changes. A lot of the doors are heavy fire doors so we've had automatic door-openers installed. The canteen is on the top floor and there's no lift! Usually I bring sandwiches so I don't mind but at times people suggest chatting over a coffee and I can't be a part of that.

Getting around the office means reminding people to tuck their chairs in when they leave their desks. But everywhere's like that. Shopping is the same. People step out in front of you because you're not at their eye line.

The printer is at the other end of the office. It took too long to get there so now I have one on my desk. The thing that annoys me now is that there's only one disabled toilet and I have to share it with *Trisha Show* audiences. Then it was vandalized and had to be locked. I can't use keys, so every time I want to go I need someone to unlock it and I have to go through crowds of people all watching me – they're not even subtle about it. And you think, 'God, everyone knows how long I'm taking!' But you can't keep kicking up a fuss. I know the employers have a lot to think about on this and I don't want them to think I'm too much of a pain! Anyway, I don't want to stand out. I want to be an employee like everyone else. Actually, toilets on the road are a pain, too. I know where every supermarket in the region is because they have to have disabled access.

What can't be done

I can't produce bulletins because I can't physically press the buttons on the desk in the gallery. So directing is out … at the moment. I can't do early shifts and late shifts because of carers – they don't start work till 7 but I would need to be in at 4 am.

If I get stuck out late on a story I have to make a million phone calls e.g. to get a new carer or get one to stay late. Others don't even think about it.

I'd like to present the news but I can't use the autocue button with my foot. Even if I could, when the autocue went down I couldn't pick up the hard copies with my hands. In fact, the most technically advanced studio here which is a virtual reality studio, I can't even get in to because it's down a flight of stairs!

Advice

Don't always compare yourself with others. Don't feel aggrieved because they've been given an opportunity. Be realistic and think, 'Actually, I couldn't do that.'

Be good at the trade. That's what the job is. I did shorthand at evening classes. I'm doing voice training to get more power in my voice so that, with more experience, I stand a chance of anchoring.

Be prepared for hard work. If I took a day off for all the times I didn't feel 100 per cent I'd never be in work. Most days I don't feel well. But I work, then go home and practise my voice into a tape recorder.

Tell the employer what grants they're entitled to. 'Access to Work' will pay everything for the first year. Bosses need to know that.

You have to have a boss who is understanding of your requirements. I think it was brave of Anglia TV to take me on. They could have said I could do a few bits now and again, but it was quite different to have me here full time.

17 Top tips

By now it's clear to all that life as a presenter won't be easy or achieved swiftly. It's time, perhaps, for a 'little list' as Gilbert and Sullivan would have it, of vital attributes and objectives. As always, you can quibble and disagree because there are no set rules in this game. Here is a collection of ideas from insiders: reporters, presenters, editors, producers and even a cameraman who has to film your antics.

JON SNOW, PRESENTER, *CHANNEL 4 NEWS*

Getting in …

> *These days in broadcasting the bias is overwhelmingly towards formal journalism training. I believe it is technically possible, even today, to become a broadcaster with no formal training – although it's harder to get a job that way.*

> *A lot of your career will depend on luck. You can help things along by persevering. I had luck and determination. My first broadcasting job was when LBC was opening up. Only the BBC had broadcasters in those days but nobody there seemed inclined to apply for a job because nobody thought it would work. So people like me stood a chance. My first lucky break. I got a position as a newsreader despite the fact that I had had no training and no experience. Nothing! In fact, I read the news on Day One at 0630, just half an hour after the station opened. I can't remember what that event was like – probably just as well. I should think it was a shambles.*

> *It's tough because it's not just the camera or the microphone you have to contend with. Bosses can be cruel. You need constant*

exposure and you don't easily get it. I don't think anyone can make it first time around. I didn't.

Getting on …

You have to be completely natural. Anyone who has to work them-selves up into it, can't do it. It's something about your relationship with the camera and microphone and the viewer. It takes a while to find out what 'being yourself' means for you, but poseurs, actors, those who put on airs and graces…forget it! The camera will find you out. Only familiarity with the beast enables you to be yourself. To reach that stage you must find it's second nature to you. It's like speaking French well. You can only be a complete natural when you actually think in French. You must be scrupulously honest to yourself and to the audience. Aim at complete integrity. Set yourself high moral, artistic, creative and technical standards, and stick to them.

Be calm whatever befalls you. My most memorable moment was on September 11th 2001. I was having lunch round the corner from the London office when I got the call. We were on air seven minutes after the first plane crashed into the World Trade Center in New York. I was stretched to the outermost limits in terms of retrieving information with virtually no back-up. There was no help since the story, and such an unbelievable story, was unfolding. There was only someone in my ear talking to me and the pictures were running live. All the time I was trying to find the words, make the connections, relate the facts and pay obeisance to the scale and tragedy of the occasion.

Words of warning …

Ability at presentation is an indefinable quality that you can't detect simply by looking at someone or even by seeing them perform in front of you. You have to see through the lens or hear on the mic. It's not about physical characteristics. It's not about male or female, young or old, black or white. Even disability makes no dif-ference. Some people just have that naturalness. There are others who will never be able to do it. People talk a lot of hooey about training, making bold claims about how it can teach you the skill and put you there…but sometimes they are whistling in the wind. They are talking about training the untrainable.

EDWINA CURRIE, PRESENTER, BBC RADIO FIVE LIVE

Getting in …

I did have some training and did pilots which helped but I'm still learning. You need a quick brain, a good voice and a decent appearance. You should also be well-read and well-informed. The kind of presentation I do is more than simply being a studio anchor with no responsibilities for the content. I help to write the scripts, brief guests and have to ad lib on air.

Getting on …

Learn good English – read a lot. Read everything; you're a word-smith. Do work experience wherever and whenever you can. You won't get much cash for it … if any! But if you're free you can get lots of opportunities. You'll learn a lot and producers are glad to have you, provided you set to and work. The regions are excellent for starting off because you'll get to do more than in London. Aim for style, vigour and intelligence. Make sure it's the very best you can do.

Words of warning …

Always listen to yourself and learn from it. Watch the tone of your voice – it's very important. Pace yourself. You have to be as bright at the end as you were at the beginning. It can be a long haul and it's very tiring.

LIS HOWELL, LECTURER IN BROADCASTING

Getting in …

Do a show reel. It's not too expensive. But be aware that people aren't going to watch long slabs of it. Make it about five minutes maximum and lots of bits – 30 to 45 second bits doing different things. It needn't be done professionally but it must be well lit.

Getting on …

Doing it, doing it, doing it all the time. You can never do too much. And you can never prepare enough. Always have reserve questions.

Never be frightened to ask the difficult ones but do it politely. You don't become a John Humphrys overnight. You've got to do a hell of an apprenticeship before you can take that tone with people. Always look smart. Always talk to camera or to interviewees or to the audience or anybody at all with respect, remembering that you owe them more than they owe you!

Words of warning ...

If you think you're going to be a presenter for life you are very, very wrong. If you start at 22, you're going to be in broadcasting for 40 years, probably. That's your aim. But you can't do the same thing for all that time. You're going to be outdone by a Tara Palmer-Tomkinson or a Christine Hamilton, who never dreamt of being a TV presenter but it's come along.

BOB LEDWIDGE, EDITOR, BBC REGIONAL POLITICAL UNIT

Getting in ...

Get into production in some capacity first. Start in local radio if you can. It's almost impossible to get on air straight away. Learn to speak clearly but I wouldn't take elocution lessons! Watch lots of TV, listen to radio ... and if you have an area of expertise e.g. knowledge of sailing, dance, music or whatever ... offer to do something on that. Editors are more sympathetic to someone who has something to offer rather than someone who is simply passionate to be on air at all costs.

Getting on ...

It's a cliché but be yourself. People who set out to be an identikit presenter are unlikely to succeed. Be determined to succeed but keep the whole thing in perspective and have strong interests in 'real life' – not just broadcasting.

Words of warning ...

Unfortunately, companies are prepared to exploit those starting out because so many want to get in, so watch out and seek advice from old hands on pay and conditions! Enjoy it and get the adrenalin rush but keep control.

RICHARD EVANS, PRESENTER, BBC RADIO FIVE LIVE

Getting in ...

I joined the BBC in Cardiff as a producer of a radio show. After a few months, when the presenter took a week off, I sat in – my first stab at presenting a show. Looking back on it, the mistake I made was trying to produce *the programme as well as presenting it which caused a degree of creative tension! The content is the producer's job.*

Getting on ...

You need a good voice for radio and the right look for TV. If interviewing is involved you must have an interest in people.

Words of warning ...

Go easy on the adjectives. Don't try to overwrite the big news stories. They tell themselves. It's a fickle business to make a living at. Voices, faces and styles go in and out of fashion. At the risk of sounding like your mother, try to have another skill to fall back on whether it be reporting, production or management.

BECKY JAGO, PRESENTER

Getting in ...

I had made contact with a regional radio station and one night the MD phoned me to say that their 'travel girl' was ill and could I come in to read the traffic news? The same girl left a few months later and I got the job. I went on from there to present my own show. If you can get work as a reporter then great but that can be hard, so approach your local radio station. Make tea! Work late. Take advantage of the equipment. Get yourself a decent show reel. Having a good grasp of the English language is very important.

Getting on …

Understand your target audience. Be confident but natural and down to earth. Be prepared to work very hard for little money to begin with but know where to draw the line. As far as children's presentation is concerned, you must be at their level without patronizing them and if you don't like kids, it'll show.

Words of warning …

More and more courses are offering training for presenting or reporting. Nothing can really prepare you. Experience is the key to success.

JENNI MILLS, PRESENTER, DIRECTOR AND VOICE COACH

Getting in …

I would recommend a good voice coach (well, I would wouldn't I?) but you need one who specializes in broadcasting. Big companies may pay for your training. A good route is to start in a production company, even as a runner, so people can get to know your lovely warm personality. If you're journalistically inclined, be prepared to go in at the bottom in a regional newsroom. It's a great training and you certainly develop a nose for a story and some experience of life. The postgraduate journalism courses are a good lead in to this. A media studies degree at undergraduate level is usually not sufficiently practical.

Getting on …

Treat your audience as equals. You need intelligence, an enthusiasm and interest for what's going on around you and confidence, tempered with humility.

Words of warning …

Presenting is hard work. You can't just swan in on the day and be beautiful. You have to be able to learn scripts, read an autocue as if it's not there, sound intelligent and look presentable – all of which takes huge amounts of time and effort. You have to stand in the pouring rain doing a PTC fifteen times while the crew scowl every time you fluff a word and mutter that you look like something the cat dragged in. You have to be prepared for the embarrassment of watching yourself on TV and realizing that the director forgot to tell you your knickers show through your trousers and your bum looks huge, and everybody's laughing at you because you look such a dork. It doesn't matter if you are hungry or cold or broke up with your boyfriend last night, you've still got to look and sound bright and enthusiastic. Because you are what film crews refer to disparagingly as 'the talent', you have to sparkle every time. If on the other hand you honestly think you can do all that – and I'd suggest you wait for a morning when you have a terrible hangover, a streaming cold and your cat just died to really know the answer to that question – and you know you want to be a presenter because communicating with people is what gives you your greatest buzz in life, then it's worth going for it. And then, by God, it feels like the best job in the world.

SARAH TOPALIAN, PRODUCER AND DIRECTOR

Getting in …

Become a journalist. Do a postgrad course after Uni. Work your butt off. Have ideas. Good ideas get noticed far more quickly than people. Don't be shy – try to meet the big editors because they won't come and find you.

Getting on …

Be comfortable but, most of all, be engaged with what you are presenting. If you look bored the audience will be bored – and no puns or naff humour. Cheese isn't clever. Relax and trust your producer. They want you to look and feel good too.

Words of warning …

Don't carpet-bomb show reels – it looks desperate and is a waste of time, even counterproductive. Never do a job that you haven't thought through. Watch your rushes. Make sure you look clean and tidy. Messy hair and lousy make-up is not attractive.

JONATHAN HEWAT, PRESENTER AND AUTHOR OF *BASIC RADIO SKILLS*

Getting in ...

Start in radio where the essentials of communicating, like 'delivery', are treated seriously. Don't take elocution lessons. You either have a suitable voice or you haven't. Know who you are doing it for – the viewer or listener. Not you!

Getting on ...

Listen to others and analyse. Be totally natural – with no 'sports cadence' or other affectations. Remember, you are talking to, not reading at, only one person.

Words of warning ...

Never, ever stop trying to be better no matter how 'big' you become. Get off that ego trip ... forever. Adrenaline is OK. When it stops flowing, stop presenting.

WESLEY KERR, REPORTER AND PRESENTER

Getting in ...

Become a damn good journalist before you start thinking about being a presenter. You should be wanting to communicate stories rather than wanting to communicate your own personality.

Getting on ...

Be versatile. I've done Panorama, Newsnight, News, Watchdog, *as well as events like the Chelsea Flower Show. You should be able to do everything. So much journalism is about living – lifestyle journalism. It's as relevant to people as covering political speeches or war. Nobody should put the daytime stuff down… as long as it's made to the same exacting standards as other parts of TV.*

Words of warning…

Your best stories often get knocked off air. When the Italians had arrested a big Mafia chief in Sicily, I was sent to Palermo and got terrific stuff with widows, police chiefs etc. I phoned in and they said, 'Sorry. We're in the middle of a bomb attack on Baghdad. I don't think your piece will make it.' Another time in Croatia I spent a weekend preparing to go in to Banjaluka on a mercy mission. I was checking out my war kit, my bullet-proof vest with its extendable flap (to cover one's genitalia!), then the flight was cancelled and the story never happened.

JAN HAWORTH, PRESENTER AND LECTURER IN BROADCASTING

Getting in …

Use your contacts and keep your ear to the ground to hear of opportunities. On the practical front, practise breathing and posture at home. We once invited a voice trainer to City University who identified three really good voices amongst the students. All had had musical training. One was a flautist, one played trumpet and the other was a jazz singer. So all were trained in breath control. His advice was to learn a musical instrument! I didn't think this was terribly helpful bearing in mind all the other things the students had to do … but it's a perspective!

Getting on …

Develop 'active listening'. Think about why this person is sounding patronising. Listen to yourself. Play with voices; it helps you lose any hang-ups you might have about your own voice and you'll become a more flexible, versatile presenter.

Words of warning …

Some think it's a pathway to the stars. It's not. You'll be a much better presenter if you are a journalist or an expert etc. Don't be a 'gob on a stick' – a voice divorced from the brain. Have something to say. If you haven't got something to say in the role that you're in, then you're in the wrong job.

DAVE JONES, LIGHTING CAMERAMAN

Getting in …

Make sure you can do the basics like master the ability to walk, or do any other activity, and talk! Learn to back-time links if you need to finish in a certain position for the camera i.e. speak the words as you do the walk in reverse. Try to understand the style of the programme, regardless of whether it's to your personal liking. Styles are more varied than ever and presenters need to be more flexible than ever.

Getting on …

Work on building your confidence. Think of the camera as your friend as well as the gateway to a whole nation. Good diction. Be cheerful; we all know telly isn't glamorous most of the time. It's a team effort and we all want the project to succeed. A miserable presenter drags the whole unit down. Muck in. We love presenters who share the same grotty hotels without complaining more than the crew, carry the odd piece of equipment and stand their round at the bar! Carry your own slap. Make-up service is long gone on most jobs but you look a bit of a prat if you're shiny – the camera doesn't like it either. Bring us a choice of frocks or jackets.

Words of warning …

If it's an early call, make sure you get up early. A late presenter pisses the crew off for the whole day.

OLENKA FRENKIEL, REPORTER AND PRESENTER

Getting in …

Be informed about the world or the subject you'll be dealing with. A presentation course might prepare you for the technology and the difficulties. Be prepared. I wasn't ready for dealing with a live, fast-changing situation and underestimated how difficult it is to continue unruffled. I found myself saying the wrong things, unable to find the words I wanted, sounding silly. All one's worst fears about live presentation became real. I had failed to prepare myself with useful phrases.

Getting on …

Confidence, confidence, confidence. You either have it or you don't. The only way to acquire it is after a long career where it stems from increased knowledge or experience. That works for men but for women that can be too late.

Words of warning …

It may be a false goal. It may bring status, money and fame, but that is usually short-lived.

PAUL FREEMAN, INDEPENDENT PRODUCER AND DIRECTOR

Getting in …

You need the ability to engage an audience, a mixture of authority, presence, warmth, humour, and 'the common touch'. There's no room for blandness. TV wants larger-than-life characters.

Getting on …

Learn to handle your hands. I can't stand presenters who constantly wave their hands about or point with their fingers whenever they are trying to emphasize a point. Adopt a style that sets you apart from the rest. Develop a sense of pace to your delivery – light and shade etc.

Words of warning ...

The whole concept of presenting is changing hugely. Outside of news, presenters are being chosen for their celebrity or expert status i.e. find the character first, then hone your presenting skills (if you can). Martin Clunes and Caroline Quentin swimming with dolphins is seen as infinitely more interesting than A. N. Other presenter talking about them. For a science series, Robert Winston would always get the nod over a general presenter. It's about soft sell. There is still room for the professional presenter but the opportunities are becoming fewer. TV has become very conservative in its choices – far less prepared to take a chance on a newcomer.

PETER EUSTACE, EDITOR, TV BUSINESS AND ECONOMICS PROGRAMMES

Getting in ...

We look for people who have a very deep knowledge of the subject which can be seen in their interview techniques, in their scripting and in their confidence on screen. I have been approached by 'general presenters' – people who say they can turn their skill to any area, be it cooking or news – but I've never seen this work within our area. Be prepared to work in a lower-profile area where you can learn, make mistakes. When you are ready, get the show reel together and start selling yourself.

Getting on ...

Find you own style – you can adapt others' styles but if you are going to make it, have your own. Read what you are going to read on air before, if at all possible.

Words of warning ...

Take advice from those around you. Sometimes little things, like hairstyle, can make a dramatic difference.

SANDY WARR, PRESENTER AND VOICE TRAINER

Getting in …

Don't be seduced into heading straight for the presenting jobs. The work of a reporter, researcher, producer may be more fulfilling for you. Even if you are sure you want to be on air then these are the skills you need to learn.

Getting on …

Have a thick skin and a huge sense of humour. An ability to stay calm when everyone else is running around like headless chickens. Build team skills so you can get the best out of your support team without them feeling you get all the glory and they do all the work.

Words of warning …

A bright and endearing personality is not enough. Without technical skills it's easy to fall flat on your face. Never think there is nothing left to learn. Most presenters are left to find their own way with decreasing emphasis on journalism. That can be a problem because the casualization of the industry means a presenter can't be sure of the knowledge of the team working around them.

PETER DONALDSON, CHIEF ANNOUNCER, BBC RADIO FOUR

Getting in …

It was week one of a two-week training session. I was in the studio waiting for the presenter, looking through listeners' letters thinking "thank goodness I won't have to read them on air", when there was a loud bang on the glass window between the studio and the cubicle. It was the presenter's arm encased in plaster! He pressed the talk-back and said 'The arm's broken, you're on your own tonight!' I duly 'presented' the programme but feel sorry for the people whose requests I played. I was very nervous and I'm sure it showed!

Getting on ...

Talk to your listener as though he or she were sitting opposite you. If you are interviewing, know something about your subject and don't assume others will. Let your subjects speak and listen to their answers!

Words of warning ...

I take the job seriously – but not myself. The money is never enough – on radio, at least. And there's no stardom – but that's probably a bonus. It beats working for a living! It's fun and 'we' are very lucky to be doing what we are doing. As for the future, will we be needed at all or will we all be automated or synthesized?!

Glossary

Analogue Video or audio analogue signals are those where the signals are directly analogous to the information that they are trying to represent. Therefore a loud sound or a bright picture is represented by a big signal wave; a quiet sound or a dark picture will be represented by a small signal wave. This contrasts with digital signals, where the information is represented by numeric information. Because digital signals never need to carry any more complex information than 1 or 0 (binary code), they are much more robust than analogue signals and suffer far less degradation during copying from tape to tape (generation losses) and suffer from less interference during transmission.

Anchor The main presenter responsible for linking the programme. Frequently studio-based but not necessarily.

Atmos Atmosphere. Used to describe background sound during a recording e.g. 'Take an atmos track of general street noise.'

Autocue A device allowing the presenter to read script whilst looking at the camera. The words scroll in front of the lens but are invisible to the TV viewer. Other machines that do the same are Teleprompter and Portaprompt.

Avid Company that has developed a widely used computer-based digital tape editing system.

Back-timing Counting the duration of a series of programme items or a script from the end back to the beginning so that you can be sure it will fit the available time. For example, starting to speak your piece to camera whilst walking *away* from the camera to find where you will have to be standing when you start it and wish to walk *towards* the lens.

BCU Big close up. A very close shot of an object. If it's of a person, it would cut off the top of the forehead and the lower part of the chin.

Caption generator Equipment that displays text on screen, such as names and designations.

Catchline   Also known as the 'slug'. The name or title that identifies the item and which is written on everything relating to it – the disc, the tape, the tape box, the computer scripts, the cues etc.

Clip   A short excerpt from a longer item, usually involving speech, for use on either a TV or a radio broadcast. For example, 'Get me a clip of the Queen's speech and we'll voice round it [write a script in which it will be included].'

Copy story   A scripted item that has no added film or audio to accompany it.

Copy tasting   Checking through written material (copy) to assess it for inaccuracies and relevance.

CSO   Colour separation overlay, sometimes referred to as Chromakey. A method of electronically replacing a screen of one colour with pictures, either moving or still, which is used a lot in newscasts. The pictures are invisible to the presenter but are seen by the audience.

Cue   Used either to refer to the introductory information to an item that is read by the presenter, as in 'cue material', or simply as a warning that something is about to happen, as in 'cue programme' (meaning the programme is starting) or 'cue Janet' (meaning Janet should start speaking immediately). Similarly, the cue light is the lamp in the studio on the desk, the door, the wall or table that alerts everyone that the studio will go live imminently.

DAB   Digital Audio Broadcasting.

Digital   See **Analogue**.

Down the line   An interview or presentation that is made in vision, with good quality sound, but without the interviewer present. The questions are heard via an earpiece and the interviewee will look directly at the camera – one of the few occasions this is done during an interview. The interviewer hears through an earpiece and usually sees the interviewee on a monitor.

Dubbing   A number of meanings:

       1. To transfer or copy recorded material from one tape to another
       2. To record the final soundtrack of a film, including the commentary
       3. To create a foreign language version of an item.

Empty-chairing   The situation where one of the expected or desired participants in the debate does not appear. It can happen innocently due to the interviewee's full diary or it can be contrived, for all sorts of reasons, by either side.

Fader   The switch or lever used to bring in or take out sound or vision in a graduated way on a sliding scale.

FX   Sound effects.

Gallery   The operational heart of the TV programme. The darkened room (not necessarily adjoining the studio) where the director and producer sit with other technical operators, watching the studio action on monitors whilst also checking the output.

GV   In TV terminology, a general view shot of a location or action frequently used as 'an establisher' i.e. to set the scene.

Hot board   A table generated by computer graphics to detail information, often facts and statistics. For example, of market prices in a business programme.

In words   The first words spoken on the film or sound tape/disc that are transcribed onto the programme script to identify the start of the item and ensure it's the correct item (see also **Out words**).

ITC   Independent Television Commission.

Links   The script between inserts and interviews in a package or in a programme.

MFR   Moray Firth Radio, broadcasting to the Highlands and Islands of Scotland and based in Inverness.

Noddies   The reaction shots of the interviewer nodding, smiling or looking quizzical. These are usually filmed after the interview and are used to cover any edits.

OB   Outside broadcast. A TV or radio programme or item presented away from base, often with the aid of an OB van in the OB location.

Out words   The final words of an item on TV or radio that indicate the end is coming. These are transcribed onto the script to warn that a piece is about to finish.

PA   Production assistant.

Package   An item involving the presenter as well as pre-recorded inserts, as in 'news package'.

Pan Short for panoramic view. A shot achieved by a horizontal sweep of the camera from left to right or right to left.

PDP Personal Digital Production. The BBC's terminology for a video journalist – namely the lone presenter/reporter who researches, fixes, shoots, edits and presents.

Post mortem The discussion after a programme or item which reviews all aspects of the broadcast.

PTC Piece to camera. A section of a film where the presenter addresses the camera directly, also known as a stand-up.

Radio mic Radio microphone. A microphone attached by a thin wire to a battery-operated power pack and with a short aerial lead that can slip into your pocket or onto your belt, allowing free movement.

RDS Radio Data System. A means of transmitting text normally accompanying audio output.

Re-take Another attempt to get the recording fault-free, done either for better sound or for better pictures.

Record as live The programme or item will be recorded as if it were going live. There will be no stopping and it will run for the correct length of time. A method used increasingly to achieve a 'live feel' and also to save money.

Running time The time in minutes and seconds noted on the right-hand side of a film script at key points (at each change of location and after each interview or PTC), allowing you to see at a glance how far into the item you are.

Rushes The uncut filmed material that will be edited to make the final cut story.

SCU Single camera unit. The production technique requiring only the reporter/presenter and the camera operator.

Self opping Where the presenter operates the broadcasting output equipment him or herself. Most DJs and radio newsreaders do this. Increasingly, regional TV news studios are self op.

Sig tune Signature tune, referring to the opening music for a programme.

Sound bite A short excerpt from an interview to be used on its own, either on film or in audio. Particularly used with reference to news bulletins.

Static   A TV shot where the camera stays still and the framing is not changed.

Strap   The label put on the screen identifying the person speaking or detailing other information.

Subs   Sub-editors. The people who write and re-write news stories.

Talkback   The sound link between the gallery and the studio floor, heard in earpieces by the crew and the presenters.

Tilt   A shot achieved using a vertical movement of the camera downwards or upwards.

Time code   An automatic numbering system of each frame of the tape in hours, minutes and seconds. It may be set to the real time of day or to the time elapsed since filming began. It's displayed on editing machines so you can identify which bits should be cut. Some cameras will burn the time code onto the tape if the settings are wrong which will make the tape useless for broadcast.

Track   1. This can refer to the spoken script or a section of it which may or may not be numbered or lettered e.g. 'Read your opening track' or, 'Read track 3 again' or, 'Lay the track' (meaning record all of the script).
2. It also denotes the different sound layers that can be recorded at the same time or added later e.g. a track for the interviewer on one microphone, a track for the interviewee on a different microphone. In post-production, more layers or tracks can be added e.g. music.
3. 'Track' is the verb describing the camera's movement across the ground following the action, often on a platform running on a track.

Two way   An interview involving only the presenter and one other.

TX   Transmission e.g. 'The TX is on Thursday.'

VJ   Video journalist. The common term for a lone presenter/reporter who shoots and edits his or her material with no other crew (see **PDP**).

Voicepiece   The radio equivalent of a piece to camera – an uninterrupted monologue by the presenter, often setting the scene or giving background information.

VT   Video tape.

Index

INDEX

Focal Press

www.focalpress.com
Join Focal Press on-line
As a member you will enjoy the following benefits:

- an email bulletin with **information on new books**
- a regular **Focal Press Newsletter**:
    - featuring a selection of new titles
    - keeps you informed of **special offers, discounts and freebies**
    - alerts you to **Focal Press news and events** such as author signings and seminars
- complete access to **free content** and reference material on the focalpress site, such as the focalXtra articles and commentary from our authors
- a **Sneak Preview** of selected titles (sample chapters) *before* they publish
- a chance to have your say on our **discussion boards** and **review books** for other Focal readers

Focal Club Members are invited to give us feedback on our products and services.
Email: worldmarketing@focalpress.com – we want to hear your views!

Membership is **FREE**. To join, visit our website and register. If you require any further information regarding the on-line club please contact:

Lucy Lomas-Walker
Email: l.lomas@elsevier.com
Tel: +44 (0) 1865 314438
Fax: +44 (0)1865 314572
Address: Focal Press, Linacre House,
Jordan Hill, Oxford, UK, OX2 8DP

Catalogue
For information on all Focal Press titles, our full catalogue is available online at www.focalpress.com and all titles can be purchased here via secure online ordering, or contact us for a free printed version:

USA
Email: christine.degon@bhusa.com
Tel: +1 781 904 2607 T

Europe and rest of world
Email: j.blackford@elsevier.com
Tel: +44 (0)1865 314220

Potential authors
If you have an idea for a book, please get in touch:

USA
editors@focalpress.com

Europe and rest of world
focal.press@elsevier.com